Cover design by Lin Cao
Foreword by Marc Atlan

INTERNATIONAL VISUAL COMMUNICATION

Edited by Jie Zhou / Muzi Guan / Zhe Gao / Liying Wang

DESIGN MEDIA PUBLISHING LIMITED

This edition published in March 2011

Design Media Publishing Limited
20/F Manulife Tower
169 Electric Rd, North Point
Hong Kong
Tel: 00852-28672587
Fax: 00852-25050411
E-mail: Kevinchoy@designmediahk.com
www.designmediahk.com

Editing: ZHOU Jie, GUAN Muzi, GAO Zhe & WANG
Proofreading: Catherine Chang
Design/Layout: ZHOU Jie

ISBN 978-988-19508-9-5

Printed in China

Contents //

Preface //

"Design is like creating small architectures. From visual identity & branding to graphic systems & packaging design, from signage to window displays, everything you design can and will provoke emotion and induce substance from nothing. What you will find in this book will inspire significance, uniqueness and meaning."

—— Marc Atlan

Editor's Note //

With the unique composition of point, line and surface as well as different textures and various colour matchings, visual arts always create intriguing images and give people fresh feeling. Along with the rapid development of the photography, graphic art, computer technology and the material technology, the expressive form and medium of visual arts are also undergoing tremendous changes. They are gradually transformed into symbolic and independent design vocabularies from the simple surface decoration features, and have directly set up connections with different societies, races and cultures.

This book themed with the cohesion and expression of the visual arts has carefully selected 347 remarkable masterpieces from over 30 countries, referring to the packaging design, layout, VI design, poster design, illustration design and guides design. We believe that it will provide readers with an excellent feast visually, and meanwhile, encourage them to think over the unique creativeness of each project by juxtaposing different projects.

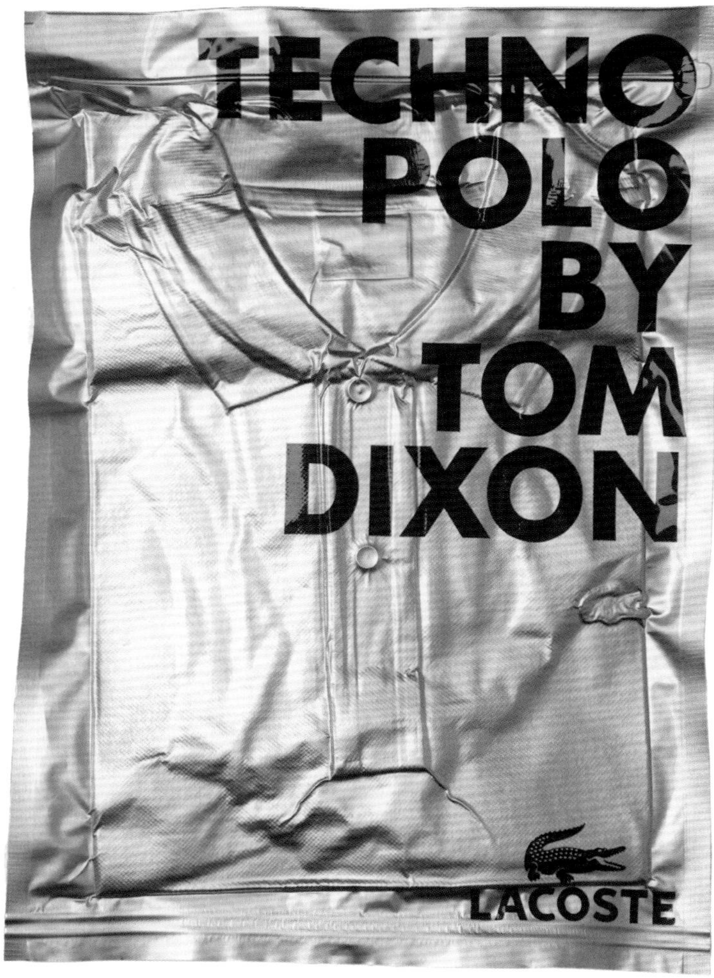

Lacoste Eco – Techno Polo by Tom Dixon

Design Agency: Mind Design

Concept: Tom Dixon

Designer: Holger Jacobs

Client: Tom Dixon

Creating Date: 2007

Information: Collaboration with Tom Dixon. Packaging and launch graphics for two special edition polo shirts commissioned by Lacoste. Tom's concept was to explore two very different materials and the technology used in the production process of the garment. The most eco-friendly way to package the eco polo was not to print on the packaging at all but to use embossing instead. The techno polo is vacuum-packaged in screen-printed foil.

LACOSTE

ECO
POLO
BY
TOM
DIXON
LACOSTE

Promotional Japanese Denim Packaging

Design Agency: Boy Bastiaens

Creative Director: Boy Bastiaens

Photography: Bert Jansen

Client: Atelier LaDurance

Creating Date: 2008

Information: The promotional Japanese Denim packaging is used as a site specific medium and developed for the retail environment. Its design is associative by means of an elegant simplicity that shows product and packaging, becoming one object.

Leather Belt Packaging

Design Agency: Boy Bastiaens
Creative Director: Boy Bastiaens
Photography: Boy Bastiaens
Client: Atelier LaDurance
Creating Date: 2008
Information: The leather belt packaging is actually a sheet of 300 grams white machine coated board, folded around the belt and attached with two brass splitpens (attaches parisiennes).Easy to open and easy to close. With just one single print run for the logo and sizechart (marked with ballpoint pen) the simple result is nothing short of a premium packaging.

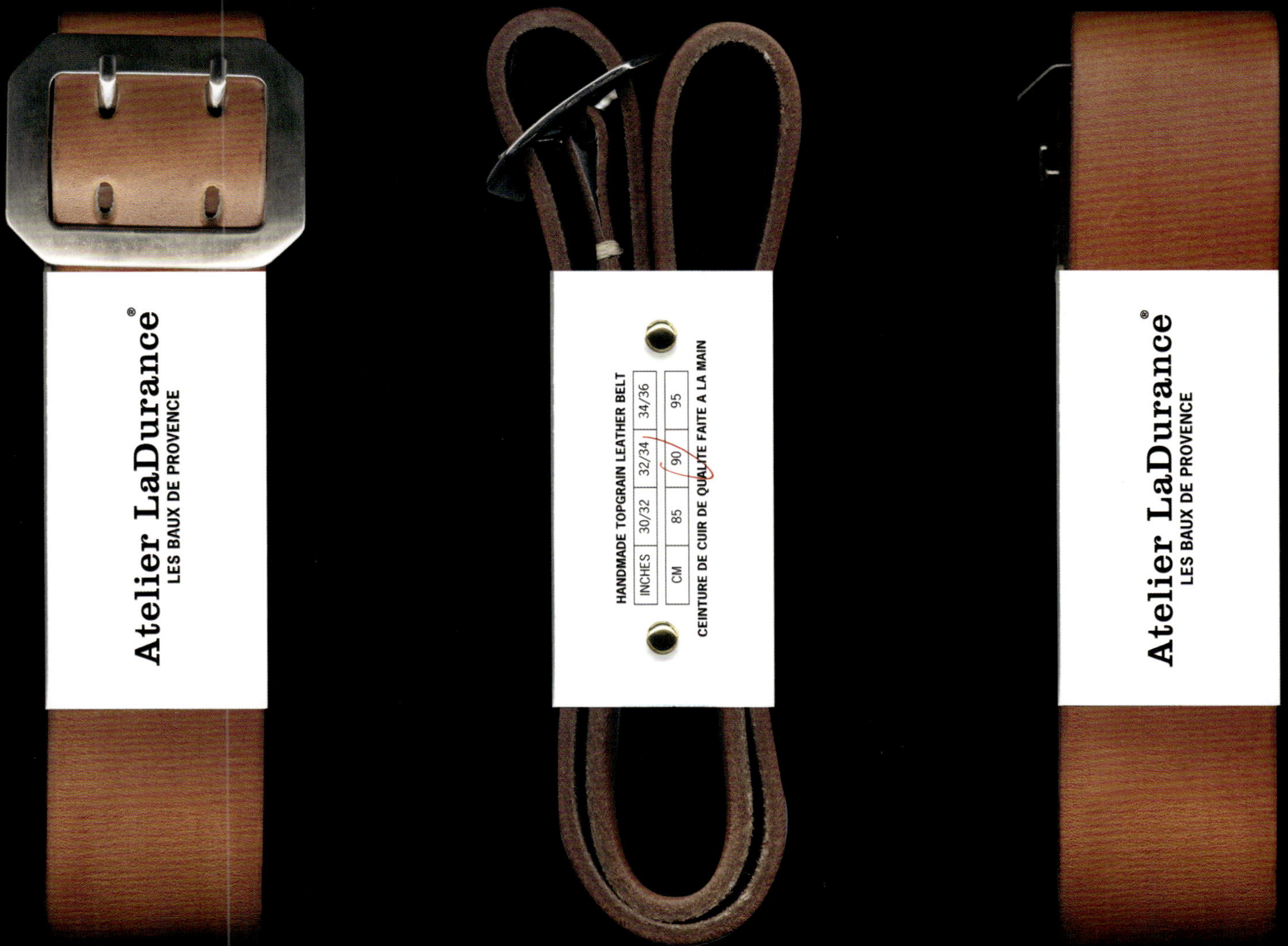

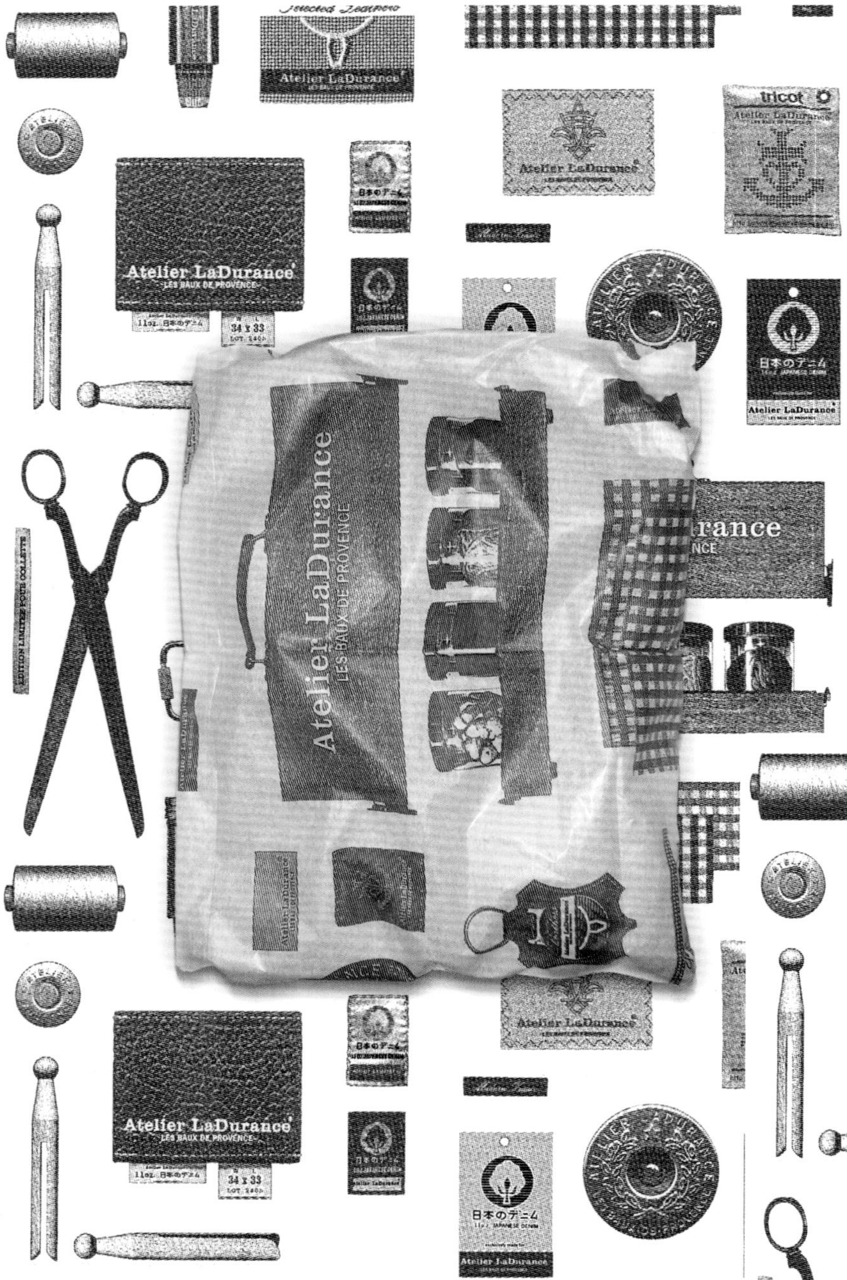

Wrapping Paper

Design Agency: Boy Bastiaens

Creative Director: Boy Bastiaens

Photography: Bert Jansen

Client: Atelier LaDurance

Creating Date: 2008

Information: The printing of the repeating pattern of 20 big images of different Atelier LaDurance branding items on a 22 grams Italian sulphite paper was a delicate job. However, the bitmap conversion into "scraperboard like" images, helped in keeping the repeating pattern crisp while printing. and avoiding the ultra thin paper from absorbing too much ink and getting too stiff.

Polo Packaging

Design Agency: Boy Bastiaens
Creative Director: Boy Bastiaens
Photography: Bert Jansen
Client: Atelier LaDurance
Creating Date: 2008
Information: The idea for the polo packaging was to develop a re-usable packaging. The choice of material is a very inexpensive loose woven cotton cloth. known as cheesecloth which was originally used as a wrapping for pressed cheese. Today it is available in seven different grades, from open to extra-fine weave. The white silkscreen print with the Fleur de Lys design and Vichy check pattern gives the envelope style bag a distinctive look.

Jordan x Levi

Design Agency: I love dust Design
Designer: Shan Jiang
Creative Director: Mark Graham & Ben Beach
Design Director: Ben Beach
Client: Brand Jordan
Creating Date: 2009
Information: The designers worked with Brand Jordan to create the packaging and illustration for the collaboration between Jordan and Levi 501's. The packaging featured specially designed Jordan and Levis illustrations and graphics, as well as an illustrated T-shirt and Perspex split box dividers. Having been sent a pair of pristine Jordans 1s and a fresh pair of Original fit Levi 501's, they went ahead, scalpel in hand, to dissect the shoes and jeans with a tear in their eye! This helped them get to grips with how each product was made and helped develop an appreciation for the details and construction. They started to design an organic, elegant hand-drawn collage, inspired by individual details from both the products and famous iconic brand elements. They created individual designs for each facet of the box and clear dividers within this. This was a really special project – and one that was great for the designers to be involved with.

Orient Design Name Card Box

Design Agency: Orient Design Pte Ltd

Designer: Ms Regina Tan

Creative Director: Mr Jackie Tan

Client: Orient Design Direct Mail Project

Creating Date: 2009

Information: The designers wanted to design a package that would be interesting and useful for their clients—something that people could keep; unlike a flyer, which is usually thrown away. They came up with the idea of a namecard holder, with dividers to showcase their portfolio of clients in alphabetical order. Made from foldable cardboard, the name cardholder also serves to reinforce a Go Green message, a cause which Orient Design believes in. At the same time, green is a gender-neutral colour which also serves to brighten up one's workspace. The name cardholder proved to be a popular corporate gift among the clients, and is also available for personalised corporate adaptation.

Attiva

Design Agency: SeventhDesign™
Designer: Bruno Siriani
Creative Director: Bruno Siriani
Client: GA.MA Italy
Creating Date: 2010
Information: GA.MA gets SeventhDesign™ services to clarify a new brand identity and deliver an integrated consumer experience. Through the introduction of a new visual expression, Attiva re-engaged their target market and also broadened their reach. The significant deliverable from the project is an impressive product image at retail, expressed through a minimalistic visual vocabulary. Packaging for the complete new line prominently features the product's unique and visually appealing design.

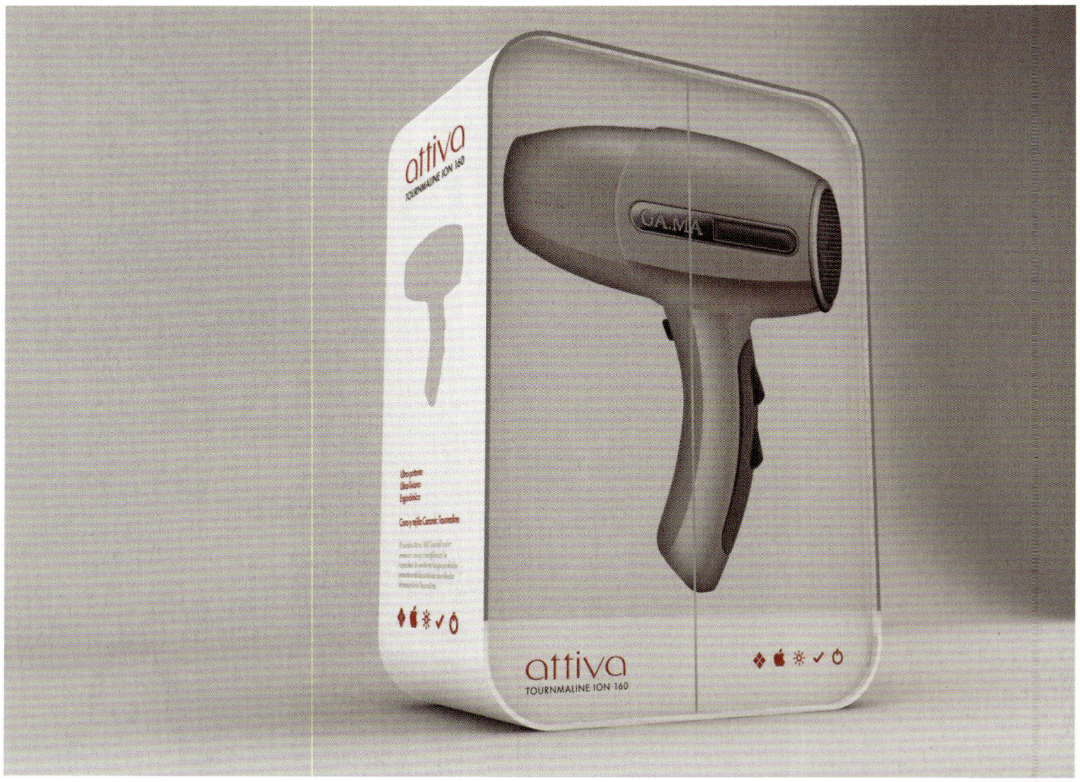

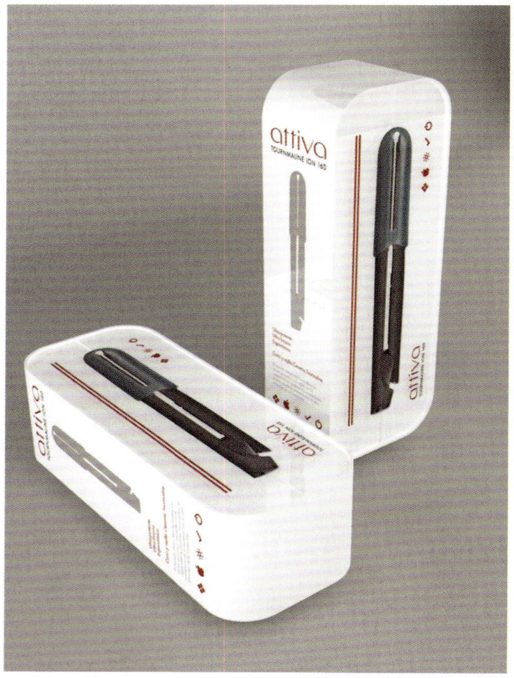

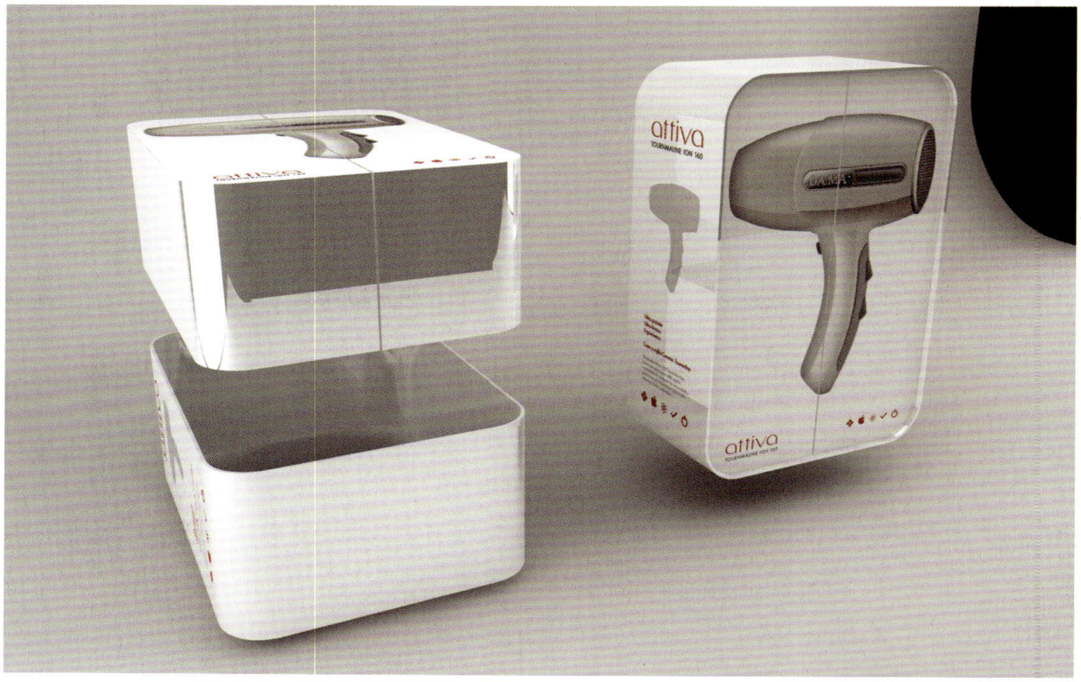

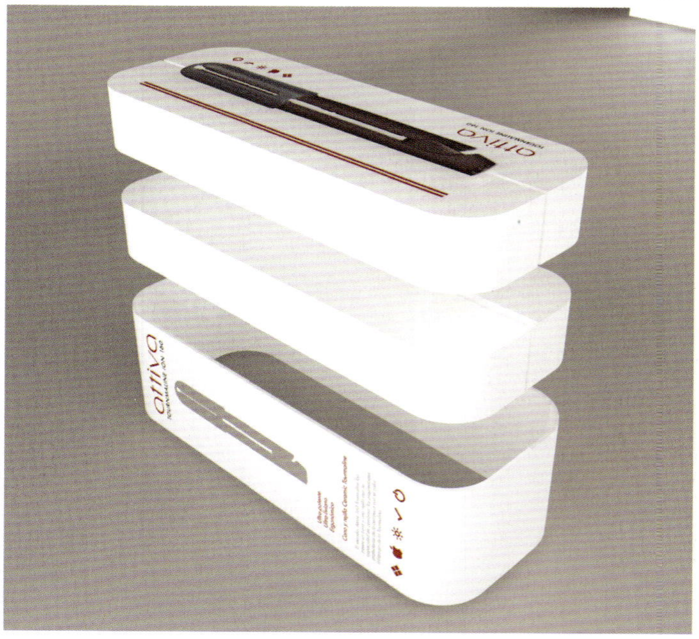

Aquatus Hygienic Products

Design Agency: Fontos Graphic Design Studio
Designer: Mate Olah
Creating Date: 2008
3D modelling: Gabor Gloviczki
Client: Aquatus

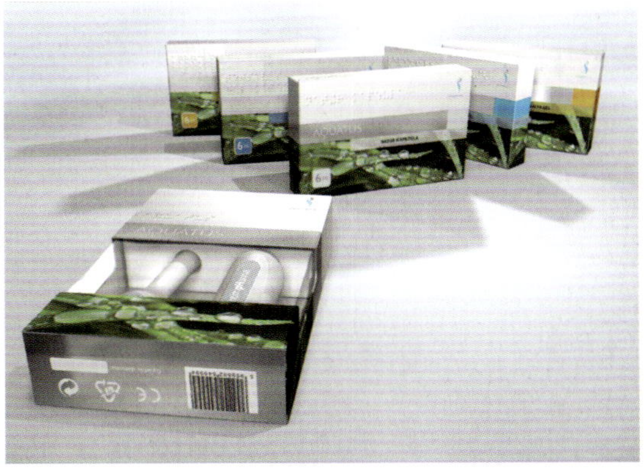

Farmetone

Design Agency: Flavia Oliveira

Designer: Flavia Oliveira

Client: Farm

Creating Date: 2010

Information: The package is used for packaging the Christmas chocolates. The original Christmas colours and graphics create a distinct visual effect.

AIWA

Design Agency: Butterfly-stroke Inc.
Creative Director: Katsunori Aoki
Designer: Katsunori Aoki
Illustrator: Seijiro Kubo
Client: AIWA
Creating Date: 2006
Information: A series of campaign posters for AIWA in October 2002, featuring boxy creatures named Copet. Elephants, bears, crocodiles, birds, gorillas and other familiar animals were turned into ultra-simple, three-dimensional characters.

Susanne Walström Catalogue

Design Agency: HeidiChisholm

Creative Director: HeidiChisholm

Design: HeidiChisholm

Creating Date: 2010

Information: Catalogue for "The Art of Wrapping Garbage"–a photography exhibition by Susanne Walström about the Japanese practice of excessively wrapping everything from candy to garbage.

THANK YOU
AND GOOD NIGHT

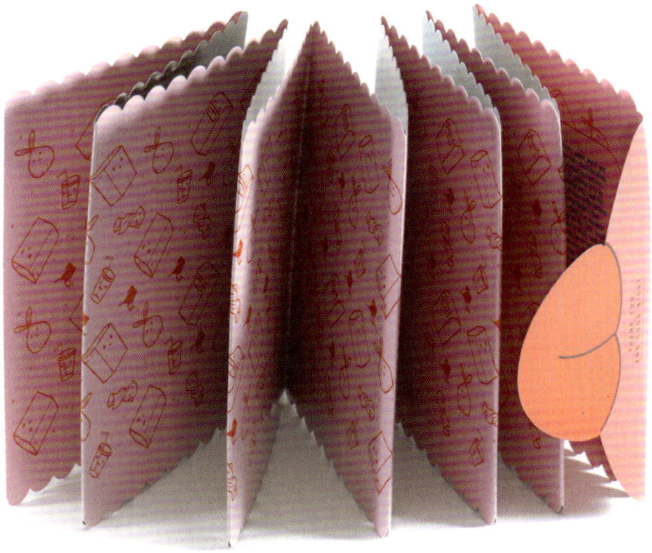

THANK YOU
AND GOOD NIGHT

THE ART OF
WRAPPING
ごみ
by SUSANNE
WALSTRÖM
THE ART OF
ラッピング
GARBAGE
by SUSANNE
WALSTRÖM

THANK YOU
AND GOOD NIGHT

Hipo Hyfryd

Design Agency: Kutchibok

Client: Hipo Hyfryd

Creating Date: 2010

Information: Kutchibok was approached by Hipo Hyfryd to create an eye–catching brand for its chocolate packaging aimed at the high-end, luxury, vegan, organic market with a strong Welsh identity. There were many challenges to this brief – namely a tight budget for materials, productions and print costs. Hipo Hyfryd was adamant that all work would be done by ethical companies using best practices. The packaging had to be 100% recycled and biodegradable–causing therefore least amount of damage to the environment. To add to this the box had to be constructed without the use of glue.

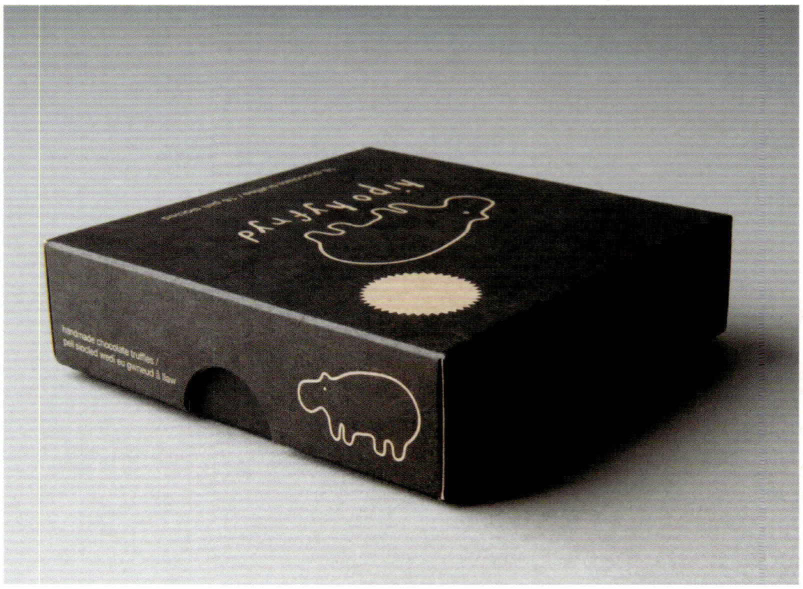

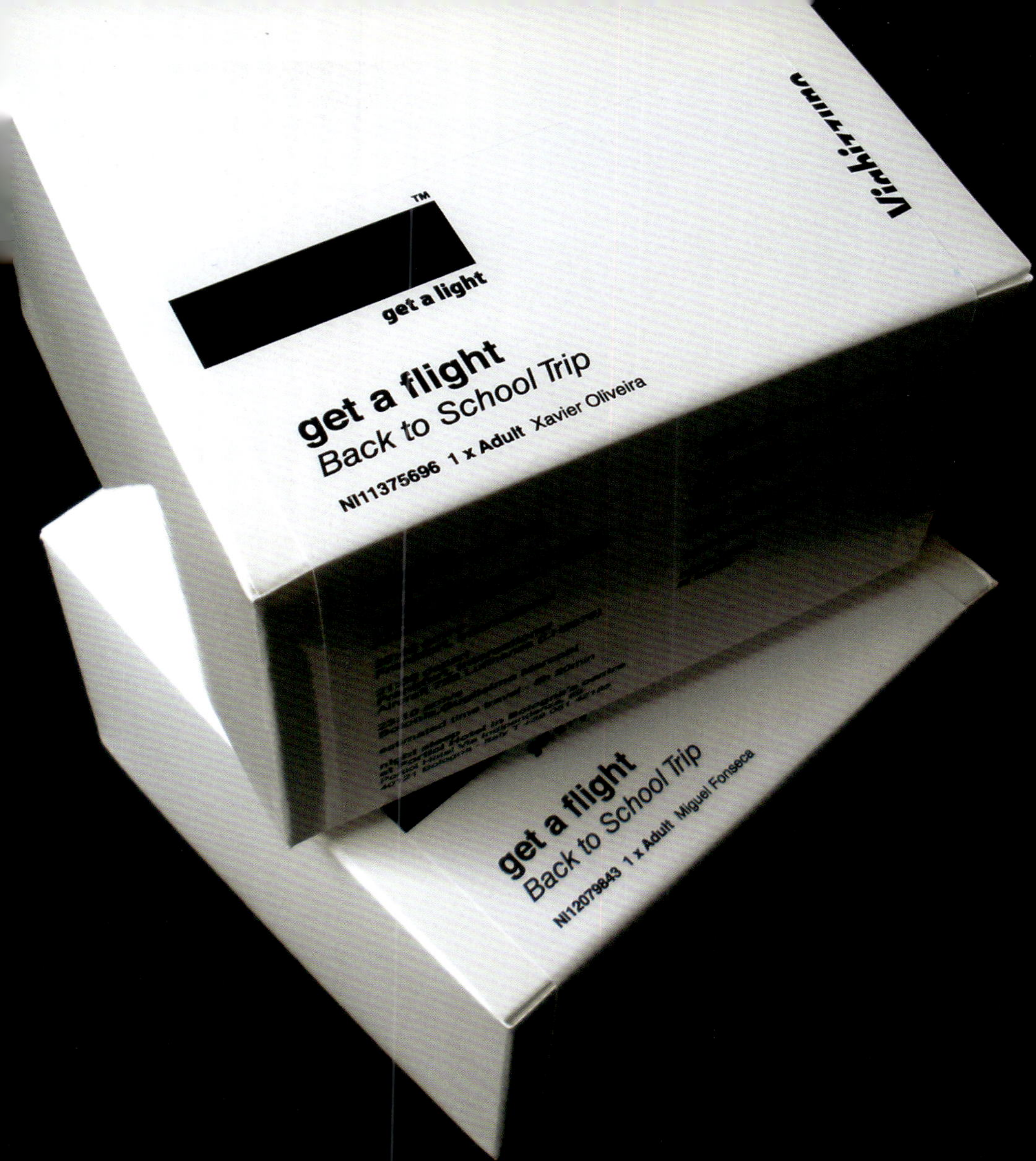

Get a Flight

Design Agency: Thisislove studio

Designer: Joana Areal

Creative Director: Joana Areal

Photography: This is love studio

Client: get a light

Creating Date: 2009

Information: Gift made especially for getting a light employees to take on a field trip. Plastic square box sealed with a sticker and filled with cotton fibers to hold inside a paper airplane with the trip schedule.

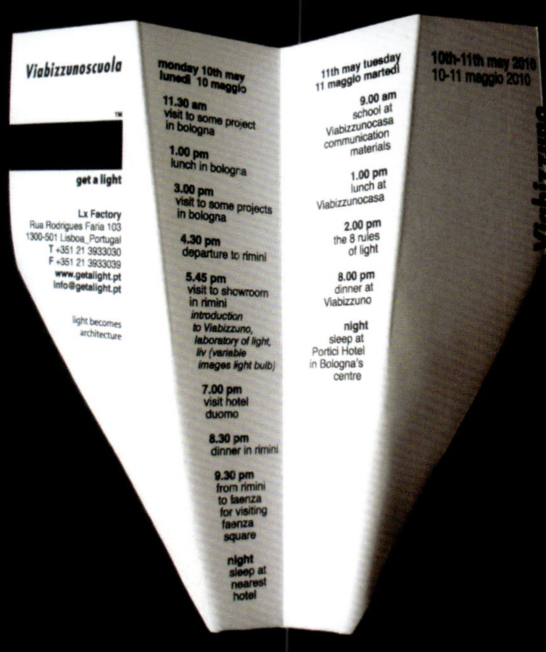

Get a Tree

Design Agency: Thisislove studio
Designer: Joana Areal
Creative Director: Joana Areal
Photography: This is love studio
Client: Get a light
Creating Date: 2009
Information: Christmas gift made especially for get a light. A limited edition object consisting in a postal package that contains a small vase cup, closed with a lid and filled with sand and pine seeds, and a leaflet with detail information about caring and maintaining Pines Trees.

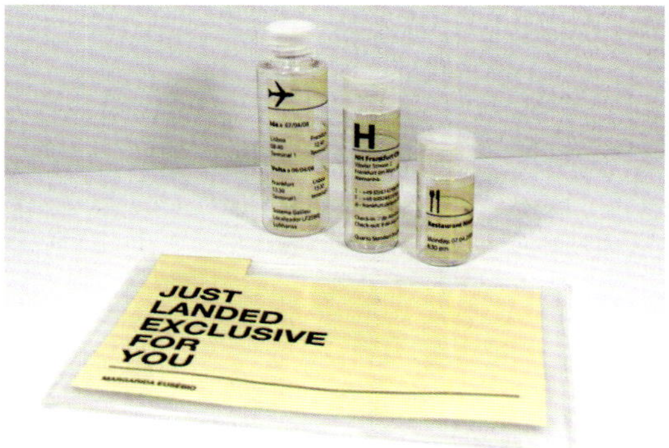

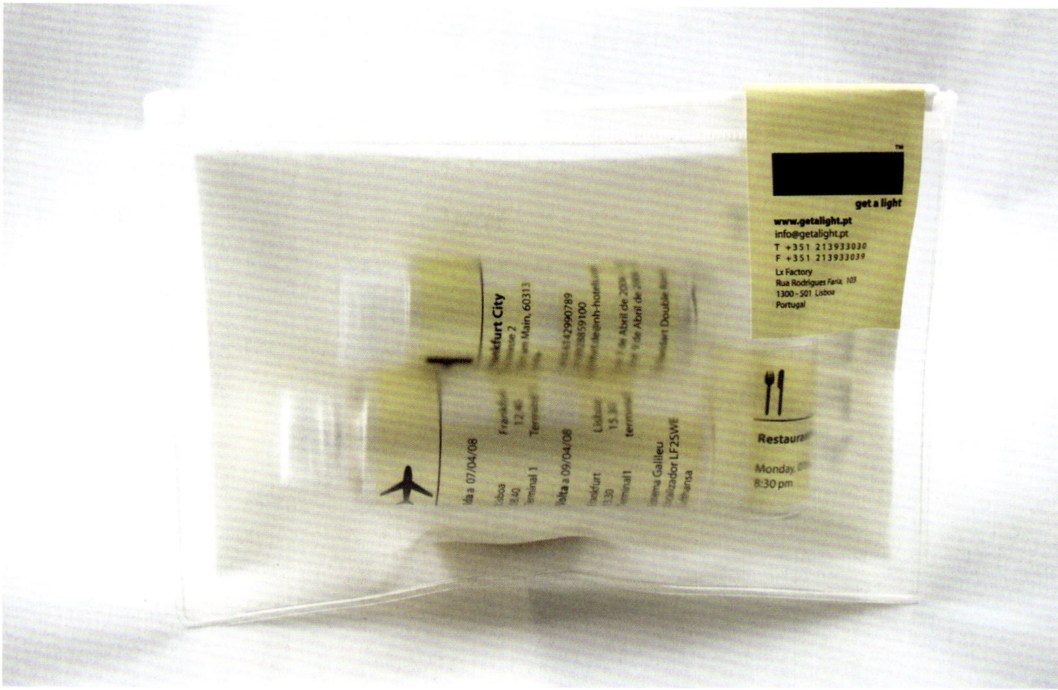

Get a trip

Design Agency: Thisislove studio
Designer: Joana Areal, Inês Veiga
Creative Director: Joana Areal
Photography: This is love studio
Client: get trip
Creating Date: 2009

Angel Eyes

Design Agency: Menta

Creative Director: Raúl Climent

Designer: Xavi Calvo & Elisa Gómez

Client: CTAV

Creating Date: 2009

Information: For the "Art and Architecture" collection promoted by the Valencia Architects Association, Menta designed this limited edition package for the "Angel Eyes" jazz album by the guitarist Louis Stewart. This special and numbered edition was limited to 200 copies and all of them contained a signed score from the author inside.

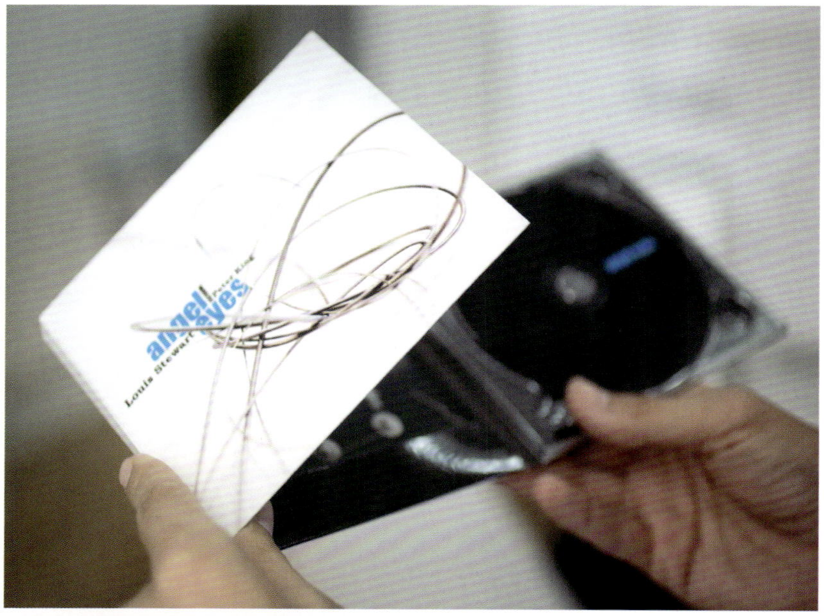

Muslimgauze – Remxs

Design Agency: PLAZM

Creative Director: Joshua Berger

Designer: Joshua Berger

Client: Soleilmoon Records

Creating Date: 2006

Information: Double CD limited edition fur-covered package. The music is a re-issue of two long out of print disks.

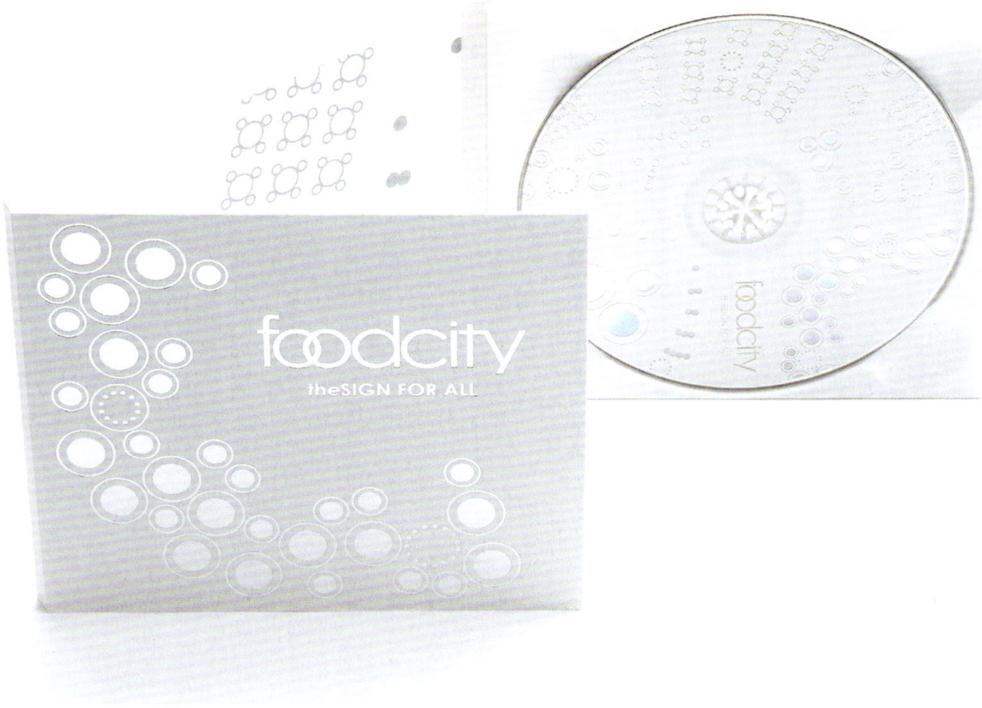

Foodcity Packaging

Design Agency: 3group

Designer: Ryszard Bienert, Slawomir Lukuc

Client: Agapes

Creating Date: 2008

Information: Package CD, envelope and poster created as direct mail campaign for Agapes. Designed for Architecture Fair in Cannes. Envelope consists poster and DVD with digital presetation. Printed with 2 Metallic Panotones–Silver and Gold. Cover of the CD with Silver and Hot Staming.

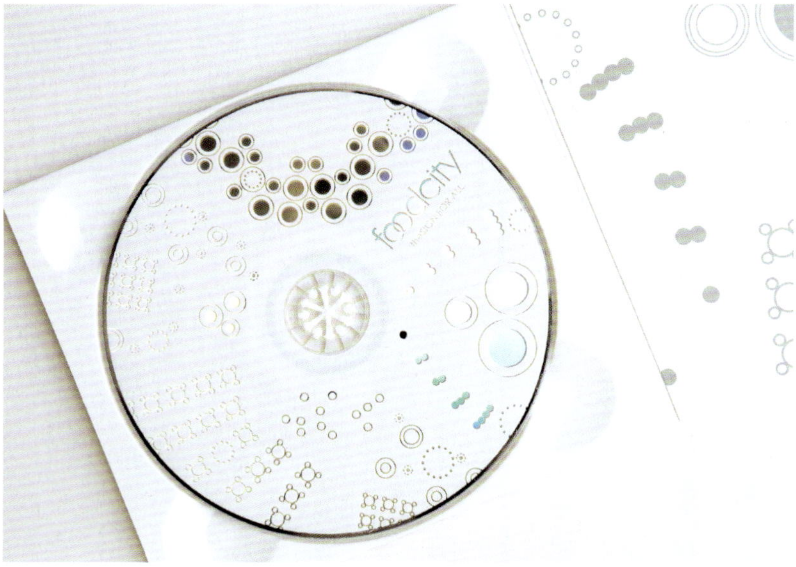

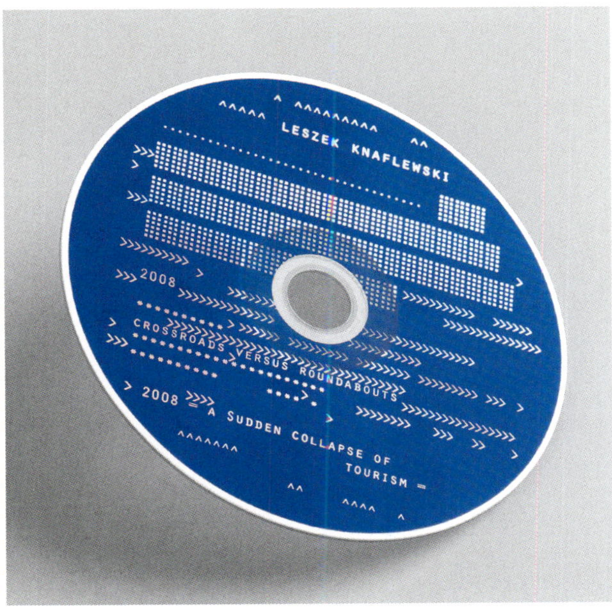

Crossroads Versus Roundabouts

Design Agency: 3group

Designer: Ryszard Bienert

Client: Leszek Knaflewski

Creating Date: 2008

Information: The work includes a cover made from corrugated cardboard with a text silk printed on it. The text is coded in a cipher known only to the artist. Two sponges to be found in the Box along with DVDs are placed in profiles cut out in the lower sponge. The dimensions of the Box: the length of 35cm, the widths of 35cm and the highs of 10cm are supposed to stress its row and monumental character. The whole piece is kept in monochromatic tone. However, to contrast it, each of the DVDs has its own strong colour, which follows the colours used to divide the catalogue into sections.

LUNATIC AGE
THE MONTH OF
MISFORTUNE
AUGUST

LUNATIC AGE
AUGUST

Lunaticage

Design Agency: Moreyellow

The creative director: Fabien Barral

Designer: Fabien Barral

Photographer: Fabien Barral

Creating Date: 2010

Information: One of my first projects was to design their second album, back in the 90's... For the fourth album, I had an opportunity to work with the photos of Eric Canto... The first design featured an old and broken music cassette tape (you can see it on the last image here). When the band asked me to design a promotional album, I wanted to do something different and used Eric's band photos... We eventually decided to keep this new design for the commercial album. I also designed a promotional single.

Aquatus Plus Hygienic Products

Design Agency: Fontos Graphic Design

Designer: Mate Olah

Client: Aquatus

3D modelling: Gabor Gloviczki

Award: Design and Design International Design Award

Creating Date: 2009

Tazaa Soap

Design Agency: How design

Designer: Jesse Kirsch

Client: Tazaa Soap

Creating Date: 2009

Information: Strong typography and a sharp colour palette define this packaging system for a line of 6 scented soaps. The bright white of the sleeve evokes a feeling of cleanliness, while the interior box conveys the colour of the ingredients used to make the soap. The initials of each scent's name, die cut on the outside sleeve, allow the colour of the box below to show through. A small narrow opening at either end invites the consumer to smell the soap without having to open the box.

Cleansing Tonic – Moistening / Stimulant

Design Agency: 3group

Designer: Ryszard Bienert

Client: Soraya

Illustarator: Eboy

Creating Date: 2008

Information: According to the characteristic of the product, the package features an appealing profile, applying the digital illustration designs to express the animated and lively nature of the product.

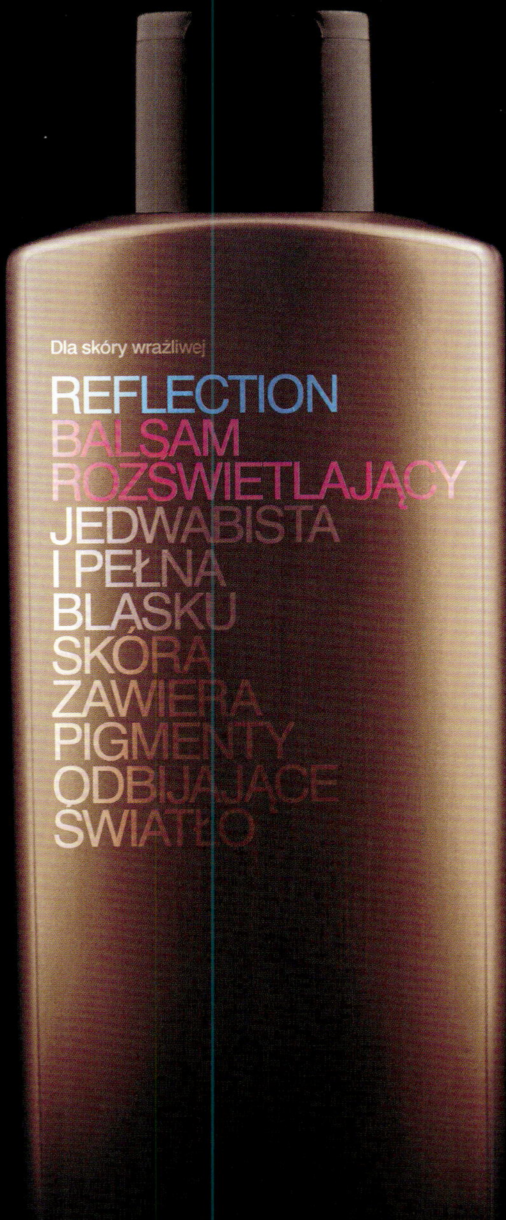

Moinstening Balm

Design Agency: 3group

Designer: Ryszard Bienert

Client: Soraya

Creating Date: 2008

Information: Packaging for Moinstening Balm – a series of skin cosmetics. There are 4 different scents in the series, each of them has its different distinctive colour.

3CAMEL Packaging

Designer: Amy Sprague

Client: Agapes

Creating Date: 2009

Information: A sustainable amenities package for a lodge in Mongolia. Vibrant photographs reveal the stunning landscape of Mongolia in hopes to inspire its visitors to want to keep it this way. Aiming to maintain the lowest environmental impact, the box that holds the products folds out into a map of Mongolia. The lid tears apart into postcards. All plastic is made from post consumer waste and all labeling is easily removable for structures to be reused or recycled.

CHAKRAS Packaging

Designer: Amy Sprague

Client: Chakra Essentials

Creating Date: 2010

Information: Chakra Essentials is a line of body oils created to satisfy the seven chakras of the body.

To clarify and highlight the benefit of each body oil, each bottle is very unique to display it's purpose. The line is inspired by Indian silks and hand – drawn artwork.

HOME Packaging

Designer: Amy Sprague

Client: Home

Creating Date: 2009

Information: HOME introduces domestic cleaning products targeting a new market. Men. Using has a masculine appearance, humour and encouraging commentary, HOME communicates that household cleaning is not just for women.

CONCEAL Packaging

Designer: Amy Sprague

Client: Conceal

Creating Date: 2009

Information: Conceal aims to raise the bar in mass market women's hygiene, to redesign a category typically hidden, and transform it into a product consumers want to show off in their homes.

Scientifica Skincare Packaging

Design Agency: Lemonyellow

Client: Scientifica Skincare

Creating Date: 2010

Information: Scientifica is a NY-based skincare line with a celebrity following. Lemon Yellow was asked to revamp its identity and packaging to create a design that would speak to its exclusive clientele. The intention was to colour code the products in a subtle way to reflect the intended usage. A pattern was created from the "S" in the Scientifica name that carried on to the various products in a playful but elegant way.

Belmacz Beauty

Design Agency: Mind Design

Creative Director: Holger Jacobs

Client: Belmacz

Creating Date: 2009

Information: Packaging and promotional material for the Belmacz Beauty range. Products include a lip gloss with real gold leaf and a powder with crushed real pearl. The packaging makes use of different textures, prints and embossing effects.

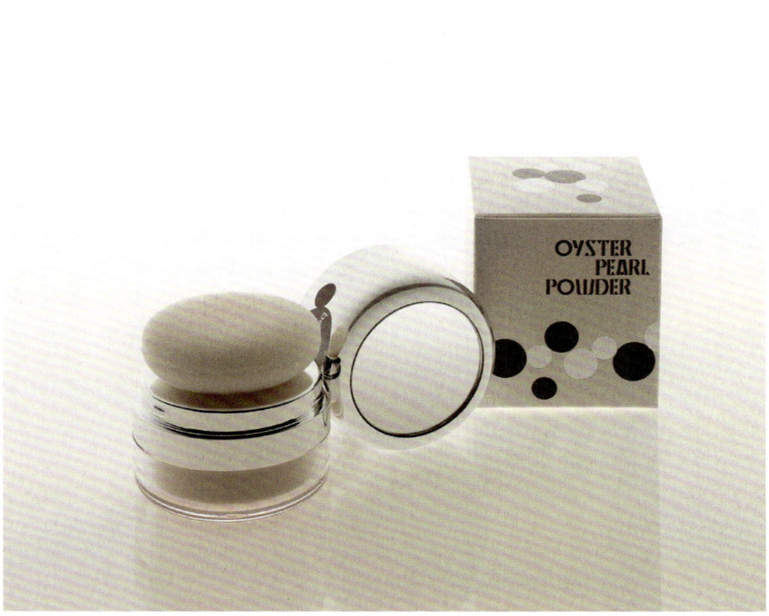

Lizhara Packaging

Design Agency: Tridimage

Client: Lizahara

Creating Date: 2009

Information: Tridimage positioned Lizhara´s skin care line through an exclusive and sophisticated image. The balance between science and emotion, glamour and effectiveness, translates into their package design resoundingly. They achieved the final goal: to trigger the desire of possession at first sight.

Buta'I

Design Agency: Dan Alexander & Co.

Client: BUTA'I

Creating Date: 2008

Information: Dan Alexander & Co. is an Israel based branding. BUTA'I, combines 100% natural ingredients with cutting edge "nano drop"technology, which has situated them on the thin line between nature and high-end technology, and so, the visual language must combine the two variables visually. The package aims to enhance women's beauty, while being kind to the planet, to enable women's radiance, by means of safe and healthy products, to offer women pure and natural alternatives to standard cosmetics.

CHIC-Water Bottle

Design Agency: Upstairs Design Studio

Designer: Manuel Vital,Pedro Novo

Photography: Frederico Martins

Client: Sociedade da Água de Monchique

Creating Date: 2008

Information: Chic is a water bottle for moments of pleasure and glamour. Its sensual outline, transparency and clear typography certainly stand out at any table. The designers made the label transparent to strengthen its impact. The project has been a huge success and the water is exported into several international markets.

Perfume for Mother's & Father's Day

Design Agency: Rpure studio

Designer: Grégory SIDOINE

Creating Date: 2008

Infermation: Packaged for the perfumes for the Mother's & Father's Day. Warm colour goes harmoniously with the delicate shape.

The Six Scents Global Fragrance Initiative

Design Agency: 3deep design

Creative Director: 3deep design

Design: 3deep design

Client: Six Scents Parfums

Creating Date: 2009

Information: Six Scents: Series Two is the second year that 3 Deep Design has collaborated with Six Scents Parfums on this amazing initiative. Annually, the project presents a distinct group of six prominent artists and perfumers to develop a limited edition series of fragrances to help raise money for charity. The collection represents a worldwide spectrum of contemporary perspectives on creativity, culture and consciousness.

SixScents Series Two
Ende/Anfang
Damir Doma
& Yann Vasnier

JCDecaux

Twigs Packaging

Design Agency: Lindsay perkins

Client: Student project

Photography: Omar mendez

Creating Date: 2010

Information: The objective was to brand Twigs Plant Boutique, a company specializing in plants for the home,and to design the packaging for their "gourmet" line featuring herbs and spices, perfect for the heart of the home – the kitchen! The "gourmet" line is inspired by olive oil and vinegar bottles, and the design aesthetics that come with modern packaging of cooking ware. The leaf-shaped images resembling a plant bring feelings of spring, happiness, comfort of the home, fresh air, nature and health – similar to a home cooked, balanced meal.

twigs
twigs

twigs
CHIVES
HERBAL SEEDS
GOURMET PLANTS FOR YOUR HOME

twigs
twigs
twigs
twigs
twigs

twigs

AND SOMETHING WITH IT LIKE A COOKIE OR
NTENT. FIKA BRINGS YOU A TOTALY NEW WAY OF
FIKA" WILL BE AS CONVENIENT AS THE WORD.
FIKA
COOKIES:
NOUGAT
CHOKLATE

Fika Choklate

Designer: Johan Hemgren

Client: Fika

Creating date: 2010

Information: On a course on packaging design Johan Hemgren was given the assignment to create new packaging for cookies. He tried to combine both nostalgia and an up-to-date function and came up with this idea were the box becomes a serving plate. The name, Fika, comes from the Swedish word for "Having a cup of coffee."

World Expo 2010 Food Packaging

Design Agency: Mattmo | Brand Value Creators

Client: World Expo 2010 in Shanghai

Creating Date: 2010

Information: For the Dutch pavilion of the World Expo 2010 in Shanghai, Mattmo created the food packaging design commissioned by Maison van den Boer, the Dutch catering company responsible for all the food and beverage at the Dutch pavilion. This design was translated into all kinds of deliverables, from all the menus to the cups and plates. Mattmo did research to minimise the footprint for the environment. The design is a modern illustrative twist of the traditional image of the Netherlands with its typical landmarks like the windmills, the canal houses in Amsterdam and the Dutch agricultural landscape.

Ilovedust Meat Packing In-house Promo

Design Agency: Ilovedust

Creative Director: Mark Grham

Art Director: Johnny Winslade

Designer: Jodie Silsby

Photography: Liz Bick

Client: Ilovedust

Creating Date: 2010

Information: Ilovedust recently moved into an old butchers workshop so their shop facing identity naturally began to lend itself to that. They hand screen printed butchers aprons and tea towels and wrapped those, along with a perfect bound book full of their latest work, in light-weight news print, secured together with twine. These were sent to new and existing clients to showcase their talents – and the response they've had so far has been great!

Nou no Mai

Design Agency: E. Co., Ltd
Creative Director: Kenichi Matsumoto
Designer: Kenichi Matsumoto
Photography: Tadashi Tomono
Client: Matsudai Noubutai
Creating Date: 2009
Information: Packaging for white and brown rice. A design to reflect and give thanks to nature for the blessing.

Laminate Film Packaging

Design Agency: E. Co., Ltd
Creative Director: Yosuke Kobayashi
Designer: Mika Nittsu
Photography: Tadashi Tomono
Client: Kaunet
Creating Date: 2009
Information: Packaging for 4 sizes of Laminate film, using fruit as a motif.

What On Earth Cake Packaging

Design Agency: Mind Design
Creative Director: Holger Jacobs
Art Director: Craig Sinnamon
Illustrator: Craig Sinnamon
Client: What On Earth
Creating Date: 2009
Information: New packaging concept for the organic food producer "What on Earth". The design uses linocut illustrations that can be arranged in many different ways. It was important not to use computer generated but hand made images which relate to the hand-made and organic aspect of the product.

Bella Barista Packaging

Design Agency: Housemouse

Client: Bella Barista

Creating Date: 2006

Information: A brand new company that provided high-quality drive thru coffee needed a strong, progressive, fun brand to be developed to reflect its mission. Housemouse were commissioned to take on the task and develop a brand for the new coffee chain.

Gubble Bum

Design Agency: How design

Designer: Jesse Kirsch

Client: Bubble gum

Creating Date: 2010

Information: A fun and twisted approach to packaging for a line of flavored bubble gum. The characters are comprised of nothing more than full and half circles; yet despite this extreme simplicity, their faces still manage to convey a wide range of emotions. Beneath the cutesy exterior, however, lies an unexpected twist: removing the outer box reveals the skeleton of each "bum".

4 your Baby Baby Products Concept

Design Agency: Fontos Graphic Design Studio

Designer: Mate Olah

Client: Bubble gum

Creating Date: 2009

3D modelling: Gabor Gloviczki

Breakfast Tea
Organic Premium Ceylon Black Tea
15 Pyramid Bags

100% ORGANIC

MILK

Organic Porridge
with Honey

LE Pain QUOTIDIEN
wine
le pique-nique
Cheese
Salads
Bread
www.lepainquotidien.co.uk

Le Pain Quotidien Packaging

Design Agency: Mind Design

Creative Director: Holger Jacobs

Illustrator: Aude van Ryn

Client: Le Pain Quotidien

Creating Date: 2010

Information: Various packaging items designed for Le Pain Quotidien London, including cotton bags, picnic and tea boxes.

Ceylon Organics Packaging

Designer: Lindsay perkins

Photography: Kristin Callahan

Client: Ceylon

Creating Date: 2009

Information: The objective was to create a package that reflects the companies sustainable values and ethics. A 100% compostable tea container redefines the traditional tea drinking system by creating the package out of the product. It is constructed by a series of layers that tear apart and release the tea bag with the string and tab. The layers are sealed with food grade wax to keep the tea fresh. As the tea is used, the package is used, so there is very little package left when the product is finished. In addition the packaging is 100% biodegradable so the user can toss the entire tea bag, string, and tab into their compost when they finish.

Fair Trade Chocolate Packaging

Designer: René Clément

Creative Director: Louis Gagnon

Art Director: René Clément

Client: Galerie au chocolat

Creating Date: 2010

Information: Galerie au Chocolat believes in beautiful packaging and in an intelligent design at all times. From a classic line of fine black chocolates to a big pot of fair-trade hot chocolate, every product deserves the best, which we strive to provide.

Jasztej Zrt. Milk Products Concept

Design Agency: Fontos Graphic Design Studio

Designer: Mate Olah

Client: Jasztej Zrt.,Inc

Creating Date: 2010

3D modelling: Gabor Gloviczki

Infermation: Packaged for the milk products, each flavour has its different distinctive colour. The simple design goes harmoniously with the characteristic of the product.

UHT
2·8
tejmilk
UHT
3·6
tejmilk
UHT
1

itt nyílik
open here
10
tehéntúró
jásztej
250 g
itt nyílik
open here
25
tehéntúró
cottage cheese
250 g

1·5
tejmilk
UHT
1·5
tejmilk
1 Liter
2·8
2·8
tejmilk
1 Liter
3·6
tejmilk
UHT
3·6
tejmilk
1 Liter

The no bs Drink

Design Agency: Saffron Brand Consultants

Creative Director: Saffron

Designer: Design Team Saffron

Client: Coca-cola

Creating Date: 2009

Information: Saffron worked with Coca-Cola Spain from the concept phase creating a vibrant expression for this great little drink. These joyful illustrations will not go unnoticed by those thirsty for new flavours.

Paper Bottle

Design Agency: Brandimage—Desgrippes & Laga

Client: Innovation

Creating Date: 2009

Information: The 360 Paper Bottle is a sustainable vision of the future. It's a first totally recyclable paper made from 100% renewable resources.

Sugoi Kuro Daizu

Design Agency: E. Co., Ltd
Art Director: Takeshi Nagata
Designer: Yutake Hirose
Photography: Tadashi Tomono
Client: Otsuka
Creating Date: 2008
Information: Packaging for a milk replacement drink.

Long's Packaging

Design Agency: Creative Spice Up

Creative Director: Olga Cuzuioc

Designer: Olga Cuzuioc & Christie Craven

Photography: Christie Craven

Client: Long's

Creating Date: 2010

Infermation: The designers developed the brand identity and packaging system for the relaunch of Long's, a gourmet brand of pure handcrafted flavored sauce. The brief was to create a unique food brand centered on homemade products made with natural, premium ngredients. The label is contemporary, yet elegant, bold and fun.

Bill's Dairy Milkshakes Packaging

Design Agency: Ilovedust Design

Client: Bill's Dairy Farm

Creating Date: 2008

Information: Featuring strawberry, chocolate and vanilla flavours, each individual graphic features its own character and specific colour palate. The fun, candy shop style packaging is designed to appeal to a young target market remit of 12 – 25 year olds.

Ei-SHO-GEN "Shin Lu Chu"

Design Agency: GK Graphics Inc., Japan

Client: Kirin Brewery Co., Ltd., Japan

Creating Date: 2005

Information: Shin Lu Chu is liquor made from plums by traditional Chinese steeping method. The illustration of plum was focused on for easy-understanding of the contents. Through these works, Shin Lu Chu had created the expression leading to the next generation of the liquor.

Sea Cider

Design Agency: Ilovedust design

Designer: Matt Howarth

Creative Director: Mark Graham

Design Director: Johnny Winslade

Client: Sea Cider

Creating Date: 2010

Information: The designers were commissioned to create fresh new packaging for a local Dorset cider company. The "Sea Ciders" packaging takes inspiration from all things maritime. Anchors and pirates mix with portholes, crabs and shrimps to create an all-over nautical narrative in this appealing design.

SAMURAI

Information: Vodka SAMURAI. Strict contours cut blow sword of vodka Samurai, effectively embodies the idea of product. Nice designer solution. As the materials to be used high-quality glass with decoration.

Cognac FLEUR DE LIS

Information: Femininity is characterised as the name and the elegance of lines and shapes.
Vertical and continuously on the three planes of bottles and boxes placed a legend about the origin of the symbol of France FLEUR DE LIS. Using uncharacteristic of cognac capping is not only convenient but also practical, design clearly distinguishes the product from the total mass of similar.

Vodka STARLEY

Design Agency: StudioIN
Designer: Arthur Schreiber
Client: Vodka Starley
Creating Date: 2008
Information: Customer has chosen a modern, clean and simple design, red logo on a background of matte aluminum characterising masculinity. The label is executed on the metal material of flex-printing.

Éxtasis

Design Agency: Series Nemo Design

Designer: Own Team

Client: Destilerías MG

Creating Date: 2010

Information: For all kind of animals. Éxtasis, energy drink with Vodka. An elegant image for an "inappropriate" message.

Wine Packaging

Design Agency: Tridimage

Creating Date: 2009

Information: Tridimage payed homage to the rocky soil that nourishes these wines, and to the different nationalities of the winery founder´s group, designing for each varietal a capital I letter composed by different indigenous South American rocks.

C'EST LA VIE – Wine Labels

Designer: David Guarnieri

Creative Director: Louis Gagnon

Art Designer: David Guarnieri

Client: Maison Albert Bichot

Creating Date: 2008

Information: Established in 1831, Maison Albert Bichot is a well-known French wine producer with products on the market in more than 100 countries. The company awarded Paprika the mandate of creating labels that respected the Bichot family tradition while adapting to new products specifically targeted for distribution in North America. Paprika created labels with a focus on French know-how and reputation, as well as on the spirit and pleasure of drinking good wine.

2010 No House Wine Giftset

Design Agency: Studio Boot

Client: 2010 No House Wine Giftset

Creating Date: 2010

Information: No House Wine packagings are designed with use of low cost materails only. The profits from the sale of this wine are used to built homes for homeless children who, due to the loss of parents to AIDS, are now "young heads cf household" caring for younger brothers and sisters.

GNLD, Tré

Design Agency: Juli Shore Design, Inc.

Creative Director: Juli Shore-Sonke

Client: GNLD, International

Creating Date: 2008

Information: GNLD produced all whole food based products, represented by the ingredient imagery on front of box. The balance of vivid colour and a cleanliness of white negative space represents the vitality this product brings along with a scientific credibility.

GNLD, Pro Vitality Dietary Supplement

Design Agency: Juli Shore Design, Inc.

Creative Director: Juli Shore-Sonke

Client: GNLD, International

Creating Date: 2008

Information: The pyramid – shaped package represents the food pyramid and the steps to a healthy diet regarding balanced nutrition from each category in the triangle. GNLD produced whole food based products, represented by the ingredient imagery on front of box.

Sundance All-Day Suckers

Design Agency: Juli Shore Design, Inc.

Creative Director: Juli Shore-Sonke

Client: Sundance Catalog Company

Creating Date: 2008

Information: JSD created unique, one-of-a-kind packaging for Sundance's Holiday Gifts. The packaging reflects Sundance's artisan style and the richness and diversity that is woven into the Americana aesthetic. Inspired by Vintage candy packages and retro typography, this package tells the story of a family candy business dating back to the early 1900's.

Tea Forte

Design Agency: Juli Shore Design, Inc.

Creative Director: Juli Shore-Sonke

Client: Tea Forte Holiday Teas

Creating Date: 2008

Information: JSD created a festive holiday package for Tea Forte, for a great, giftable tea.

Gin Mare

Design Agency: Series Nemo Design

Designer: Own Team

Client: Global Premium Brands

Creating Date: 2010

Information: The design of the bottle combines the straight and curvy ways with white and blue reflexes that suggest a synthesis between sea and sky, water and foam. A singular bottle stopper wraps all the neck of the bottle strenghtening thus its Premium character.

Ginmg Packaging

Design Agency: Seriesnemo Design

Designer: Own Team

Client: Destilerías MG

Creating Date: 2009

Information: A new packaging, with marking and an exclusive customization, containing the original gin of Destilerías MG. The design of the new bottle of Gin MG has been awarded with a Best Pack Award.

Balblair Single Malt Scotch Whisky

Design Agency: NTGJ studio

Client: BALBLAIR

Creating Date: 2010

Information: This passionately designed pack preserves the essence of premium and expensive single malt whisky. NTGJ intentionally mixed "rough" and traditional materials like real Scottish wool and cork with new and "hi-tech" ones like aluminum, used on the cap and on some details.

GINJA D'ÓBIDOS Premium Edition

Design Agency: NTGJ studio

Client: GINJA D'ÓBIDOS

Creating Date: 2010

Information: The design of the bottle is elegant and the graphics are very simple and modern. The simplicity of the design contrasts with the complexity of the product itself. The liquor contains cherries inside and that makes a very interesting visual effect. Gold and red colours have always been connected with royalty, which highlights the premium quality of the product. The logo is simple and the symbol represents the Castle of Óbidos, the village where the liquor comes from.

O Ultra Premium Olive Oil

Design Agency: NTGJ studio

Client: BALBLAIR

Creating Date: 2010

Information: The logo is an "O" with a hole on the middle from where you can see the colour of the olive oil. The bottle is made by glass and painted with a gradient, from white to transparent. On the bottom you can see the olive oil clearly, in a beautiful and interesting visual effect. The cap is made by cork, giving a traditional and "hand made" feeling to the product.

Celt Ales

Design Agency: Kutchibok
Creative Director: Alwyn Thomas, Siôn Dafydd
Design Director: Alwyn Thomas, Siôn Dafydd
Designer: Alwyn Thomas, Siôn Dafydd
Photography: Matt Cant
Client: The Celt Experience
Creating Date: 2009
Information: To achieve the sense of history and Celtic tradition, Kutchibok used distressed foiling on an uncoated craft paper, recalling the Bronze Age during which the Celts thrived, thus emphasising the historical aspect of their brewing methods. The labels had to reflect the high quality of the bottled ales, and so it was vital that the packaging stood out from the bar shelves and back-lit fridges – attracting the attention of discerning consumers.

Ch.ACO Contemporary Art Fair Catalogue

Design Agency: Base design

Client: Ch.ACO Contemporary Art Fair

Creating Date: 2009

Information: 2009 marked the first year of Ch.ACO a contemporary art fair of Chile. The design concept for the catalog relates to the way one experiences the fair itself. Upon entering, one sees the fair as a whole. Once inside, however, the various booths and exhibition sites are often obstructed, offering only hints of the work. The book is structured in much the same way, organising the works in a single horizontal axis throughout, and displaying fragmented titles in the page's margins to emphasize the idea of the contents being parts of a whole.

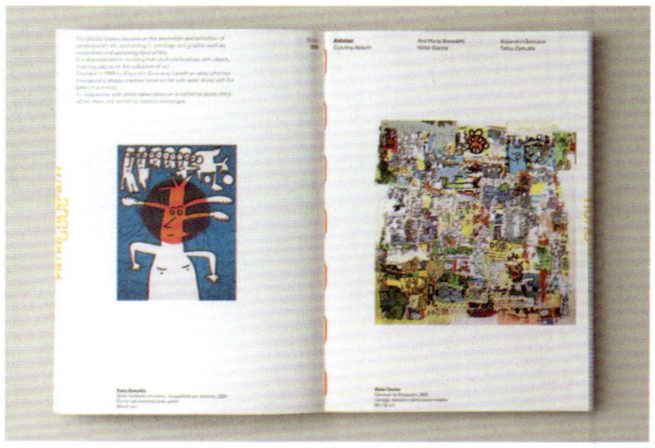

Jeff Koons Gagosian Gallery

Design Agency: Base design

Client: Gagosian Gallery

Creating Date: 2007

Information: In designing the identity for Jeff Koons's "Hulk Elvis" exhibition at the Gagosian London, Base used a square text block to convey relevant information – name of the artist, title of the show, date and location. In contrast to the reverential don't-touch-the-art approach of most gallery materials, this information was set as knock-out text, and positioned over Koons's work to reveal glimpses of the paintings underneath, and to reflect the layers in Koons's work. Base designed the applications for the show, including invitations, advertisements for major art magazines and daily newspapers, a poster, and catalog. While the show was held in summer 2007, the book was released, by Rizzoli, in January 2010.

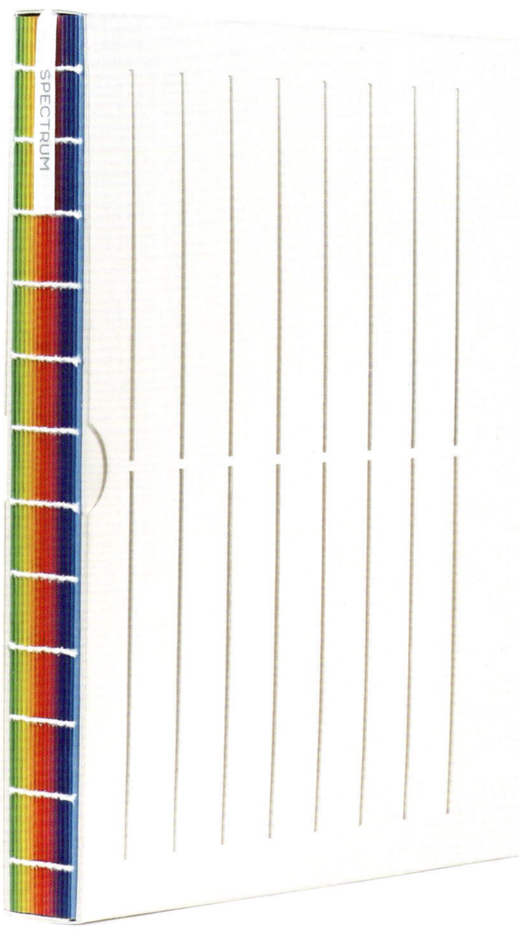
SPECTRUM

SPECTRUM
Designed by Jesse Kirsch

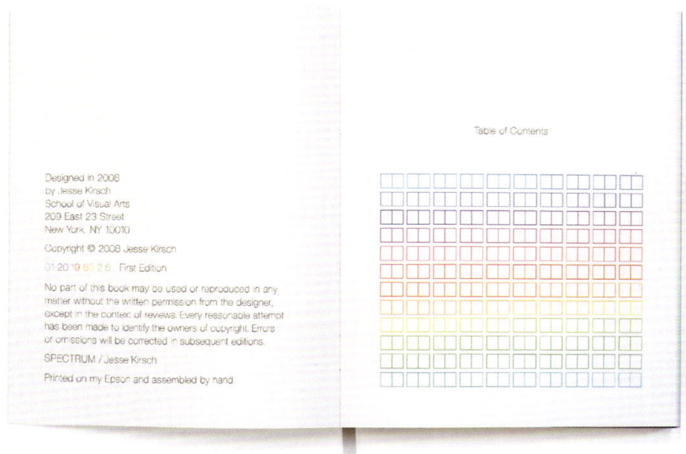
Designed in 2008
by Jesse Kirsch
School of Visual Arts
209 East 23 Street
New York, NY 10010
Copyright © 2008 Jesse Kirsch
First Edition
No part of this book may be used or reproduced in any matter without the written permission from the designer, except in the context of reviews. Every reasonable attempt has been made to identify the owners of copyright. Errors or omissions will be corrected in subsequent editions.
SPECTRUM / Jesse Kirsch
Printed on my Epson and assembled by hand
Table of Contents

Spectrum

Design Agency: How design

Design: Jesse Kirsch

Creating Date: 2009

Information: SPECTRUM is a designer's resource and a decorative art book in one. The way the book is constructed and presented serves to compliment the colour inside without overshadowing it. Each spread displays just one colour. When removing the book from its slipcase waves of color shimmer down the front and back of the case. The book is a couple hundred pages long and is a continous, linear gradient showcasing the colour spectrum from the first to final page jumping at just 5% increments from one spread to the next.

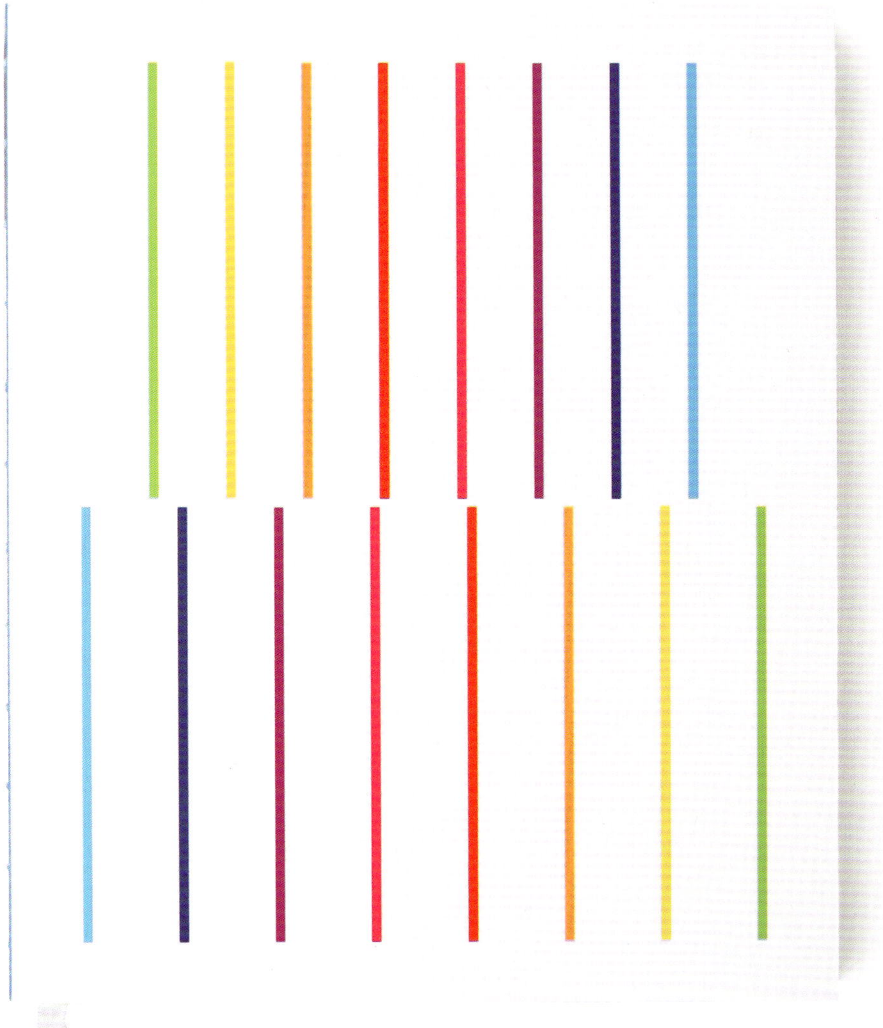

AGDA Ricky Poynor Lecture

Design Agency: TANK

Creative Director: Jim Antonopoulos

Designer: Chris Evans

Client: The Australian Graphic Design Association

Creating Date: 2009

Information: TANK were excited to be given the opportunity to develop the brand identity and promotional material for the Rick Poynor Lecture on Design Thinking and Critical Design. Rick Poynor is one of the world's leading design critics and commentators on graphic design, design thinking and its impact on business and cultural identity.

RICK
POYNOR
AGDA

Publication "Where there is smoke, there is fire"

Design Agency: Trapped in Suburbia

Client: The City of The Hague

Award: Sliver Award in the 2010 European Design Awards

Creating Date: 2009

Information: "Where there is smoke, there is fire" is a publication about the old Caballero Cigarette factory, which has been transformed into a creative work area. Where once cigarettes where made, now creative projects are carried out by architects, photographers, industrial designers, graphic designers, web designers, etc.

The back of the cover and the typography on the front is silkscreen printed with a matchbox structure, so you can actually light a match with the book. Inside the book the designers have used several different kinds of paper that represent the different architectural textures in the building.

Publication "Creative City The Hague"

Design Agency: Trapped in Suburbia

Client: The City of The Hague

Photography: Robert jan Verhagen

Creating Date: 2008

Information: The programme "Creative City" The Hague' has been up and running for 3 years. This publication gives good insight in these results. The book is a building block and all the books together make a beautiful construction, symbolizing all the creative people working together in making the "creative city".This book has won a bronze award in the International Design Award.

Publication "Hi Brand Book"

Design Agency: Trapped in Suburbia

Client: Hi

Creating Date: 2009

Information: Hi is a Dutch telecom company which aims at young adults as their primary target group. With this brand book they wanted to inspire their managers to "live the lives of their target group" instead of looking in from the outside. That's why the designers chose to make the brand book look like an agenda as used daily by a young adult. It's filled with pictures, stickers, concert and train tickets, flyers, a beer mat with phone numbers, you name it; it's is in. The book contains several scratch ink tests, 5 double blind fold out pages, stickers, a letter of resignation (in case you fail the scratch tests), lots of illustrations, UV spot ink and a huge pop-up. All in all a fantastic project to work on.

week 60
61
maandag
Met Hi hoef je helemaal niks te missen
Wij hebben altijd alle lijnen open om niets te hoeven missen. De behoefte aan contact is grenzeloos. We geloven dat de onderlinge band binnen de Hi Society alleen maar hechter wordt naarmate we meer en vaker contact met elkaar hebben
52

PERSOONLIJKE GEGEVENS
NOTITIES
JOUW PERSOONLIJKE MERKBOEK

30
31
ONS MERK
IS MEER DAN ALLEEN ONZE PRODUCTEN

ADRESSEN
Welke proposities passen echt bij Hi?
VANDAAG ONLINE

10
11
FAVORIETE
andere
MERKEN
Hi SOCIETY
Kras op de volgende pagina's het vakje met jouw antwoord open.
GO!

Object Magazine

Design Agency: Naughtyfish Design Studio

Client: Object Magazine

Creating Date: 2010

Information: This was a guest-designed issue of Object magazine. The theme of the issue was "Patterns, prototypes and blueprints".

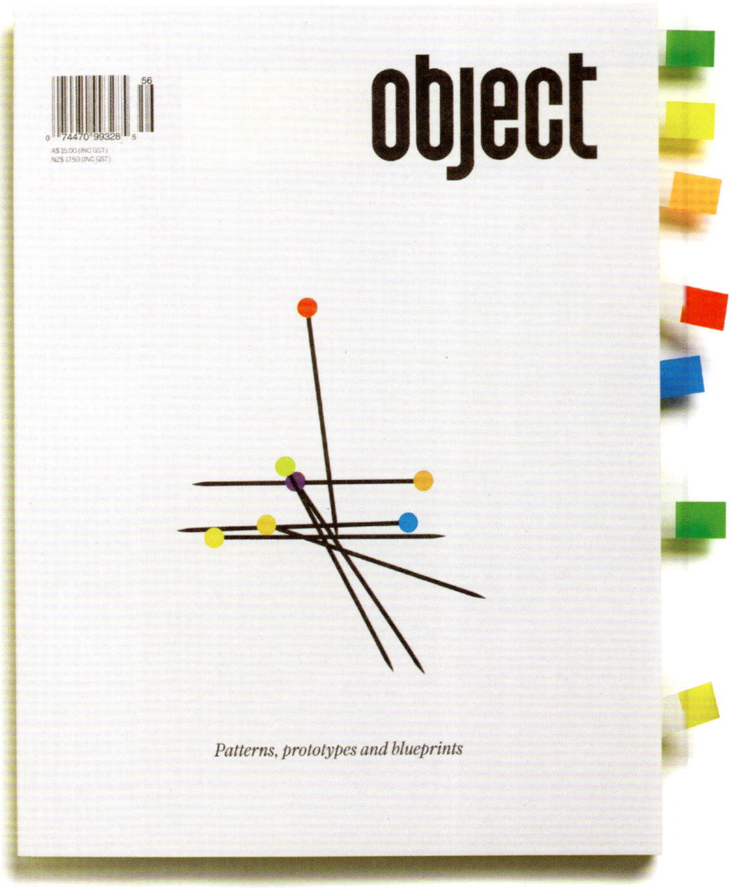

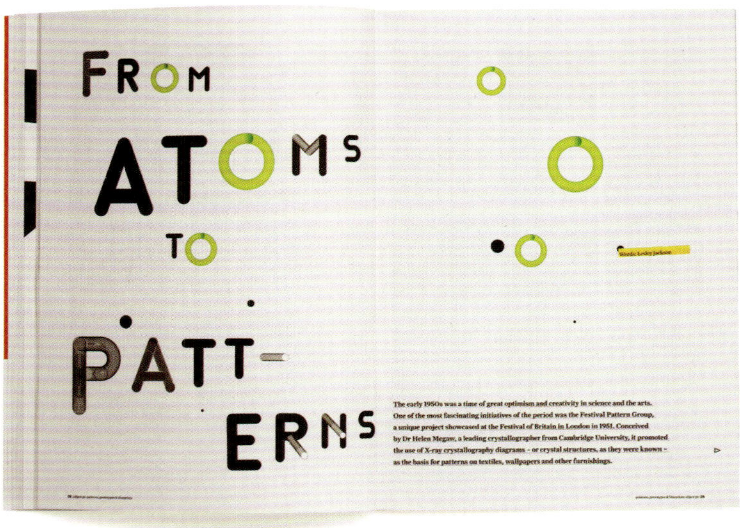

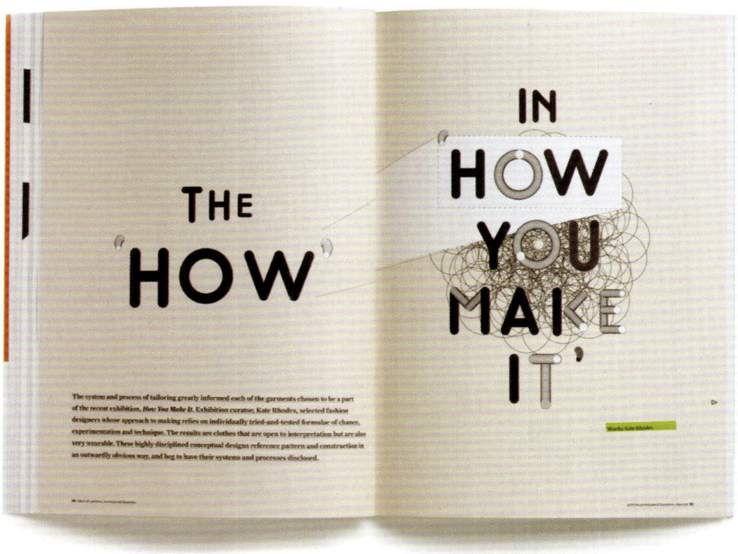

Show & Tell: Naughtyfish Self Promotional Mailer

Design Agency: Naughtyfish Design Studio

Client: Naughtyfish

Creating Date: 2010

Information: This piece was created to give to potential and existing clients. It serves as a glimpse of the studio's recent projects and provides an overview of the designers as a studio. They chose the loose leaf to allow for easy updating.

Mercedes Matter

Design Agency: Studio Kudos

Client: Mark Borghi Fine Art

Creative Director: John Kudos, Kiki Katahira, Studio Kudos

Designer: John Kudos, Kiki Katahira, Studio Kudos

Creating Date: 2009

Information: Catalogue for a retrospective exhibition of Mercedes Matter (1913-2001), a New York–born abstract expressionist painter. Matter is a frequent photographic subject of her husband, Herbert Matter, the Swiss graphic designer and photographer, whose work is shown on the cover. By printing her name along the edges of this large format book, Kudos intend to capture her understated life and career being close friends with Jackson Pollock, Lee Krasner, Franz Kline, Philip Guston, Alexander Calder and Willem de Kooning.

Co.lectiva

Design Agency: Menta
Client: Valencia Youth Concil (CJCV)
Creative Director: Raúl Climent
Designer: Xavi Calvo & Elisa Gómez
Photography: Robert jan Verhagen
Creating Date: 2009
Information: The first issue of this nonprofit organisation magazine is directed towards young people to promote the associationism. Each number of the magazine is a monograph on a current issue, for the first one it's about the accommodation problem for the young people, and this is the theme for the cover and the colour of each number.

ECO Message

Design Agency: Taste Inc.

Designer: Toskiyasu Nanbu

Client: Taste Inc.

Creating Date: 2008

Information: As for the paper designed by the laser cutting, the message by typeface is intertwined. The page and the page mutually influence. As for the detail of delicate paper, the sensibility of the person who touches this book is tested. A delicate structure is not damaged if it treats gently. Paper screams when violently touching. It is a message to the global environment by typographic design book.

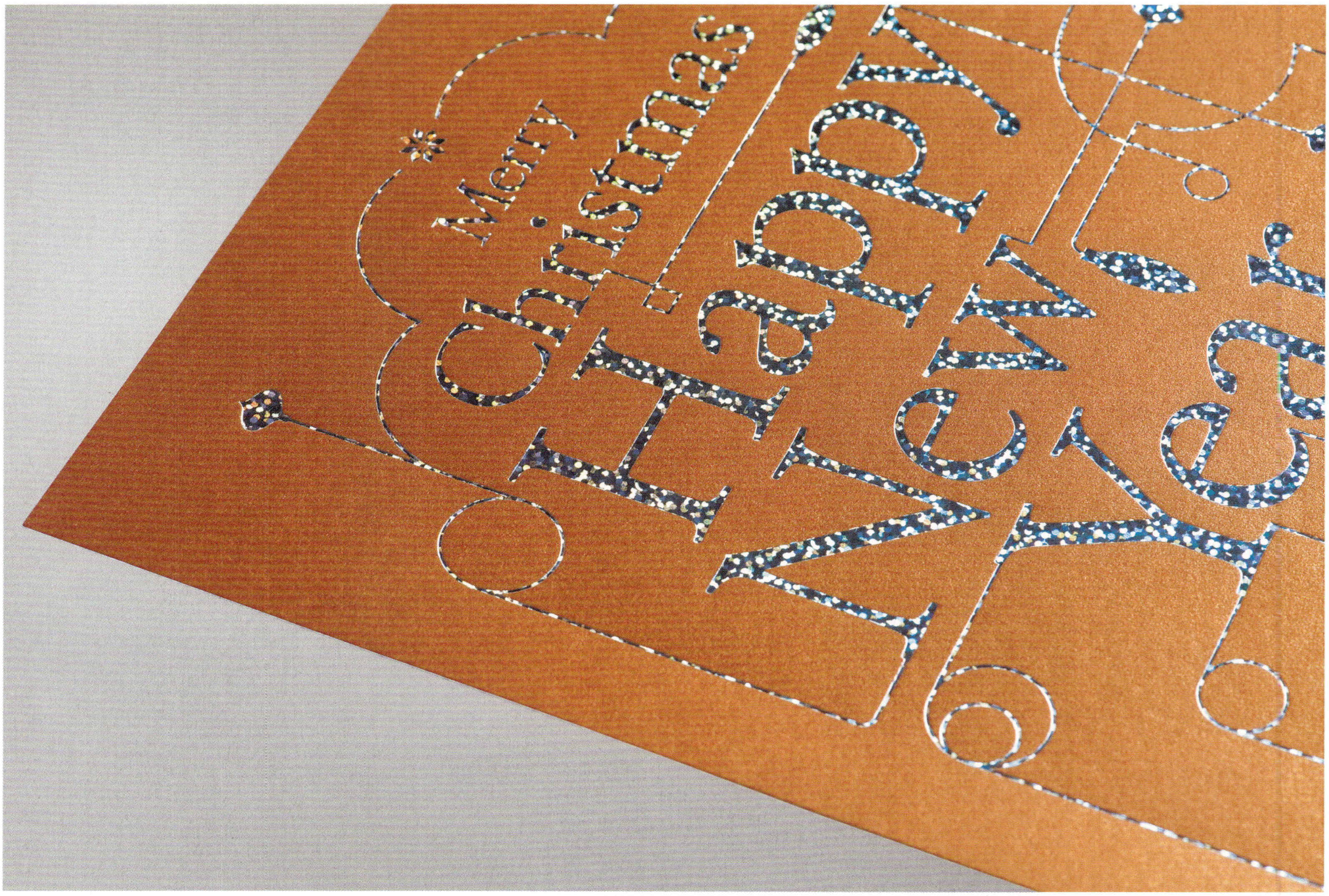

MS2

Design Agency: 3group
Designer: Ryszard Bienert
Client: MS2
Creating Date: 2010
Information: This is a New Year's postcard.

Nelec Studio

Design Agency: 3group

Designer: Ryszard Bienert

Client: Nelec Studio

Creating Date: 2008

Information: Business Cards series created for Nalec Studio of Photography. Strong, bold typography gets attention of the viewer, it's influenced by strong polish typography style of 60's. Strong metallic colour of hot stamp foil contrasts with natural cardboard. Different colours were assigned to each employee of the Studio.

Design Museum

Design Agency: Vonsung

Client: Design museum

Creating Date: 2008

Information: The design museum in London cooissined Vonsung to design their bookmark for their quarterly design overtime events. A festive night of shopping, music, and making,the SPARKLE THE DARK UP events aimed at Christmas shopping done early in the design museum shop. Vonsung also had to hignlight the current museum's showcase, celebrating the love of ceramics at the Design museum's exhibition patricia urquiola-purely porcelain.Their bookmark was deisgned to be one-part shopping bag,one-part porcelain mug.

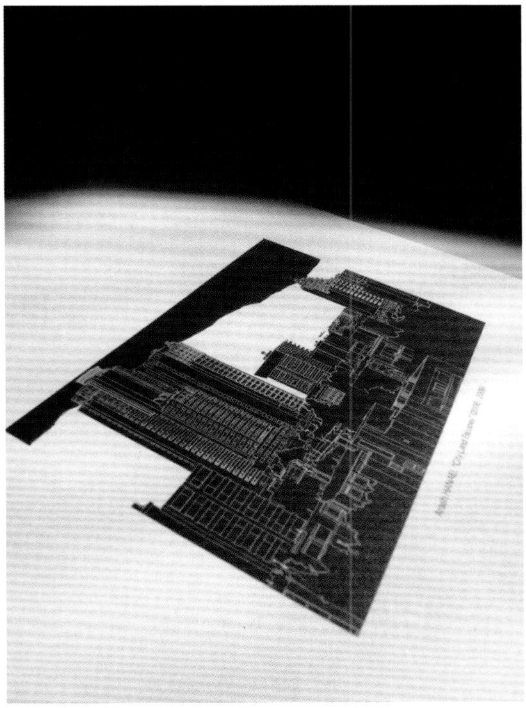

Made in Iran

Design Agency: Vonsung

Client: A&E Projects

Creating Date: 2009

Information: MADE IN IRAN was the exhibition for 7 contemporary Iranian artists. The art is very colourful and powerful, so Vonsung decided the brochure to be white canvas vis-a-vis a gallery's white cube space. They also use a bold black font for the exhibition identity, showing the strong Iranian art feel.

D2 Printers

Design Agency: Ilovedust

Client: D2 Printers

Creating Date: 2008

Information: D2 wanted to do a promotional piece to showcase their FSC accreditation and demonstrate the importance they know environmental sustainability and responsibility have within their industry.

Ilovedust came up with a unique concept using the innovative combination of layers, cutouts, illustrations and graphics to detail the journey of the paper – from the original forest the tree was grown in, through the pulp mill, the paper mill, the paper merchant – with the journey ending at the finished paper product.

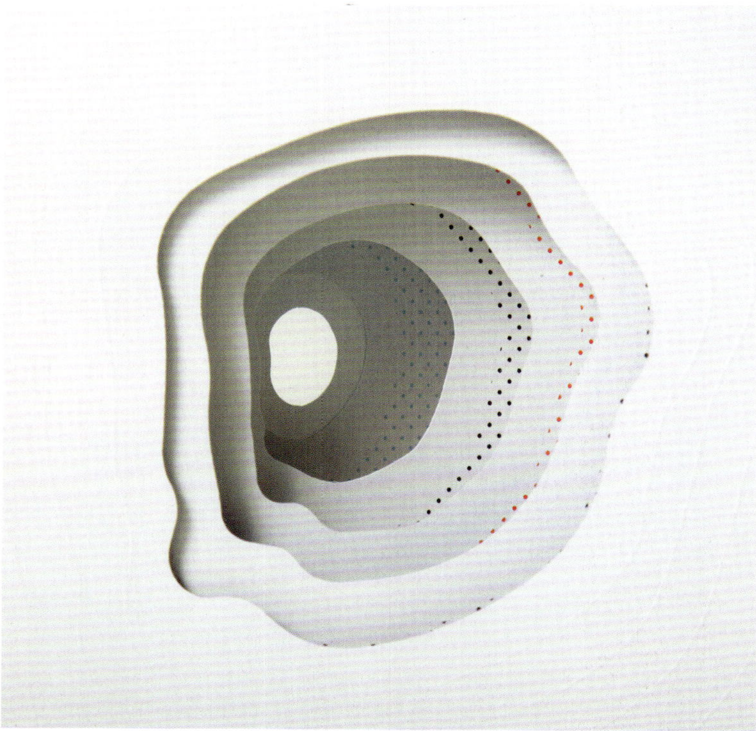

The Gift of Sound & Vision

Design Agency: Trapped in Suburbia

Client: Institute of Sound & Vision

Creating Date: 2008

Information: For the Institute of Sound and Vision the designers made a unique farewell present for their departing president. In the publication they've translated video and sound on to the 600 pages. The book contains David Bowies "Sound and vision"(single version), pop-ups, a dvd, several flip booklets and a RFID tag.

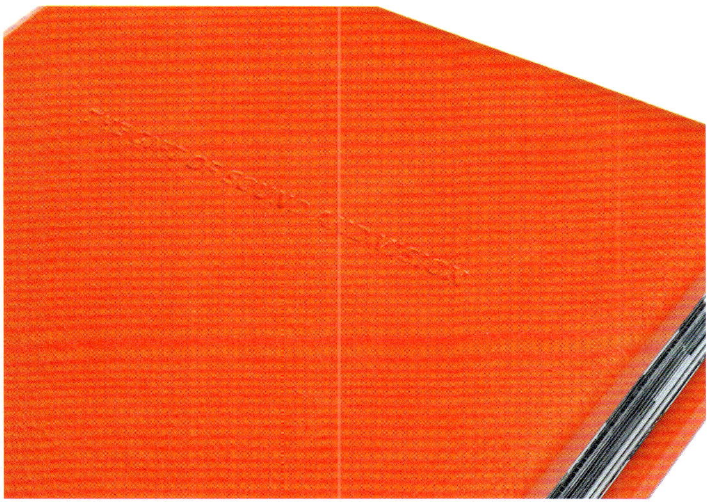

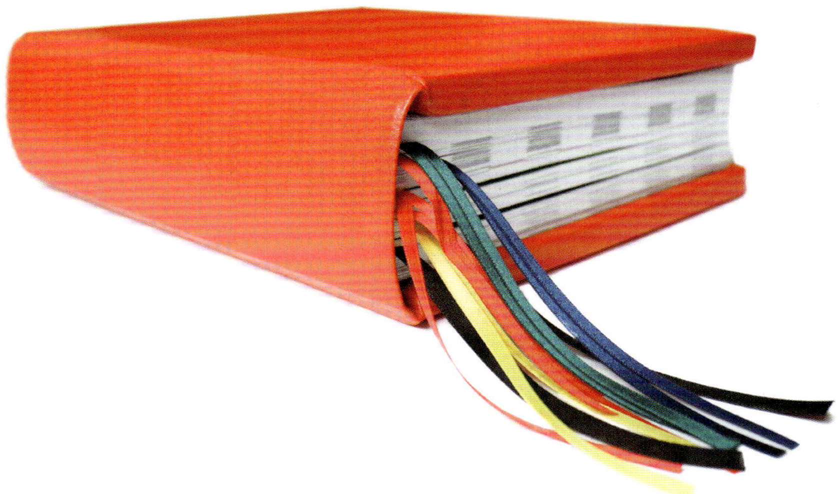

Playlab

Design Agency: Mind design

Creative Director: Holger Jacobs

Art Director: Craig Sinnamon

Illustrator: Craig Sinnamon

Client: Playlab

Creating Date: 2009

Information: Identity and stationery for Playlab, a workshop space aimed to be a creative playground for stressed adults. The Illustrations used are a mixture of scientific elements and random fun images. The stationery is printed in fluorescent Pantone colours while the actual logo is just blind embossed. The address details are filled in using a rubber stamp.

Activity 3: Colouring

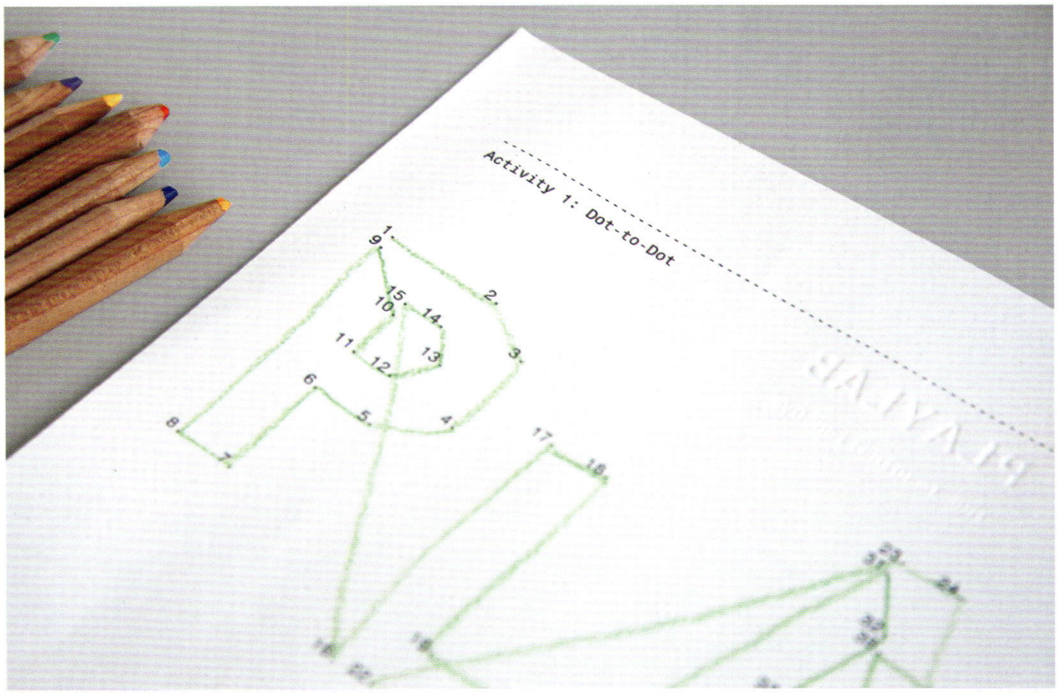
Activity 1: Dot-to-Dot

LA Earthquake Source Book

Art Director: Stefan Sagmeister

Designer: Richard The, Joe Shouldice, Mark Pernice

Illustrator: Stephan Walter

Client: Art Center College of Design

Creating Date: 2008

Information: A source book to prepare California residents for the impending "Big One". Attached to the bookmark ribbon is a self-righting wobble that just won't fall over.

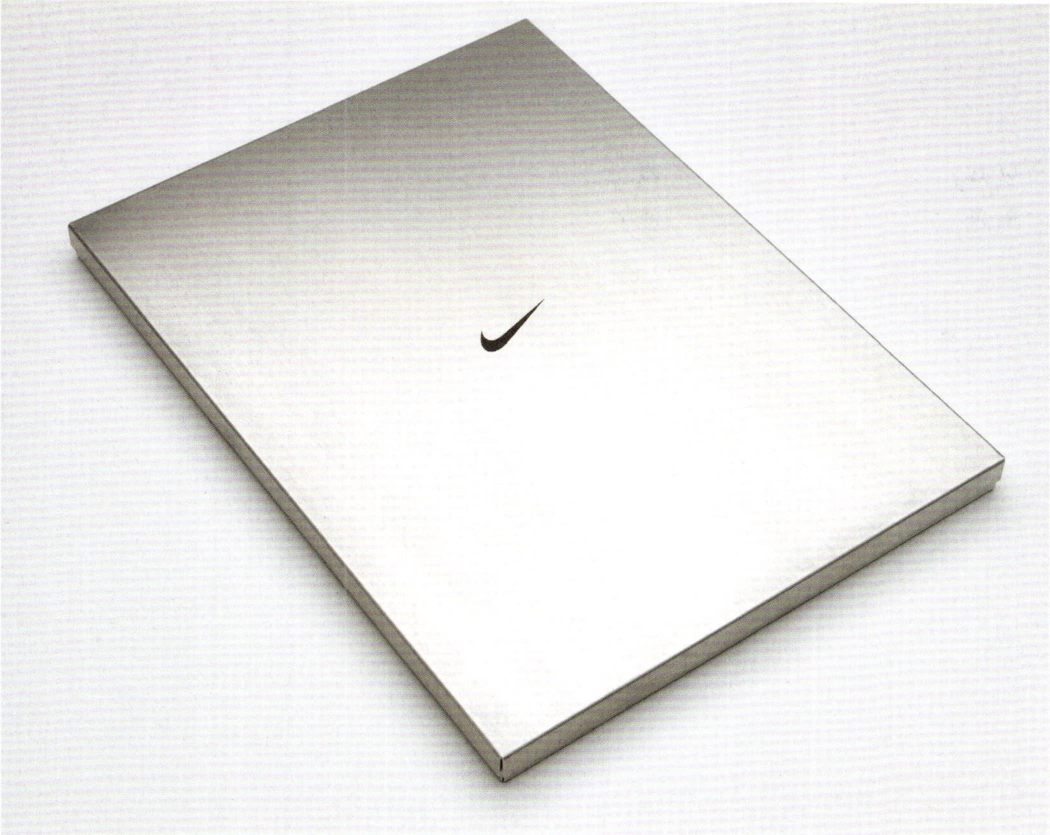

Nike Premium Performance

Design Agency: PLAZM

Art Director: Joshua Berger

Designer: Todd Houlette

Client: Nike Asia Pacific

Creating Date: 2007

Information: Custom media package to roll out a campaign focused on product innovation. Born from obsession.

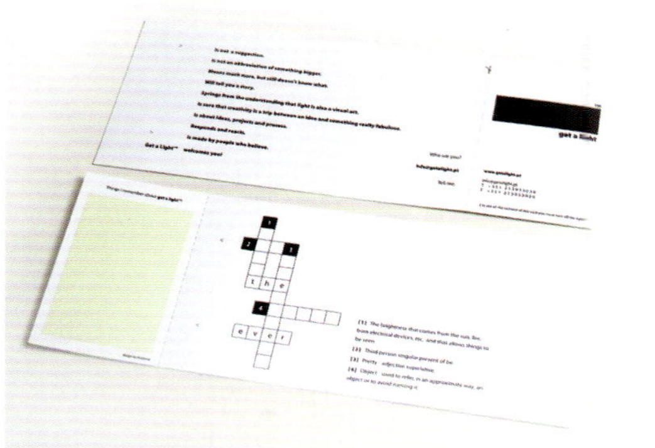

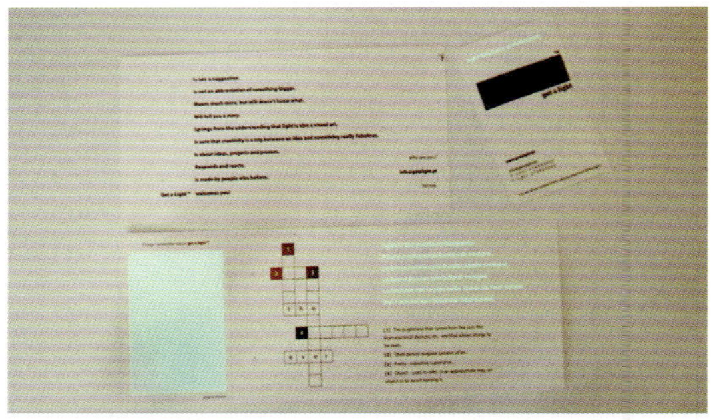

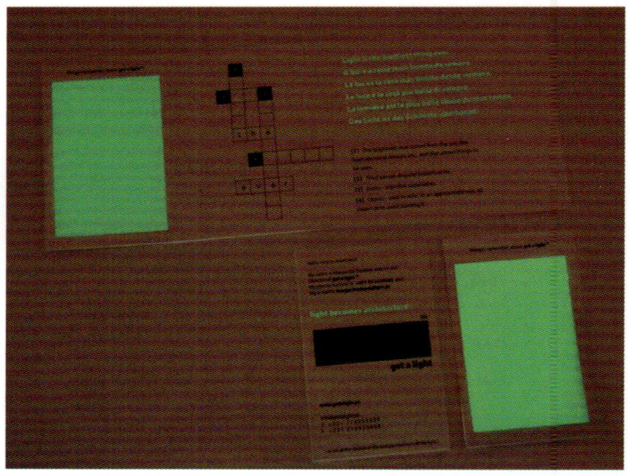

Get a Light

Design Agency: Thisislove studio

Creative Director: Joana Areal

Design: Joana Areal

Client: Get a light

Creating Date: 2010

Information: Get a Light is a Lisbon-based Light Design Studio focused on experimenting and researching new forms of approaching light and architecture.

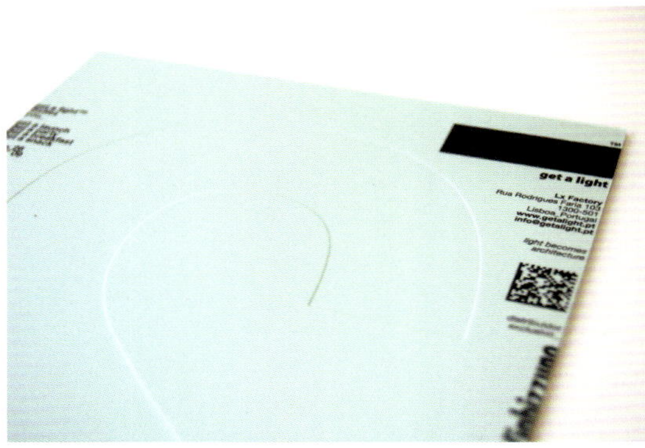

Get a Light Second B-day

Design Agency: Thisislove studio

Creative Director: Joana Areal

Design: Joana Areal

Client: Get a light

Creating Date: 2010

Information: Official invitation, microsite and wine label for get a light 2 year anniversary event.

'no no!' said the queen. 'sentence first, verdict afterwards.'
hello, I'm your notebook!
don't break my heart...
feed me!
drink to me
what's in the fridge?
oh a happy day!
inter-nacional design hotel

hello, I'm your notebook!
don't break my heart...
inter-nacional design hotel

nice to meet you!
inter-nacional design hotel

Internacional Design Hotel

Design Agency: Thisislove studio

Creative Director: Joana Areal

Design: Joana Areal, Inês Veiga

Client: International Design Hotel

Creating Date: 2010

Information: Internacional Design Hotel is a small luxury and design hotel located in the centre of Lisbon that stands for a new hotel concept, providing a personal stay for each customer within four existing scenarios from the four corners of the world: Urban feeling, Tribal setting, Zen feeling and Pop atmosphere.

Moet & Chandon Gold

Design Agency: MusaWorkLab

Designer: MusaWorkLab

Client: Moet & Chandon

Creating Date: 2008

Information: Moet & Chandon Gold party in Oporto city was a party by the Gold concept. Serralves museum was the place, a very distinct art museum. Within this gold and art concept Musa try to concept the invitation using a different size and approach.

Play More

Design Agency: Trapped in Suburbia

Client: Self Initiated

Creating Date: 2007

Award: Bronze medal for "printed self promotion" in 2007 European Design Awards

Information: The designers wanted to get their clients moving behind their desk, so they created this notebook with writing space on one side and side ball patterns on the other. Just screw a piece of paper to a ball and you can play soccer, or rugby, or throw a tennis ball in your waste basket.

HQ:D&B Flyer

Designer: Ross gunter

Client: HQ:D&B

Creating Date: 2010

Information: Flyer designed for a club night. The intent was to create a simple but appealing central graphic, reminiscent of an optical illusion. The promoters agreed to print the flyer on 100% recycled pulp board, a more tactile stock that stood out among the over-saturated market of gloss. The flyer was also printed with two spot colours, to enhance its simplicity and improve the quality of finish.

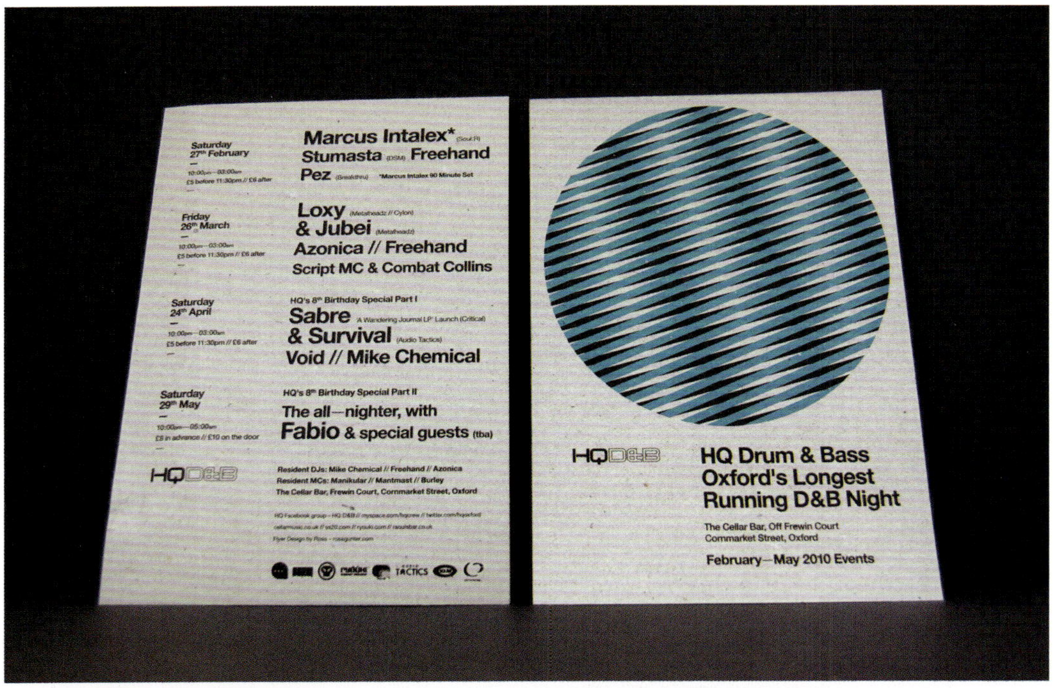

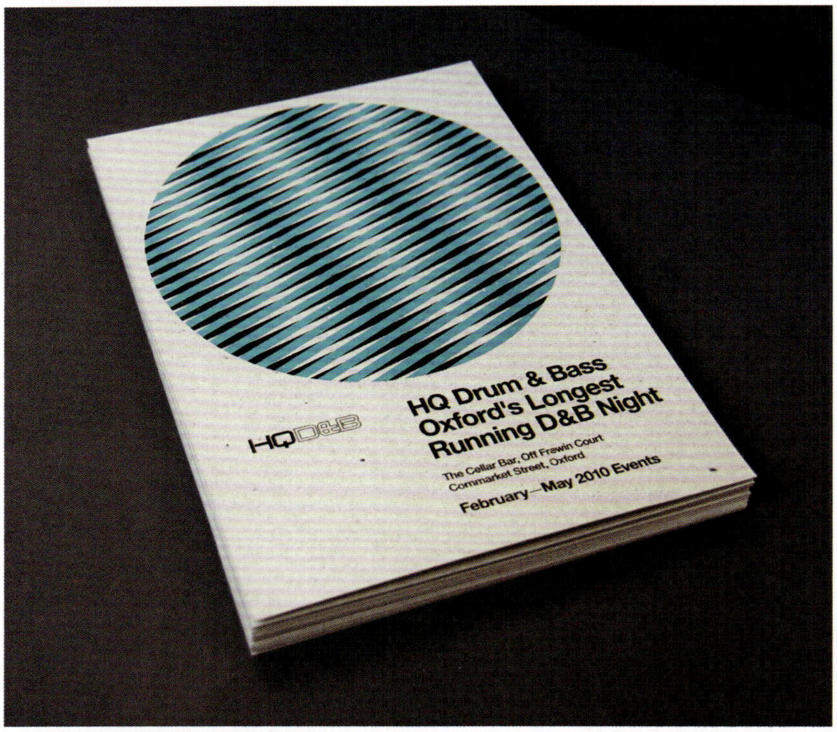

Legal Art Brochure

Design Agency: Lemon Yellow

Client: Legal Art

Creating Date: 2009

Information: Legal Art is an organisation focused on providing artists with affordable legal services and grants opportunities. Lemon Yellow was asked to produce a modular print brochure which outlined the organisation's goals in an interesting context. A fold-out brochure was created consisting of various tear out panels showcasing a selection of internationally renowned emerging and established artists. The piece allowed the reader to interact and obtain a small scale version of their favourite artwork while learning more about the vital role that the arts organisation plays in the community.

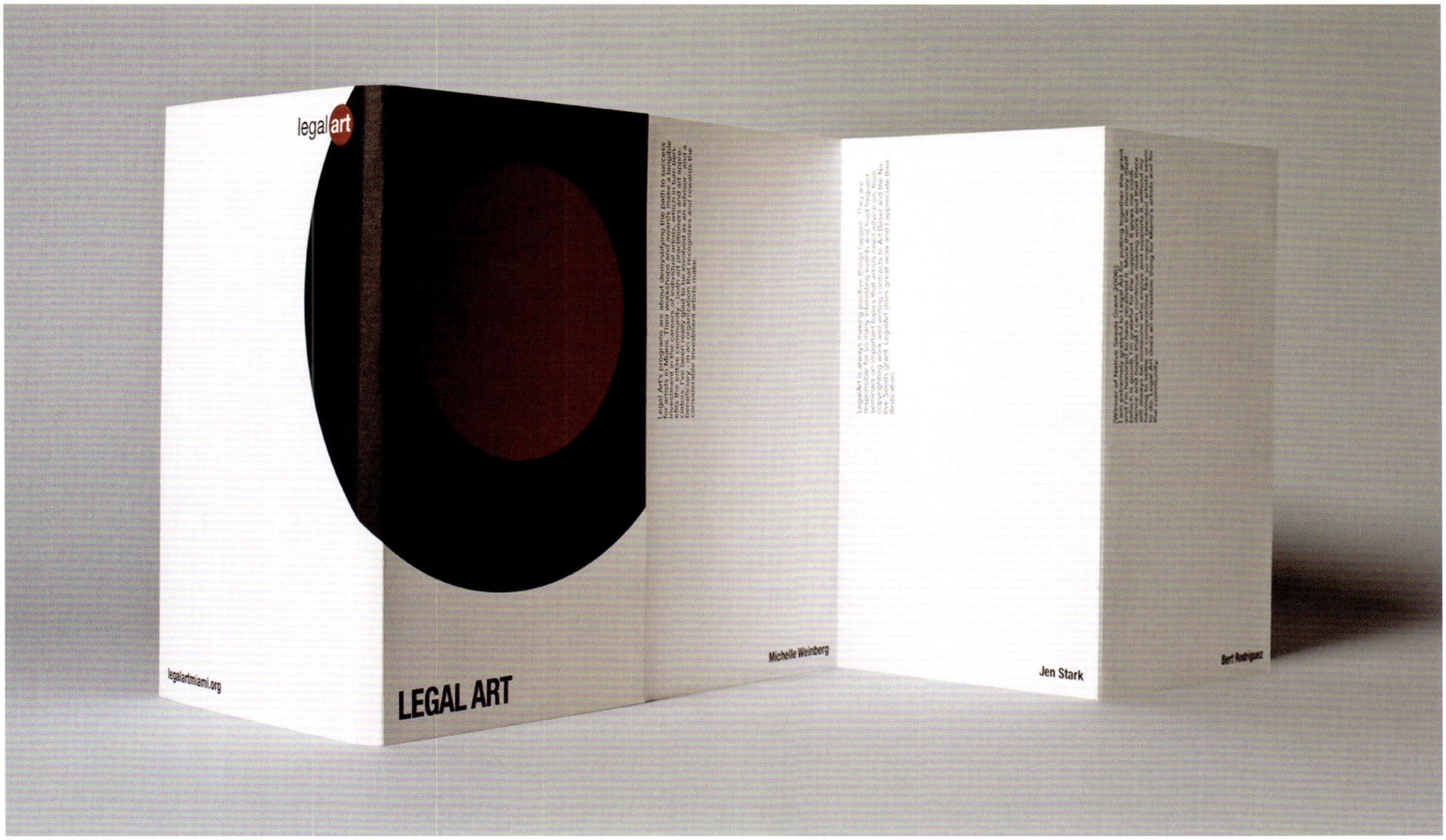

Sandra Boïls, Vocalista de Jazz

Design Agency: Menta

Creative Director: Raúl Climent, Xavi Calvo & Elisa Gómez

Designer: Raúl Climent, Xavi Calvo & Elisa Gómez

Client: Sandra Boïls

Creating Date: 2010

Information: This business card was created for a Jazz Vocalist from Valencia (Spain): Sandra Boïls. She needed something simple and elegant, so Menta proposed a monochromatic design with simple graphics and typography. But what really makes them lovely is the repeating piano key pattern that forms when the cards are layed out side by side.

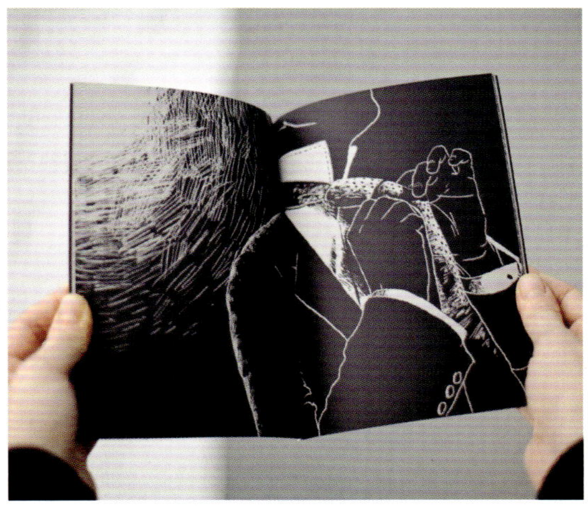

El tiempo de Basilio

Design Agency: Menta

Creative Director: Raúl Climent, Xavi Calvo & Elisa Gómez

Designer: Raúl Climent, Xavi Calvo & Elisa Gómez

Client: Menta

Creating Date: 2009

Information: In the design studio they designed an illustrated book launched with a short print run of limited copies for their clients and friends. This was a gift for Christmas and New Year, a kind of tale about the time, written by Cristina Gómez with illustrations of Raúl Climent. The white title page has a big hot stamping on it, inside the light grey pages with black ink on it puts forth a reflection about how time goes by.

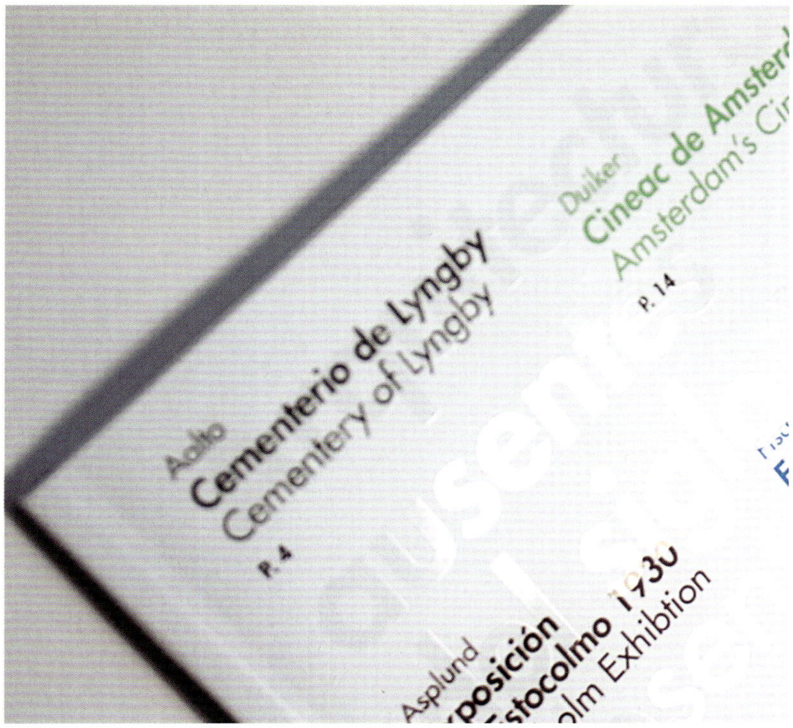

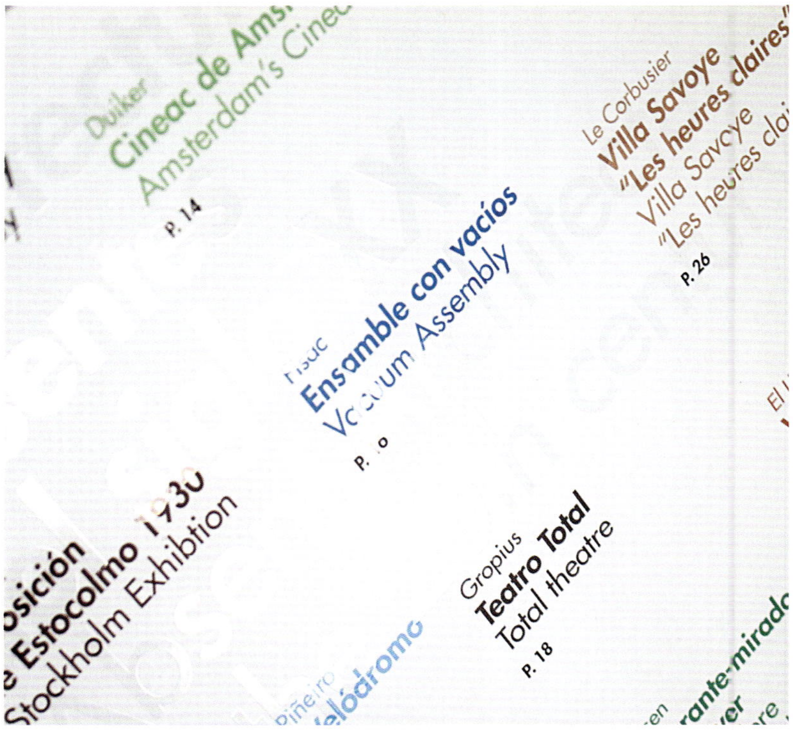

Absent Architecture of the 20th Century

Design Agency: Base design studio

Client: Absent Architectures of the 20th Century

Creating Date: 2010

Information: Absent Architectures of the 20th Century was an exhibition organised by the Minister of Housing dedicated to buildings never contructed, soon demolished or trasformed which have in common their high quality and their capacity to influence subsequent architectural through down to the present. Base designed the catalogue of the exhibition expressing the idea of "absent architectures" through the balance between white spaces and graphics: so the title on the cover has been printed with a UV varnish instead of colour to make it visible only when light shines upon the letter.

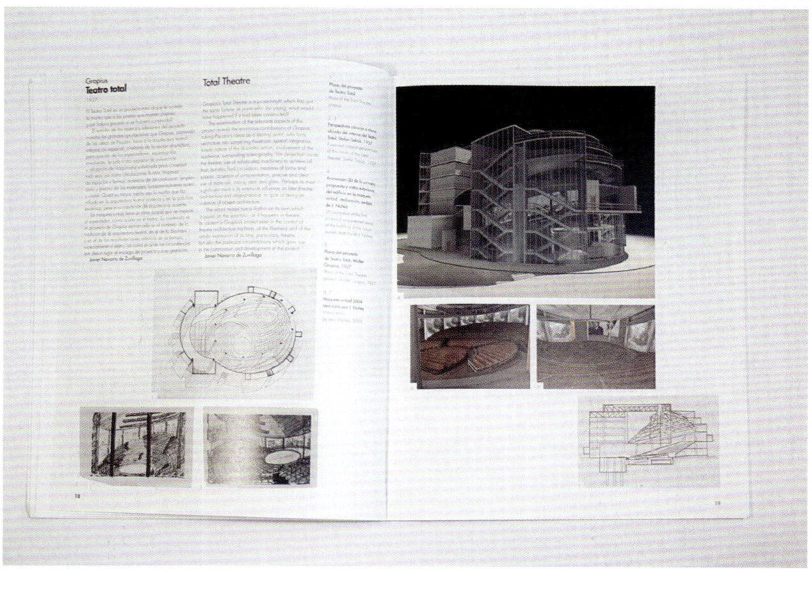

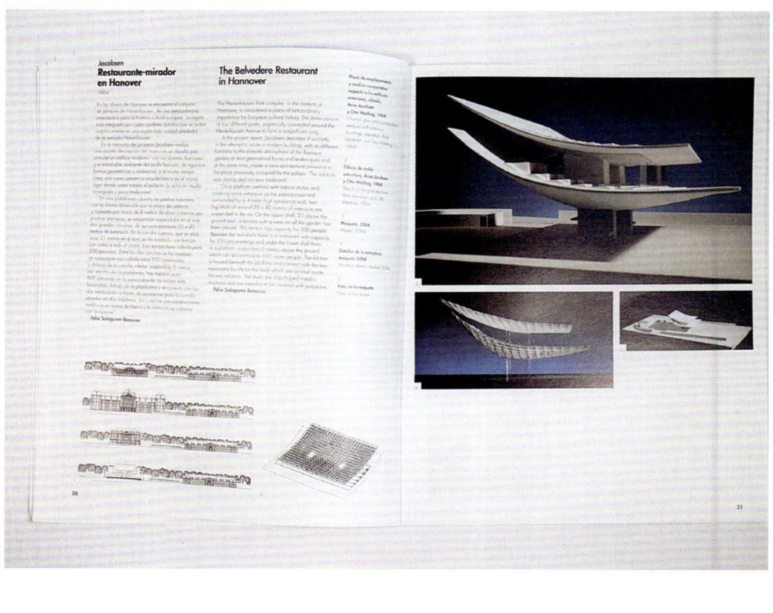

Ryan McGinness Studio Franchise Catalogue

Design Agency: Base design studio

Client: Ryan McGinness Studio

Creating Date: 2010

Information: Base worked with design the catalogue, which presents in-progress shots of the exhibition from the beginning, when the moving trucks are arriving at La Casa with the contents of the studio franchise. Also included in the catalog are essays by Paul Laster and Jordi Costa, and an interview between the curator of the show, Adam Jorquera, and Ryan.

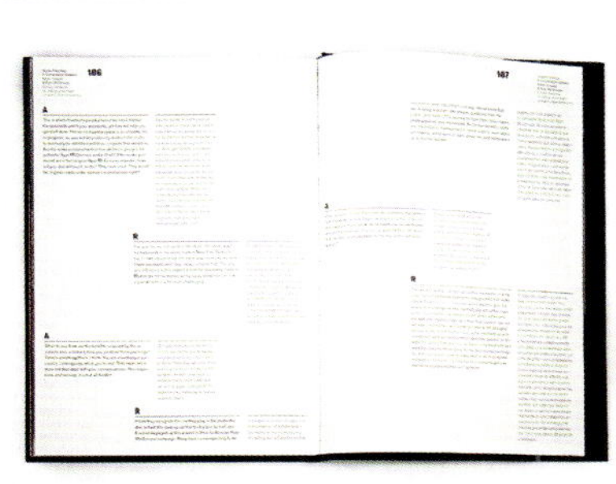

Camouflage Sights

Design Agency: Jamiedelaney

Designer: Jamie Delaney

Client: Camouflage

Creating Date: 2007

Information: Layout and information pack

55
Co. Kildare
Hill of Allen

Folk-
lore
02

The
Goddess
of Almu

CAM-
OU-
FLAGE
SIGHTS
#55

Clampdown

Design Agency: Jamiedelaney

Designer: Jamie Delaney

Client: Clampdown

Creating Date: 2010

Information: Development of typeface and identity to be used for Dublin/London collective of promoters, producers and DJ's, the typeface is the main graphic used across all communication.

3DM Edelman

Design Agency: Jamiedelaney

Designer: Jamie Delaney

Client: Clampdown

Creating Date: 2010

Information: Designed for global PR firm, the idea behind the sub brand was to appeal to the less corporate side of the market. As 3DM, main clients are high profile music festivals and youth orientated events they felt the Edelman brand too corporate for this market.

The Good Guide

Design Agency: Monique Kneepkens

Art Direction: Monique Kneepkens & Justin Overell

Designer: Monique Kneepkens

Creating Date: 2010

Information: At last, Brisbane gets its own street guide, or "the Good Guide". This is a job the designer did for the awesome crew at the Film Garden. This edition of the Good Guide is the first edition of many to come, taking you to all the best places in Fortitude Valley and New Farm. For this job the designer revolved the design around the concept of a pigeon (who knows our city streets better?) and really glorified this little street bird. Complete with a gold foil on the cover and a royal wallpaper for the inside.

Wedding Invite Jade and Tash

Design Agency: Monique Kneepkens

Art Direction: Monique Kneepkens

Designer: Monique Kneepkens

Creating Date: 2009

Information: Jade and Tash,friends of Monique Kneepkens, asked the designer to do their wedding invite. She did the invite as a folded poster, which came in a clear pocket. The pocket showed a decorative illustration that she hand drew, showing Jade's name on one side, and Tash's name on the other side. When one takes the poster out of the clear pocket, the two halves reveal one love-heart. The poster unfolds to an A3 announcement poster, with the full heart-drawing shown and the wedding information.

In Africa Sustainable Christmas Card

Design Agency: In Africa

Art Direction: Monique Kneepkens

Designer: Monique Kneepkens

Creating Date: 2009

Information: In Africa is a non for profit organisation, focussing on rural enterprise development and sustainable growth in Africa. This is the 2009 Christmas Card Kneepkens did for In Africa. The font she designed is a contemporary take on traditional African art. She then wrote the christmas message in this font. The receiver opened an envelope and found our card, an A3 poster, folded to A5. In the bottom there was a sticker with the In Africa logo, and the message "Wrapping the year with seasons greetings from the team at In Africa". The sticker was a peel-off. When the receiver peeled off the sticker the poster could be used as christmas wrapping paper, and that way the sustainable approach is reiforced.

In Africa Business Cards

Design Agency: In Africa

Art Direction: Monique Kneepkens

Designer: Monique Kneepkens

Creating Date: 2009

Information: In Africa is a non for profit organisation, focussing on rural enterprise development and sustainable growth in Africa. For the new stationery Kneepkens has used traditional African symbols. These symbols are used and recognised in the whole of Africa, and all have different meanings, such as "freedom", "iniative", "support", "co-operation", "encouragement", etc. All meanings that also agree with In Africa's work and beliefs.

Collaboration is one of In Africa's key principles. To highlight that, Kneepkens placed the african symbols on the back of the cards, but always 2 halves. Each staff member has a different back design, and only when you put the cards together (when we work together) the symbols become whole.

Design Agency: Fabien Barral
Creative Director: Fabien Barral
Designer: Fabien Barral
Photography: Fabien Barral
Creating Date: 2009
Information: Although Fabien Barral has a logo, he wanted more for his business card: a design that says something about him, and the services he offers, as well as the important "nice to meet you" greeting. New decade, new identity... or at least evolution of the existing one. He has used some of Frédérique's (his wife) textures, which is symbolic as she is very much involved in the creative process. The cards have been printed by Studio on fire.

DSO Fashion

Design Agency: Jamiedelaney

Designer: Jamie Delaney

Client: DSO Fashion

Creating Date: 2010

Information: Design and art direction for this Dublin based fashion brand combining high-quality garments with typographic slogans. This involved styling of all elements of design and photography.

Concretewave

Design Agency: Fabien Barral
Creative director: Fabien Barral
Designer: Fabien Barral
Photography: Fabien Barral
Creating Date: 2010
Information: Another project introduced by more YELLOW. Concrete Wave designs counter tops, floors and sinks in concrete. Their graphic language was based on the concept "A bold wave of expression". The final product was enhanced with metalic inks for the blue and gold spots on the brochure and buisness cards.

Parole

Design Agency: Fabien Barral
Creative director: Fabien Barral
Designer: Fabien Barral
Photography: Fabien Barral
Creating Date: 2009
Information: Eve Schütz writes poems and asked Fabien Barral to create a visual interpretation of her work the result was this "book-object", a cardboard box that contains her poems printed on cards. Some of the pictures used were found in garbage that was about to be incinerated.

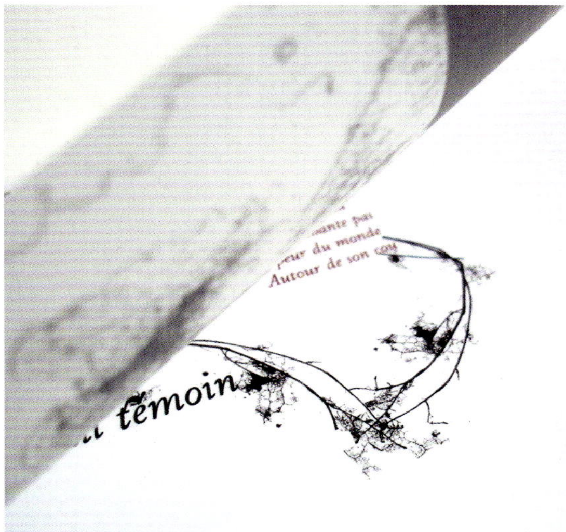

Hiltl

Design Agency: Anton Studer

Client: Hiltl Club

Creating Date: 2010

Information: The Hiltl Club in Zurich has a huge range of customers. From Tango to Hip Hop there is everything possible to happen what makes it very interesting to meet people there.

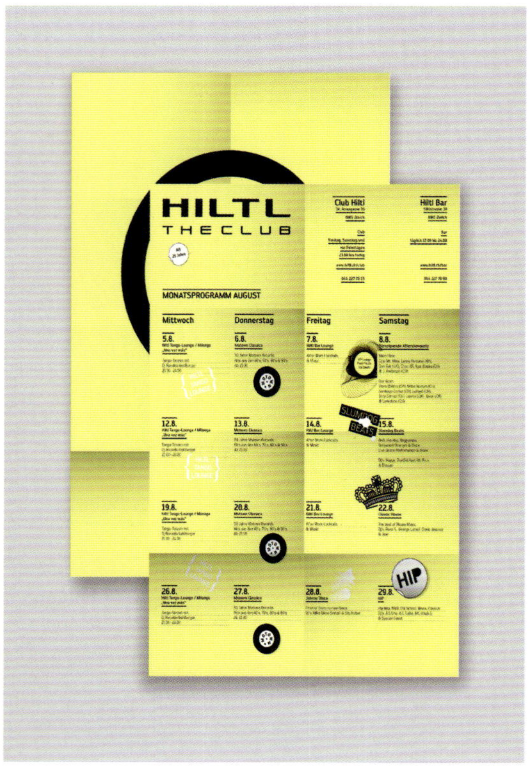

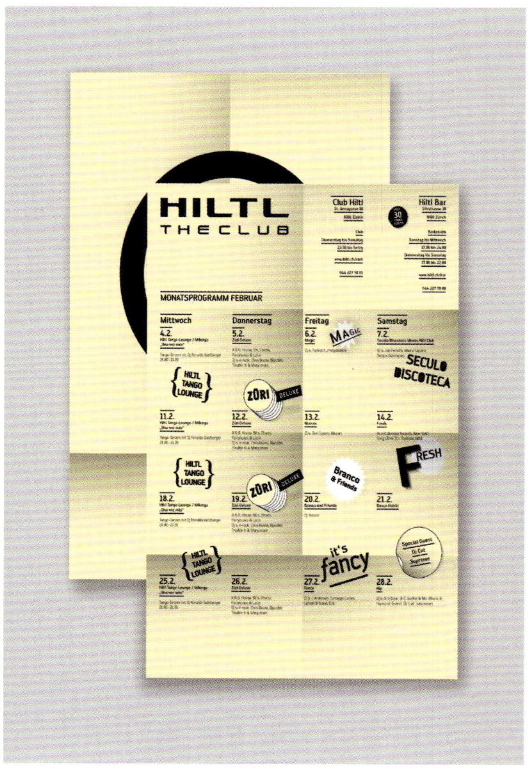

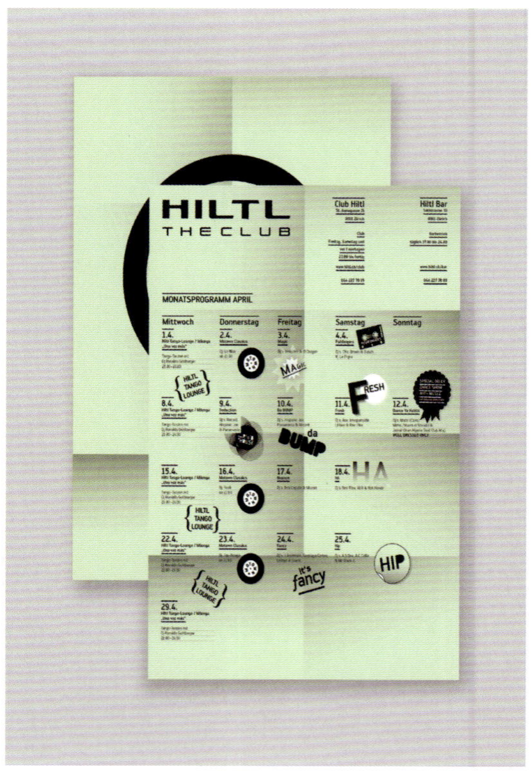

Suomi Disco

Design Agency: Anton Studer
Client: Suomi Disco
Creating Date: 2009
Information: Suomi Disco is a party label from zurich that plays justfinnish music for anybody that likes it.

Marc Ligos Exhibition

Design Agency: Raquel Quevedo

Designer: Raquel Quevedo

Photographer: Jordi Vendrell

Client: Marc Ligos

Creating Date: 2008

Information: Invitation design for the designer Marc ligos.

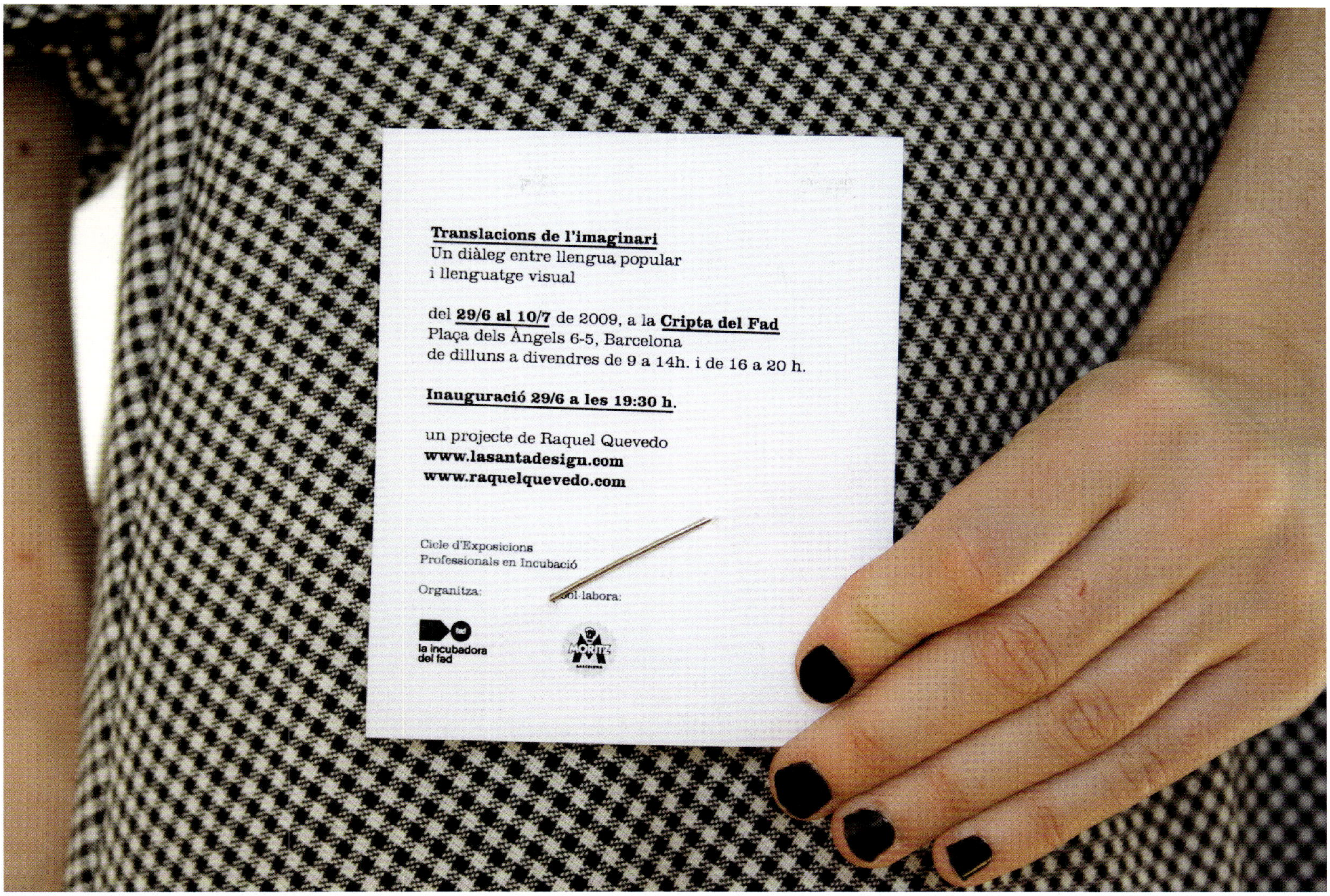

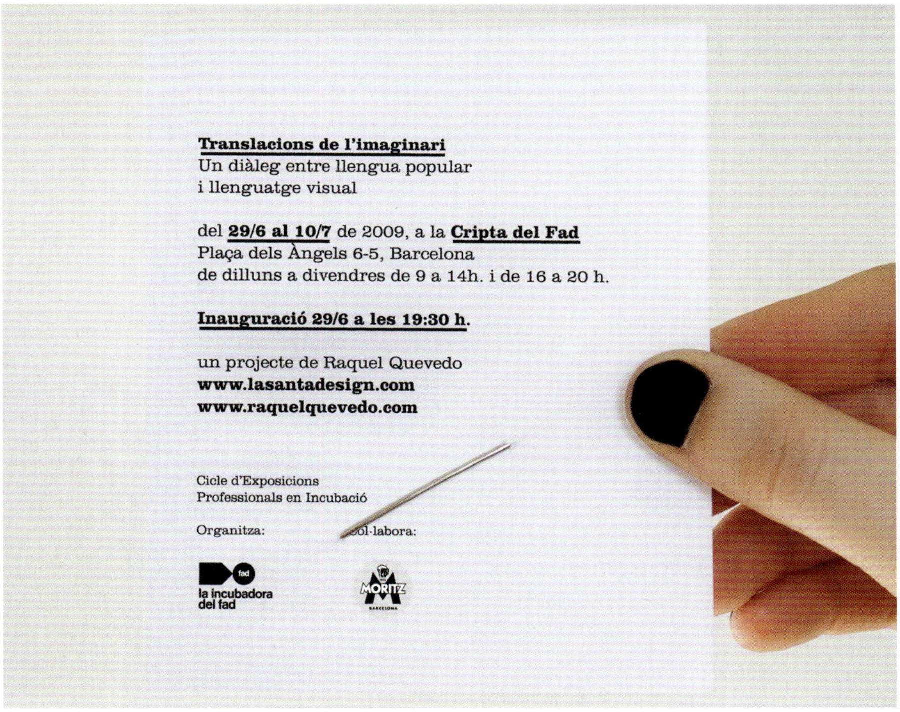

Un Buen Flyer Tiene Que Enganchar al Lector

Designer: Raquel Quevedo

Creative Director: Raquel Quevedo

Client: Raquel Quevedo/La Incubadora del FAD

Creating Date: 2009

Information: The creative concept refers to the subject of the client's exhibition. So, the communicative piece turns into a saying object. The headline refers to a popular design saying and the concept "to get hooked", with the meaning to emphasise the conceptual ambivalence. The arts design for this handmade flyer was thought to emphasise the hanger.

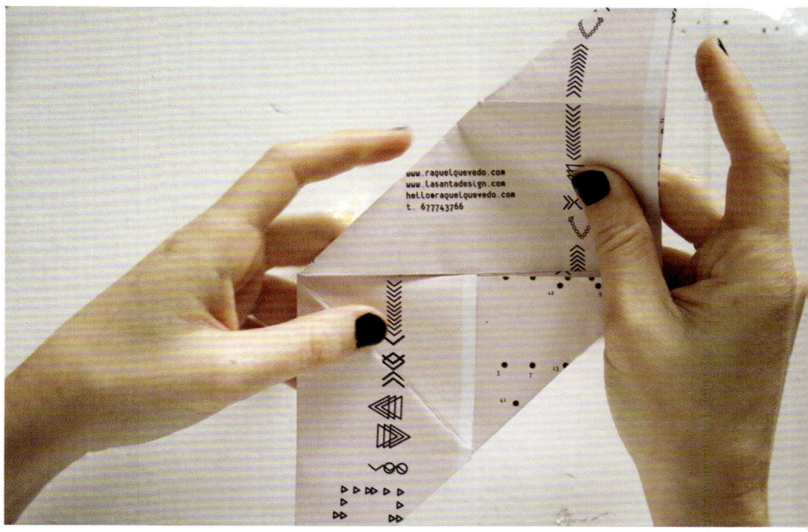

Nice to Meet You

Designer: Raquel Quevedo

Creative Director: Raquel Quevedo

Creating Date: 2009

Information: The concept for Raquel Quevedo presentation card was create a good feeling with the other person, being kindly and sincere. The card invites to participate to the receive, with a code message. This message is clear, direct and kindly, and therefore, the present contributes to create a nice and memorable meeting. The card was dolding with an origami techique, so once unfolded, it is difficult to fold again... maybe in the next meeting.

www.raquelquevedo.com
www.lasantadesign.com
hello@raquelquevedo.com
t. 677743766

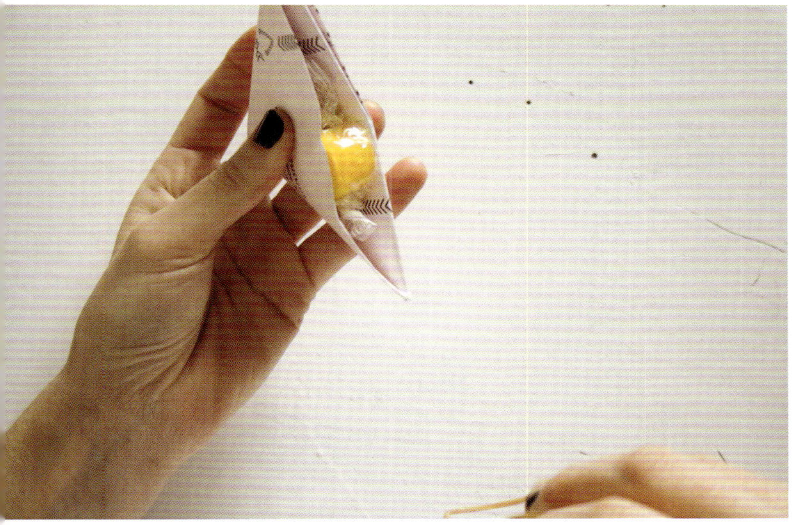

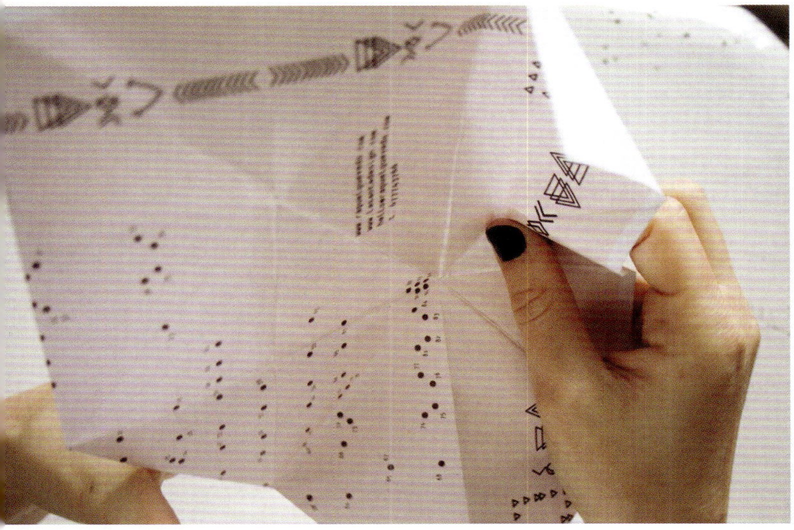

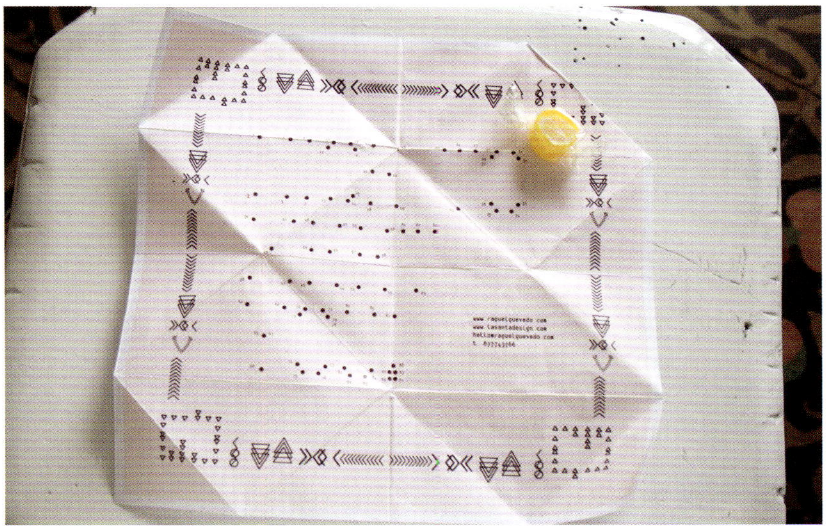

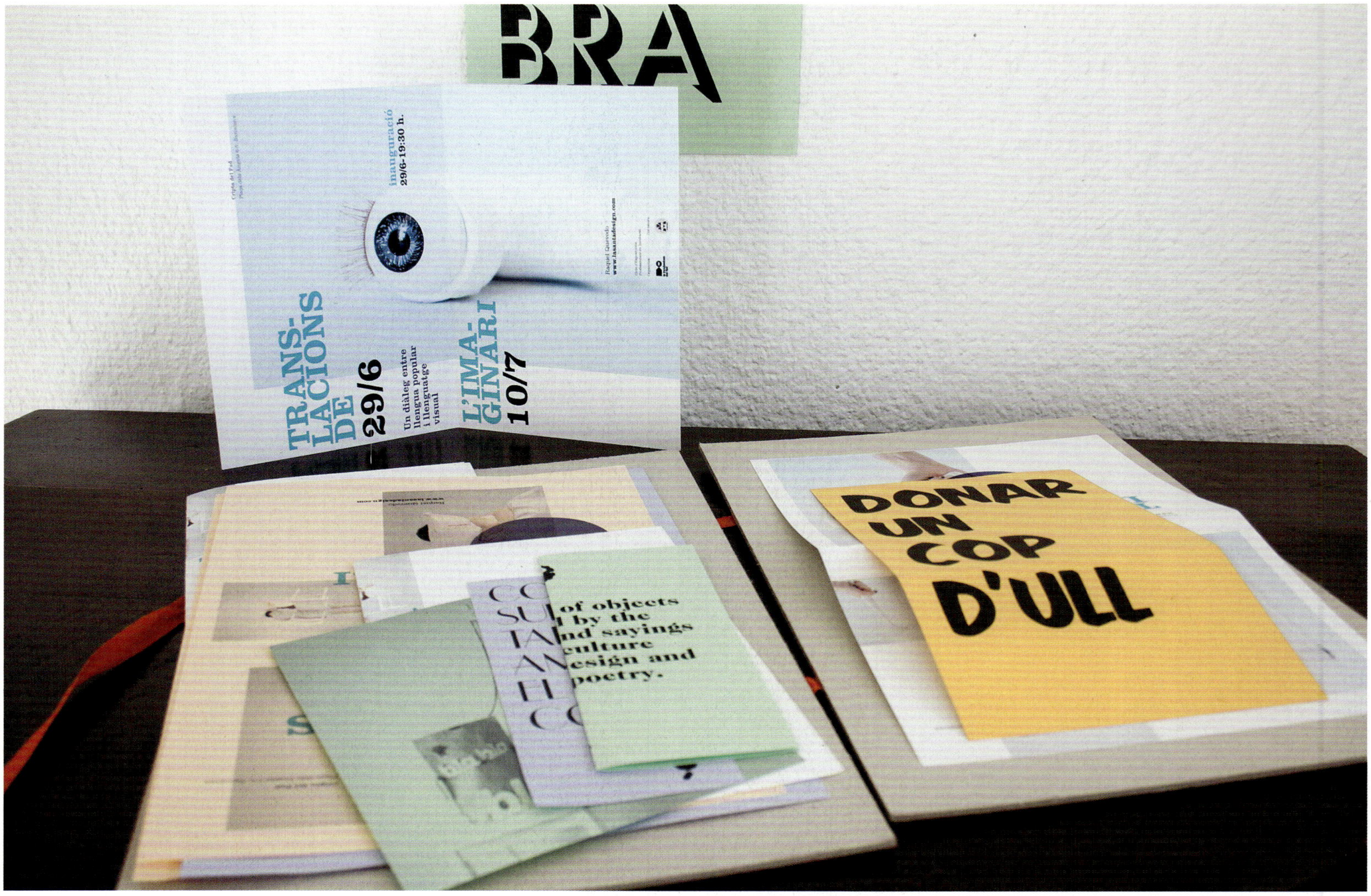

Tralattions of the Lmaginary

Designer: Raquel Quevedo

Creative Director: Raquel Quevedo

Client: Raquel Quevedo/La incubadora del FAD

Creating Date: 2009

Information: Brochure design for the exhibition "Tralations of the imaginary", a collection of objects inspired by proverbs and catalan sayings, through design and visual poetry.

DONAR
UN
COP

FER

TRANS-
LACIONS
DE
29/6
Un diàleg entre
llengua popular
i llenguatge
visual
inauguració
29/6-19:30 h.
D'ULL

Hello Card

Designer: Raquel Quevedo

Creative Director: Raquel Quevedo

Client: Raquel Quevedo

Creating Date: 2009

Information: The design for this selfpromotional typographic card was thought to impact the receive with an unusual and eye-catching card. First, it looks like a mini book, but then, when you unfold it, you can see anf touch the message "hello". The concept for this design was playing with cantent and form; the usual message "hello" change into the format.

677743766
raquel quevedo
graphic design

raquel quevedo

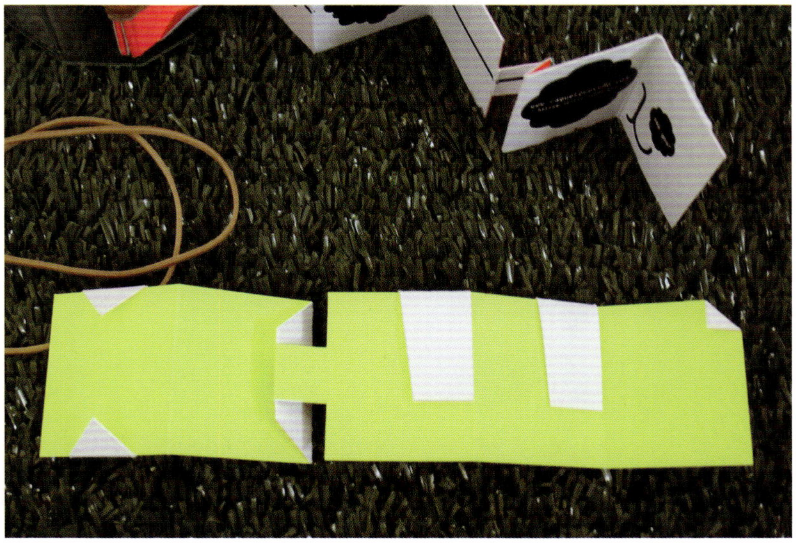

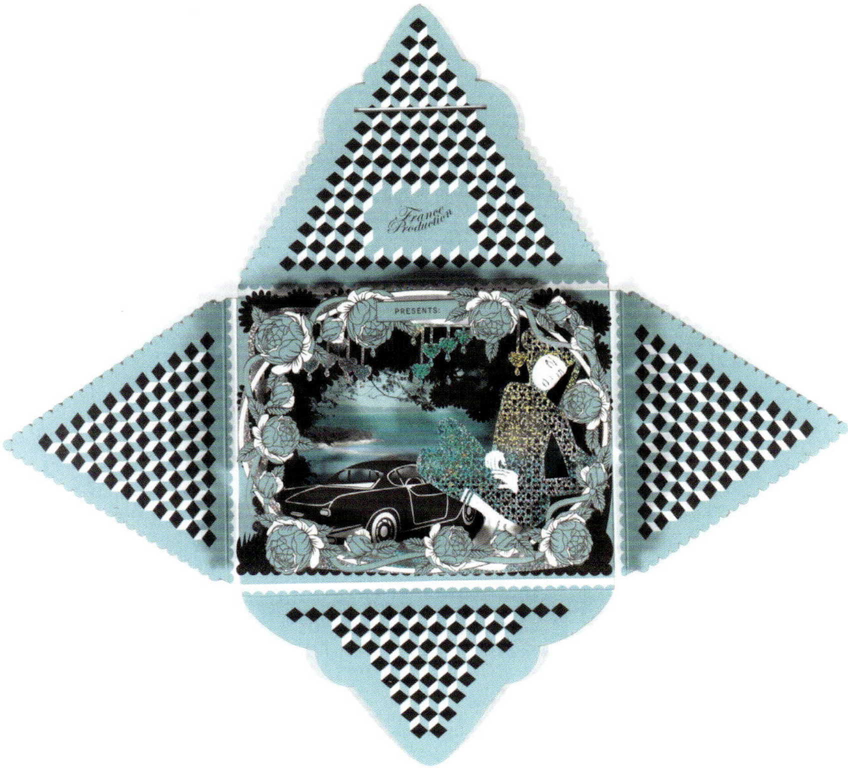

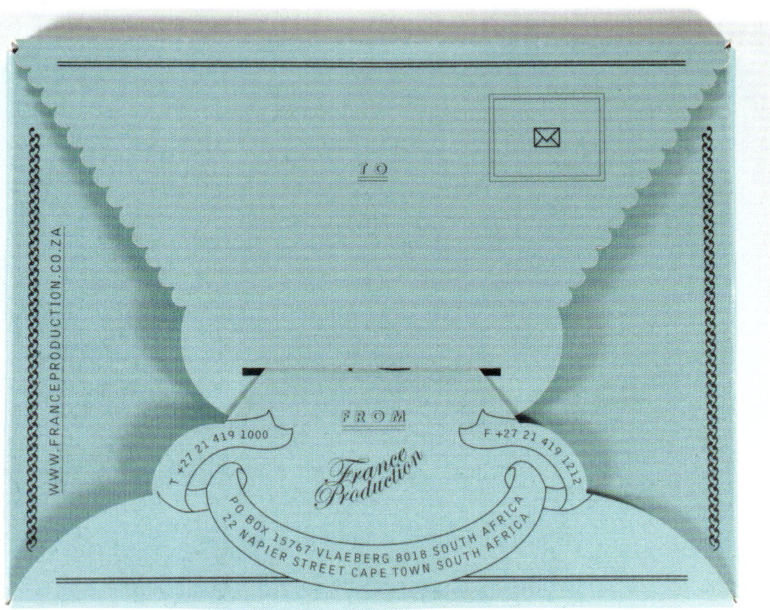

France Production Mailer

Designer: Heidi Chisholm

Creative Director: Heidi Chisholm

Client: France Production Mailer

Creating Date: 2009

Information: France Production is a stills production house serving the French fashion industry. This mailer invites potential clients to shoot with them at their South African and Indian Ocean island locations.

Extra Fancy Michelle O Bag

Designer: Heidi Chisholm
Creative Director: Heidi Chisholm
Client: Extra Fancy
Creating Date: 2010
Information: Extra Fancy produces products to celebrate Africa and it's super quirky crazy colour culture clash style. This bag captures the first black First Lady of the USA, Michelle O, hula hooping.

Snyder and the Swedes Mailer

Designer: Heidi Chisholm
Creative Director: Heidi Chisholm
Client: France Production Mailer
Creating Date: 2009
Information: Snyder and the Swedes represents Swedish illustrators. This mailer was sent to current and potential clients to showcase their work. A flocked poster is folded and wrapped around the catalogue to form an extra loose cover. Separating each illustrator's page is a short anecdotal paragraph from subwaycrush.com complementing the piece.

Polly Put the Kettle On

Designer: Kayla Jang

Creative Director: Kayla Jang

Client: Polly Put The Kettle On

Creating Date: 2010

Information: Nursery rhyme made from using only the 1975 The Hockey News type and images.

Clouds House: 25 Year Anniversary Book

Design Agency: Magpie Studio

Designer: Ben Christie, Tim Fellowes, Tommy Taylor

Creative Director: David Azurdia, Ben Christie, Jamie Ellul

Client: Action on Addiction

Creating Date: 2009

Information: For 25 years, Action on Addiction's Clouds House treatment centre has helped a diverse range of people break their addictions. To celebrate its anniversary, Magpie Studio let readers break the "addiction" belly band of our commemorative book and discover 25 stories – each one contrasting an autobiographical account of life before treatment, with a photographic case study of life after.

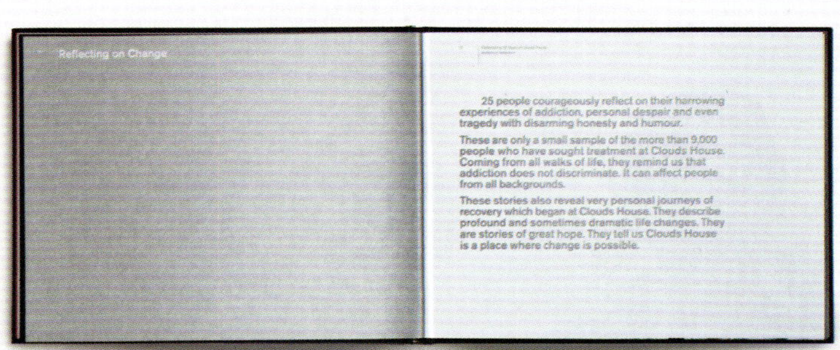

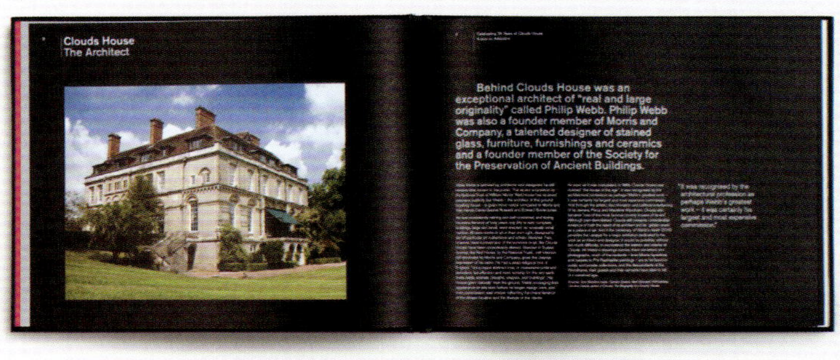

Kroppen

Designer: Johan Hemgren
Creating Date: 2010
Information: The cover is a traditional hardback but covered in tricot instead of the usual binding cloth. Holes are punched through the pages so that you get a peek preview of the picture on the following page.

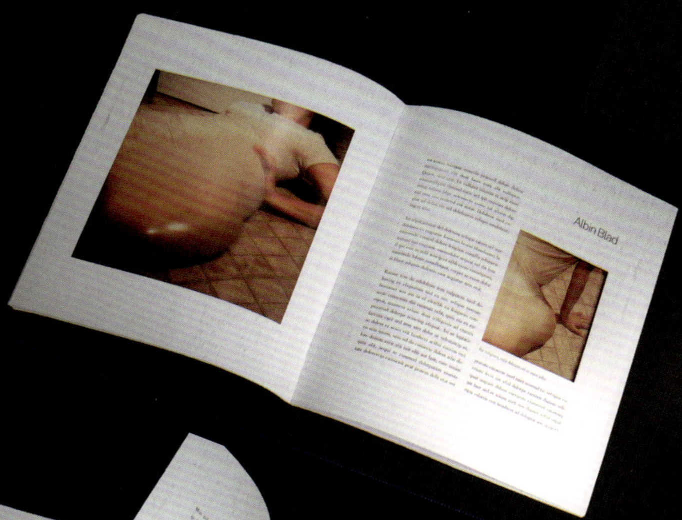

Typo Porn

Designer: Johan Hemgren

Creating Date: 2010

Information: As a way to reconcile with his own geeky interest in typography, Johan Hemgren made a number of booklets. They were aimed to make fun of people like the designer himself, who talk about letterforms as something nearly erotic.

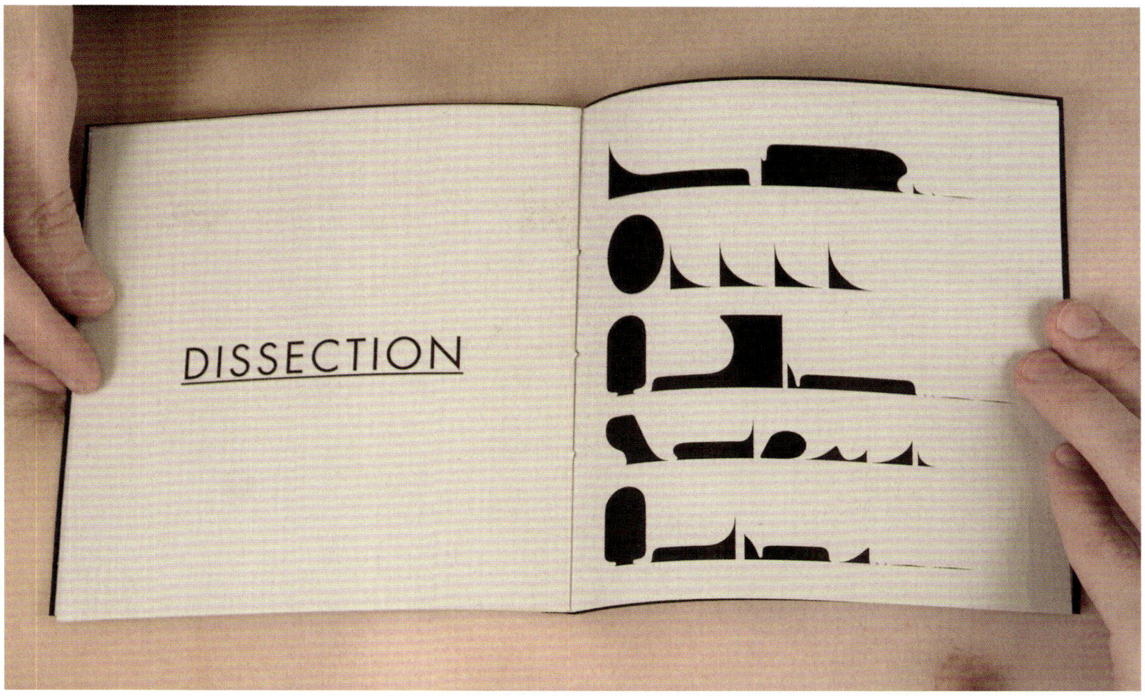

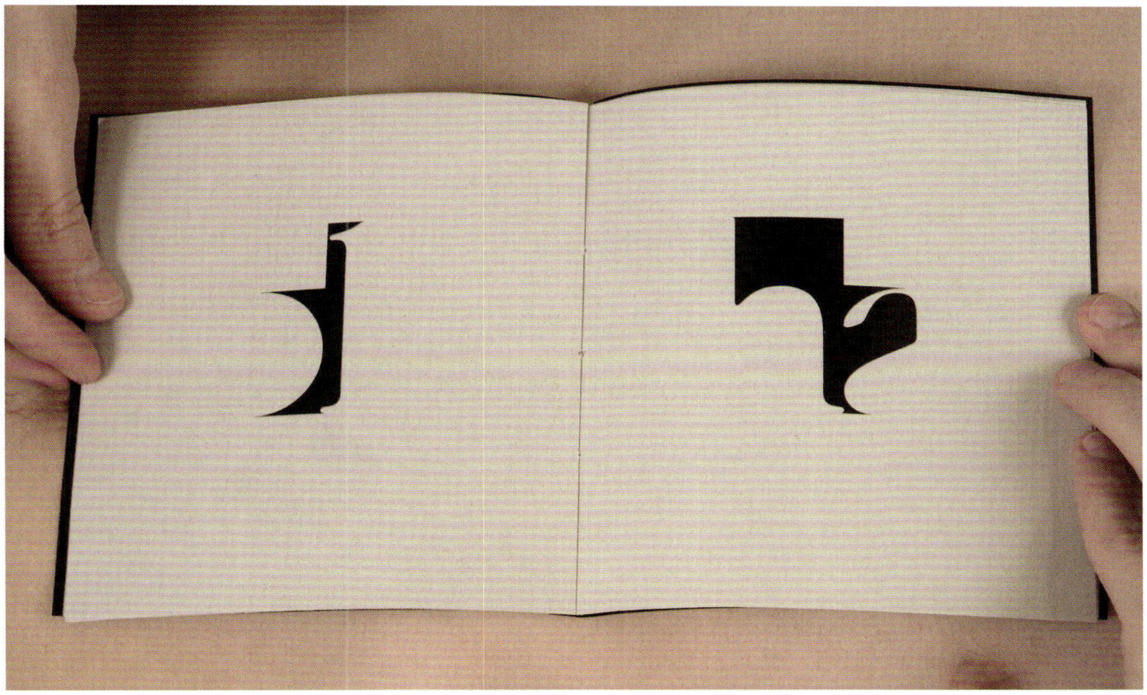

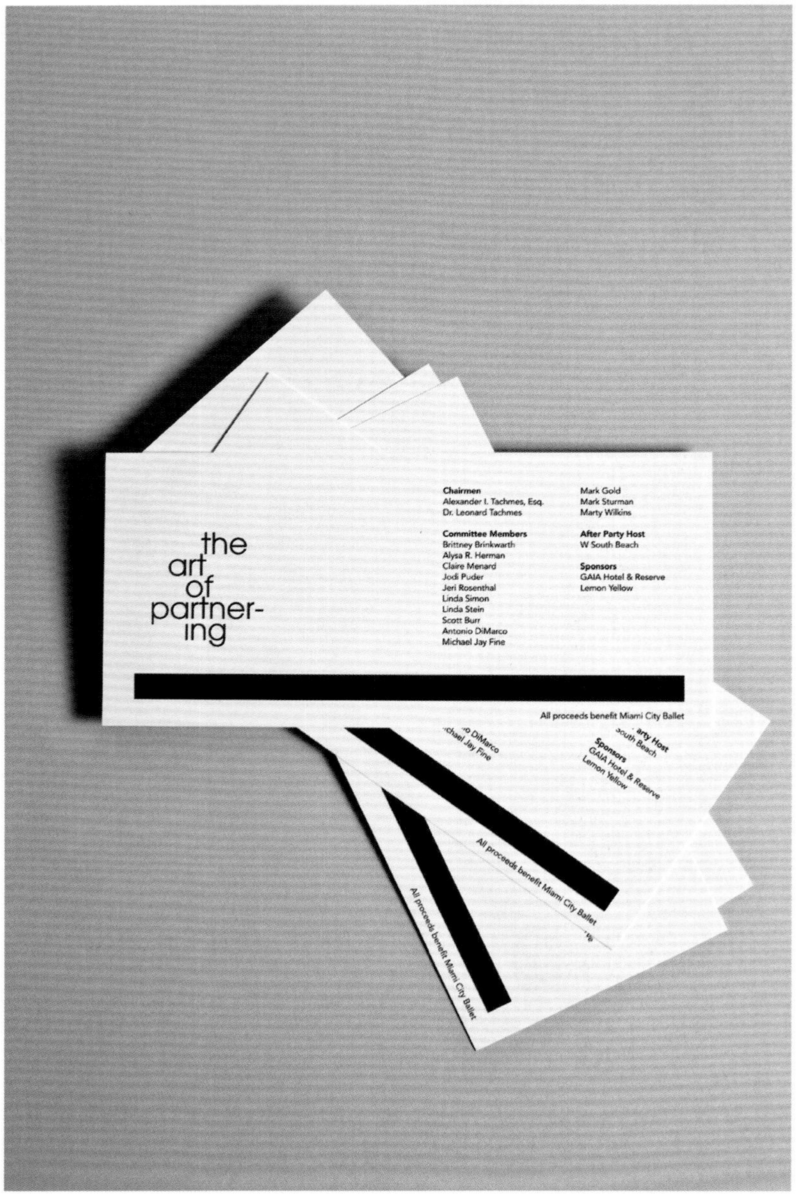

Miami City Ballet Invitation

Design Agency: Lemon Yellow

Designer: Erika Morales and Julian Martin

Creative Director: Erika Morales and Julian Martin

Client: Miami City Ballet

Creating Date: 2010

Information: Miami City Ballet asked Lemon Yellow to come up with an invitation design for The Art of Partnering, presented by the Miami City Ballet. The scope called for something minimal and elegant to promote an event for singles that is an ode to the legendary partnerships that are the foundation of ballet.

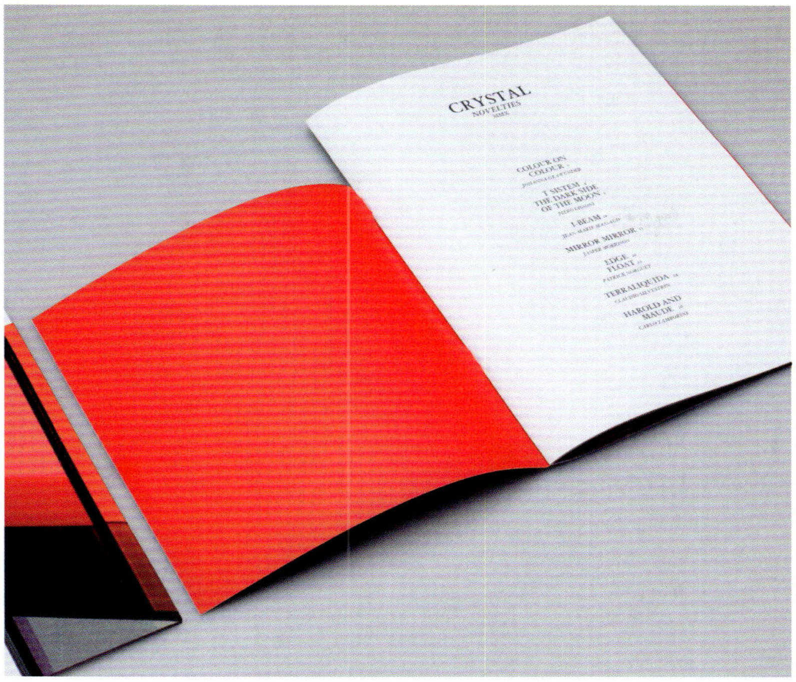

Glas Catalogue

Design Agency: Beki Bessi Karavil

Creative Director: Beki Bessi Karavil

Client: Glas

Creating Date: 2010

Information: The two smaller pages, used as cover and in mid-catalog, have been included to break the repetitive sequence and easily identify the section of technical drawings.

Inicial/08

Design Agency: Underbau Studio

Client: Culture Department. Andalusian Government

Creating Date: 2008

Information: Graphs and catalogue creation and design for this collective exhibition made up of some of the works of art purchased by Iniciarte.

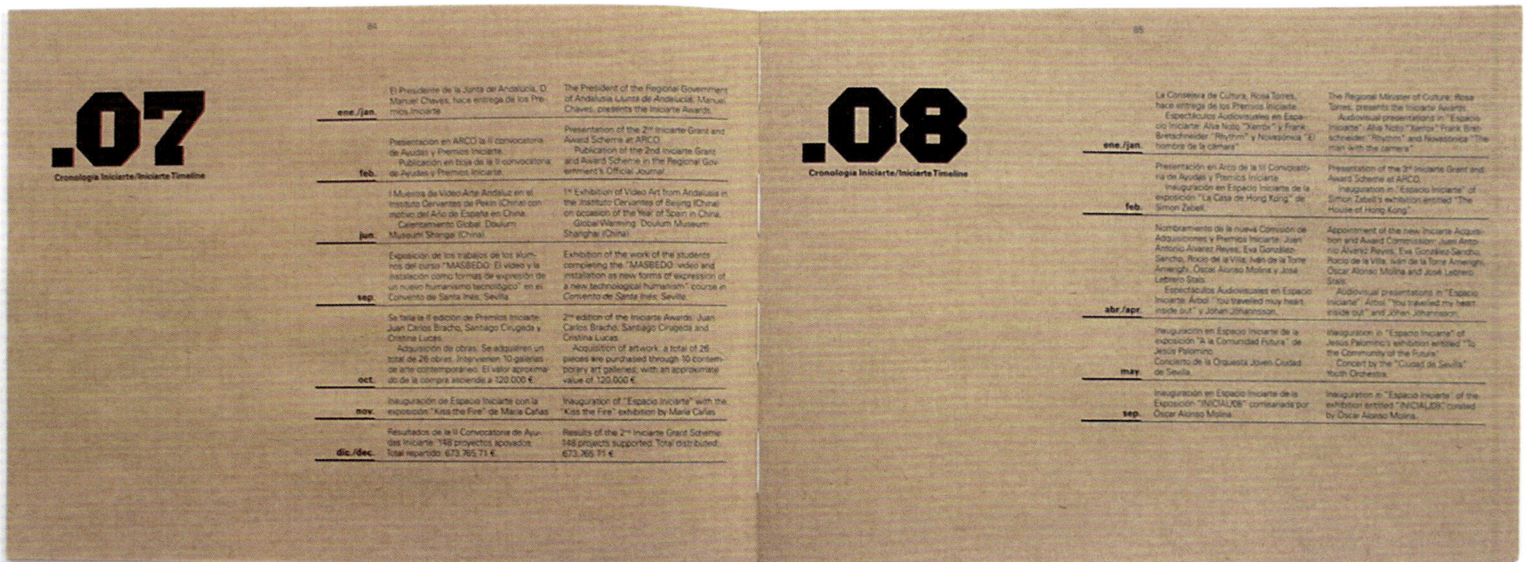

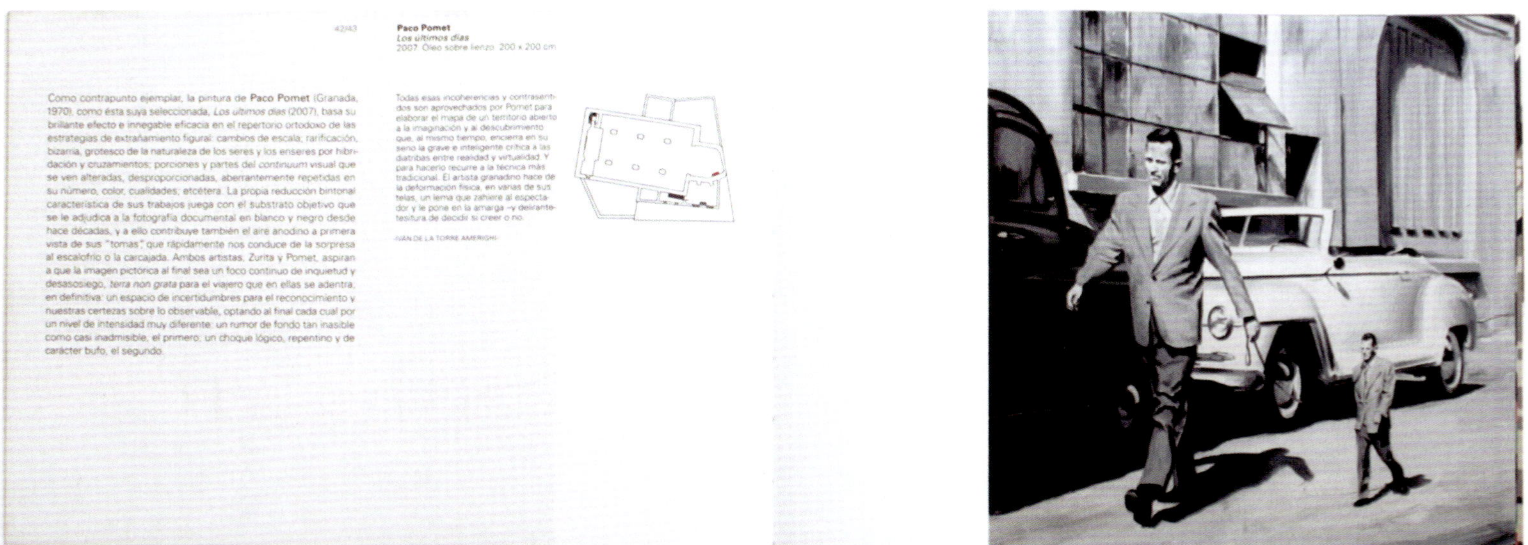

Visióndesafíos

Design Agency: Underbau Studio

Client: Instituto Cervantes

Creating Date: 2009

Information: Book/DVD for the special programme about Latin American videoart in Barcelona Loop Festival.

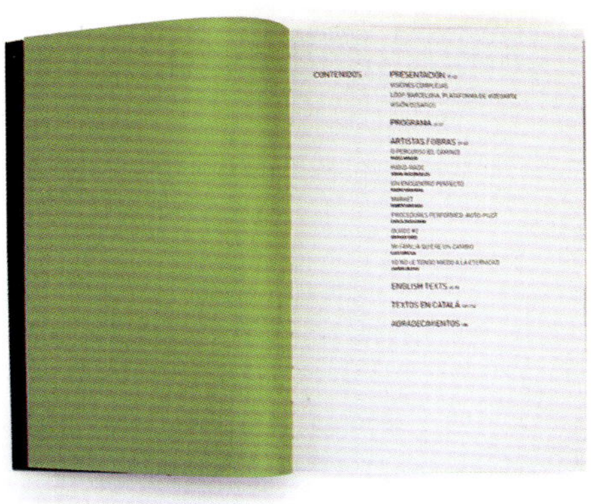

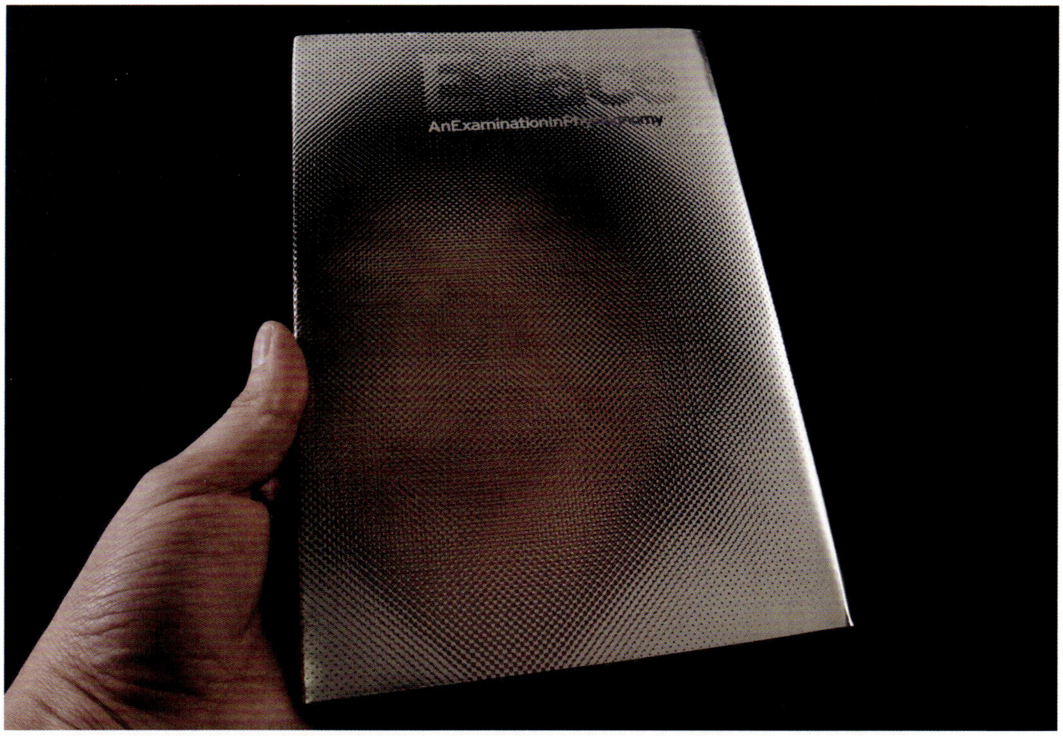

Delusions of Aviation and Land in Spain

Design Agency: ADearFriend

Designer: Chris Ro

Photography: Nojisu

Creating Date: 2010

Information: The human face is infinitely complex and in some instances extraordinarily simple. Recognition of facial expressions and features occupies both the instinctual and the systematic. Physiognomy is the analysis of the face as a potential indicator of character. Fourteen faces were constructed, de-constructed and fused in the hopes of assembling experiences that are simultaneously simple and yet very complex. The objective was to encounter the human face as one previously may not have encountered before.

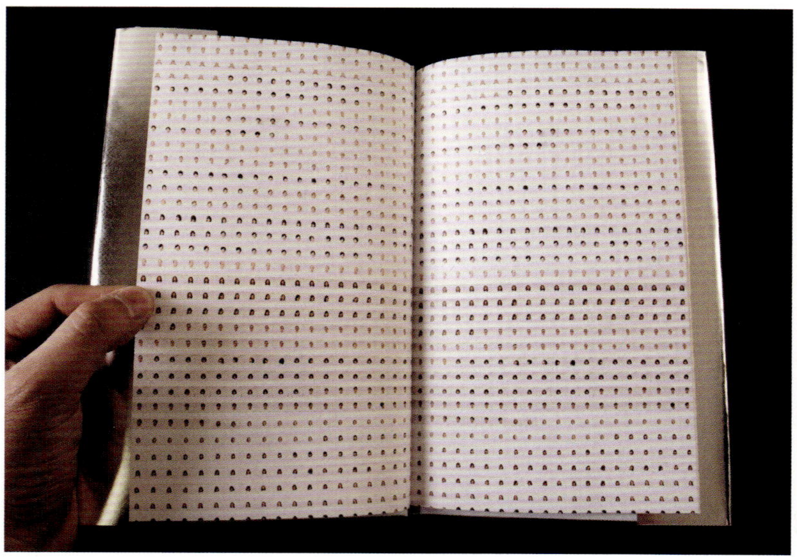

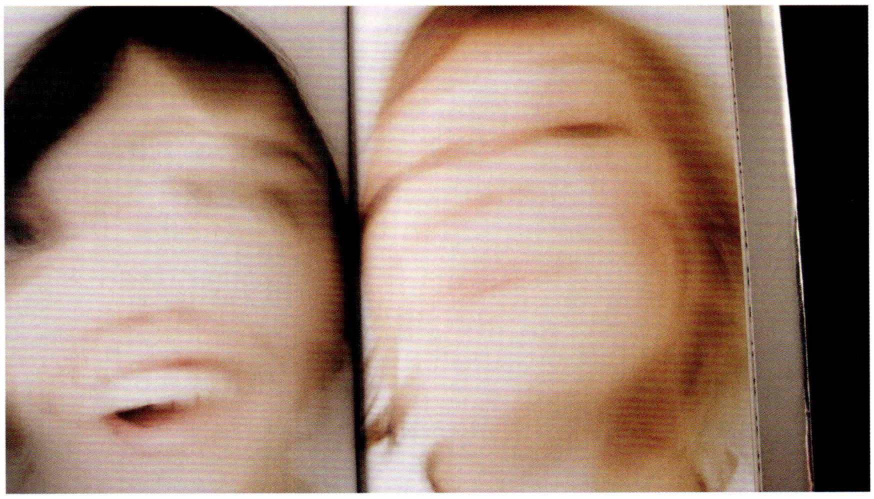

Spontaneous. A.D.D. Fast Talker.
Expressive. Jittery. Schizophrenic.
Excitable. Easily Distracted.
Contemplative. Caricature. Moving
Fast. Shifting Emotions. Animated.
A Little Schizophrenic. Sporadic.
Jolty. Inspiring. Charisma.
Spontaneous. Crazy. Dynamic. All
Over The Place. Sad Eyes. Laugh.
Thoughtful. Duality. Multiple
Personalities. Interior/Exterior.
Shifty. Constantly In Motion.
Getting Excited. Yelling About
Something. Serene. Movement.
Crazy. Laughter. Lively. Fish!
Constantly In Motion. Electric
Energy. Jazzed.

Circus Idenity

Design Agency: Mind Design

Creative Director: Holger Jacobs

Art Director: Craig Sinnamon

Designer: Andy Lang, Sara Streule

Client: Circus

Creating Date: 2009

Information: Identity for a new club and restaurant with a burlesque theme and changing performances. Since the club interior features many mirrored surfaces, the design of the logo is based on the shape of a kaleidoscope.

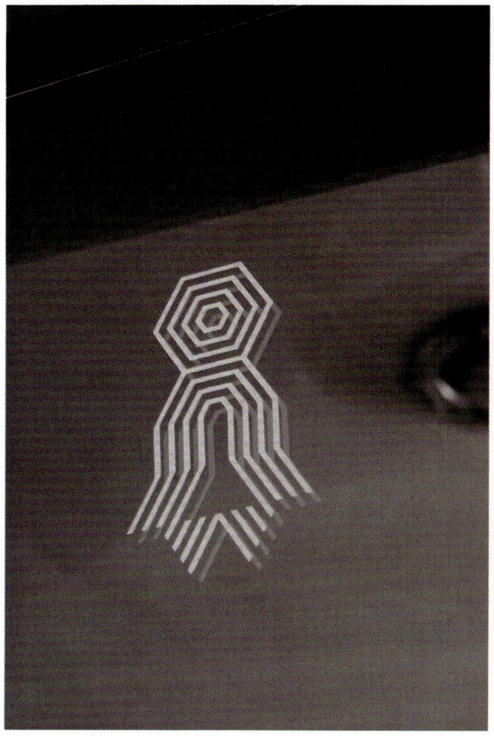

DRINKS
DRINKS

BAR MENU
CIRCUS

DRINKS
CIRCUS
MENU
CIRCUS
BAR MENU
CIRCUS
DESSERTS
CIRCUS

186
192
196
179

D100 Idenity

Design Agency: Mind Design

Client: Instituto Cervantes

Creative Director: Holger Jacobs

Art Director: Craig Sinnamon

Designer: Andy Lang, Sara Streule

Creating Date: 2009

Information: D100 is a modern dentistry at the Barbican (100 Aldersgate street). The identity is inspired by the raking patterns around stones in Japanese Zen gardens and protective layers of enamel around teeth. The pattern have also been applied to the interior going around furniture and various fixed or removable object in the practice.

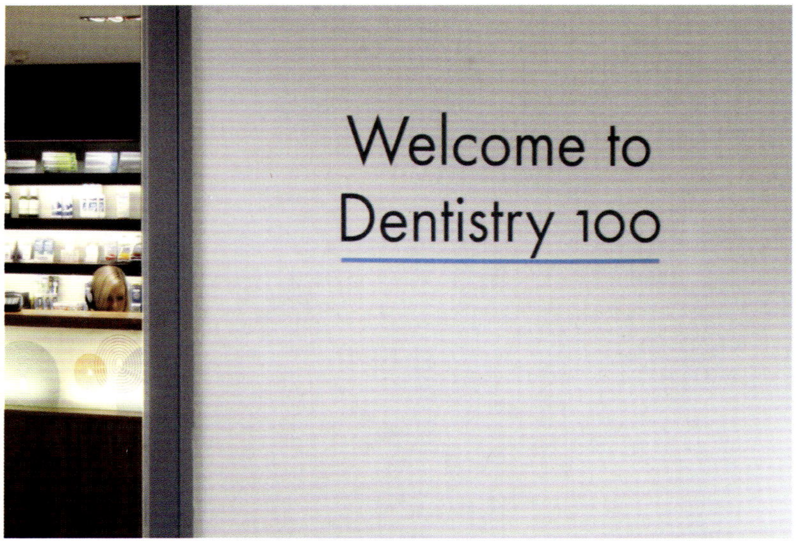

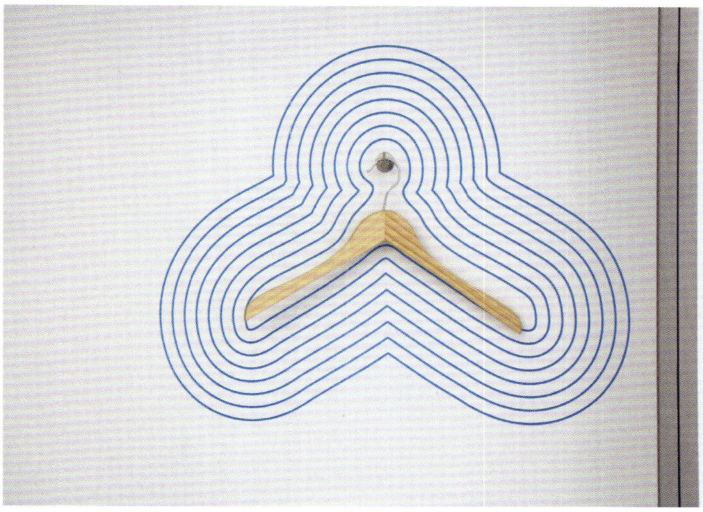

EDGE Hair Salon

Design Agency: ALPHA a.k.a Anastasia Gerali

Designer: Anastasia Gerali

Client: EDGE Hair Salon

Creating Date: 2008

Information: An identity proposal for a hair salon based in Paphos, Cyprus. "Cutting edge" taken literally, a simple graphic solution, cutting corners off things and using the "edge" shape as a feature and as a pattern. The concept is applied across print, packaging, interior and architecture of the store. The Edge hair care range uses colour coding and descriptive copy to describe the function and differentiate the products.

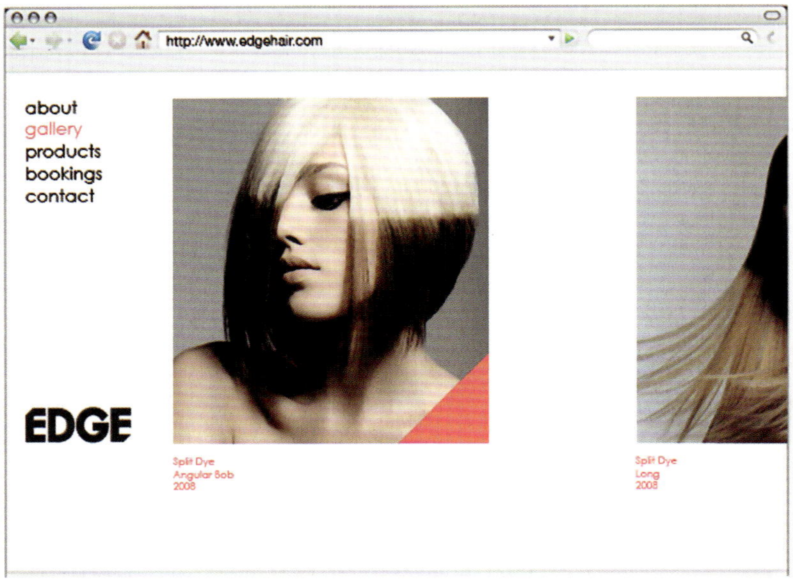

Sinfonia Varsovia Centre

Design Agency: Edgar B k & Robert Mendel

Client: Sinfonia Varsovia Centre

Creating Date: 2009

Information: Forever morphing visual identification of cultural centre in Warsaw, Poland. Logotype always fits into particular space, only one fixed thing is set of rules that can lead to design or redesign of logo. The border between logotype and rest of the materials/stationery is heavily blended.

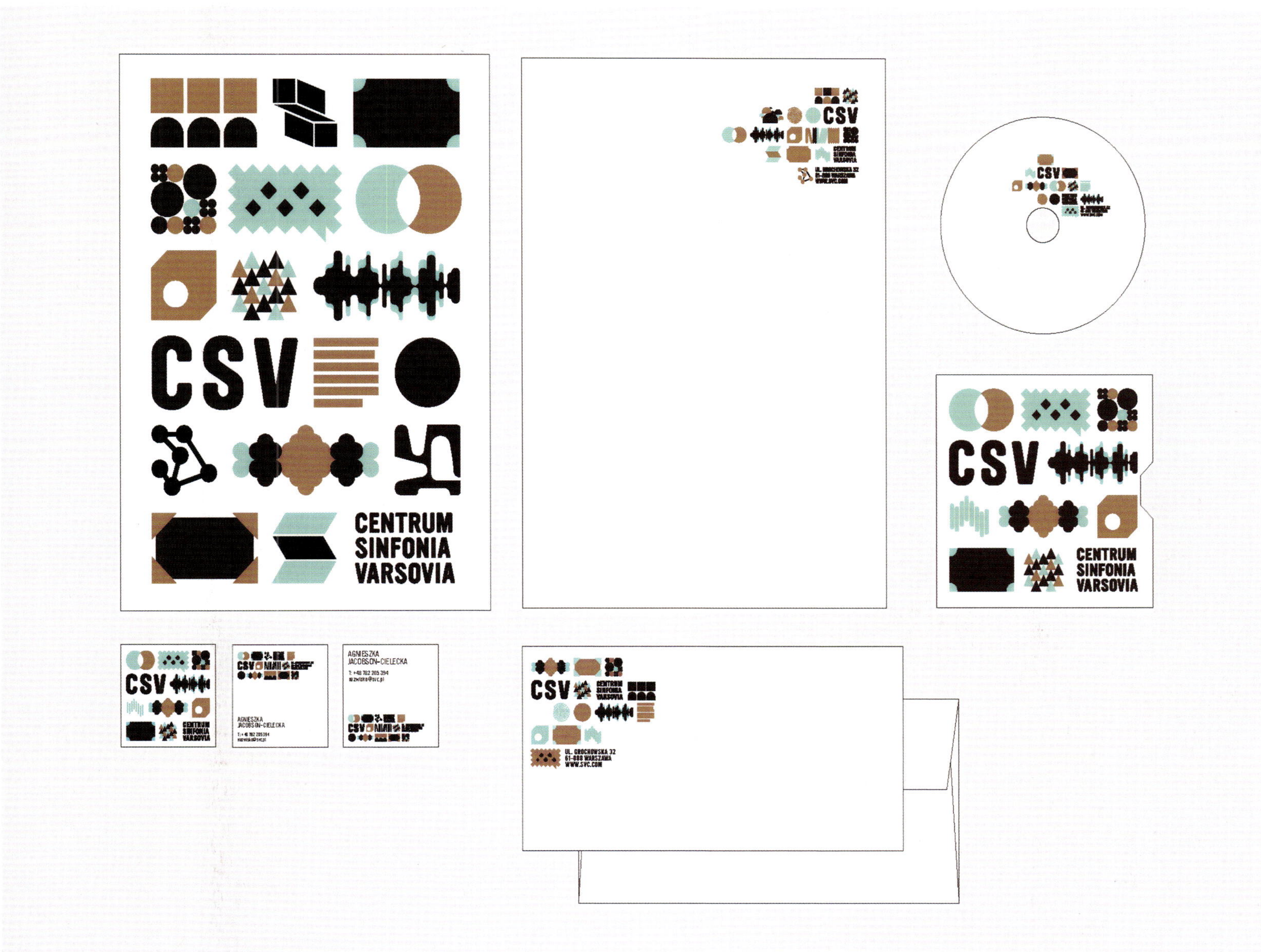

the grass is greener on our side

NEZINSCOT FARM

the grass is greener on our side

the grass is greener on our side

Nezinscot Farm

Designer: Lindsay perkins

Photography: Omar mendez

Creating Date: 2010

Information: The objective was to design a brand and packaging line that reflected the farm's eco-friendly agricultural methods. All packaging is reproduced individually, making each piece a little bit different, just as produce from an organic farm. The concept the grass is greener on the designer's side in emphasised throughout the brand and product lines by the use of biodegradable paper made with grass seeds, so where ever and however the packaging is disposed, grass will grow one way to give back to the farms free range animals.

Chocolate Festival

Designer: Lindsay perkins

Photography: Omar mendez

Creating Date: 2010

Information: The objective was to brand the Life by Chocolate Festival, a fundraiser for breast cancer. The concept was to entice the audience with chocolate references making their mouth water. All the collateral is printed on chocolate gold foil so when opening an envelope to read a letter, it feels as though there is chocolate inside.

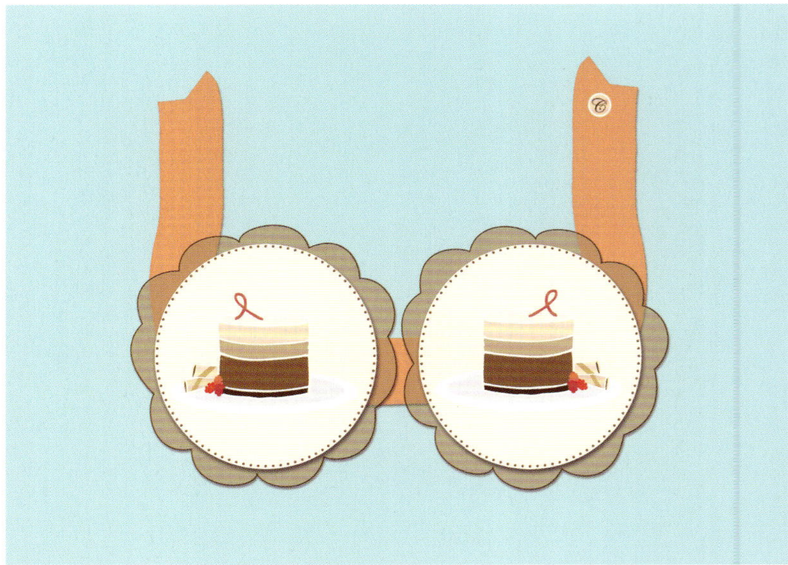

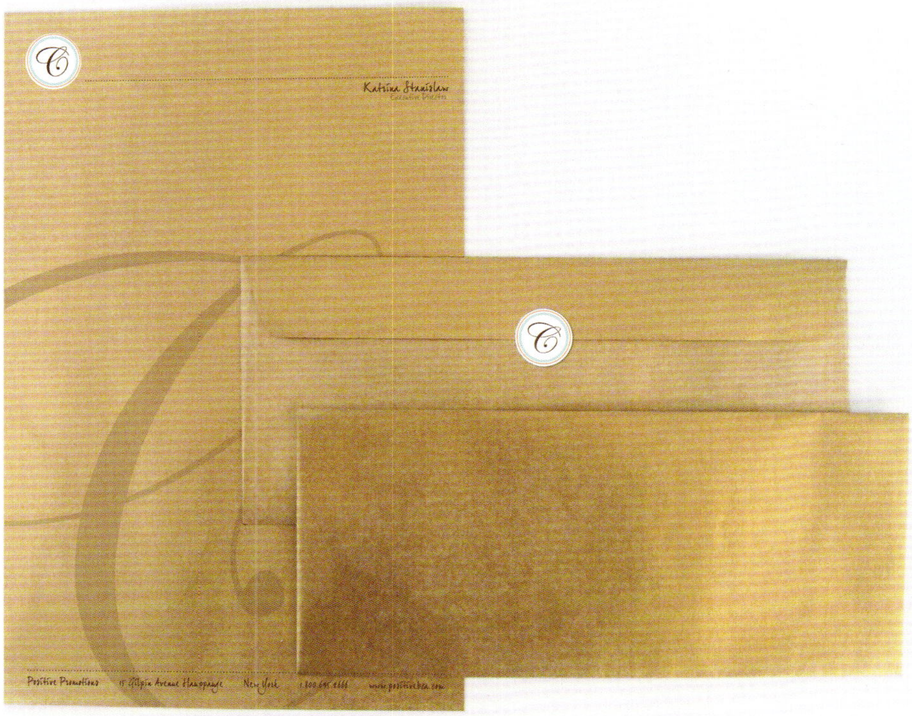

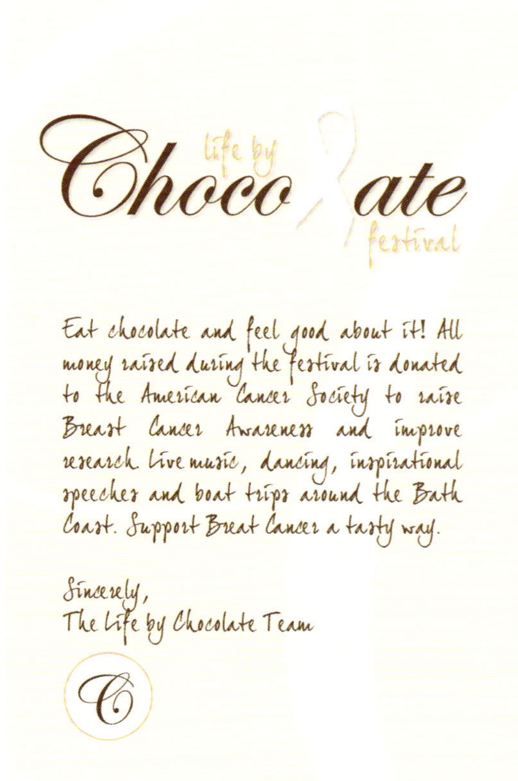
life by
Chocolate
festival
Eat chocolate and feel good about it! All money raised during the festival is donated to the American Cancer Society to raise Breast Cancer Awareness and improve research. Live music, dancing, inspirational speeches and boat trips around the Bath Coast. Support Breat Cancer a tasty way.
Sincerely,
The Life by Chocolate Team

Life by Chocolate Festival
GET TICKETS . VENDORS . SPONSORS
COMPETITION . PRESS . CONTACT US

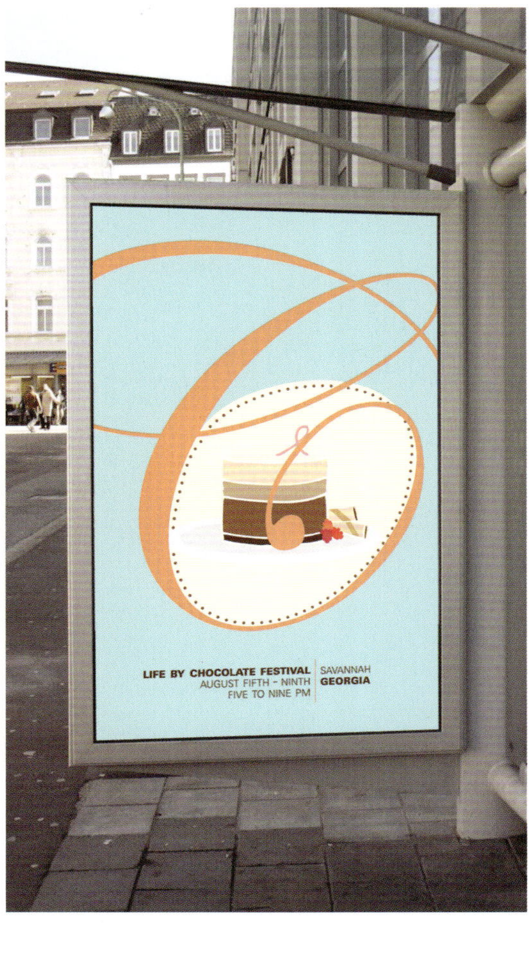
LIFE BY CHOCOLATE FESTIVAL
AUGUST FIFTH - NINTH
FIVE TO NINE PM
SAVANNAH
GEORGIA

Turn the Tide

Designer: Lindsay perkins

Photography: Kristin callahan

Creating Date: 2010

Information: The objective was to increase general awareness of the world's depleting ocean life, due to our over consumption of fish. The packaging is inspired by traditional fish wrapping and New England codfish boxes – cod being an example of the kind of damage the can come from unsustainable practices. The direct mail piece, targeted to restaurant chefs and owners, stays away from lecturing and preaching, and instead is designed to make them feel that they are part of the change to a more sustainable future.

BEST CHOICES.
BARRAMUNDI (US FARMED)
CATFISH (US FARMED)
CLAMS, MUSSELS (FARMED)
COBIA (US FARMED)
COD: PACIFIC (AK LONGLINE)+
CRAB: DUNGENESS, STONE
HALIBUT: PACIFIC+
OYSTERS (FARMED)
POLLOCK (ALASKA WILD)+
SALMON (ALASKA WILD)+
SCALLOPS: BAY (FARMED)
TILAPIA (US FARMED)
TROUT: RAINBOW (FARMED)
TUNA: ALBACORE/SKIPJACK
(TROLL/POLE)
GOOD ALTERNATIVES.
CLAMS (WILD)
COD: PACIFIC (US TRAWLED)
CRAB: BLUE*, KING, SNOW
CRAB: IMITATION/SURIMI
FLOUNDERS, SOLES (PACIFIC)
HERRING: ATLNATIC
LOBSTER: AMERICAN/MAINE
MAHI MAHI/DOLPHINE (US)
OYSTERS (WILD)*
SCALLOPS: SEA (WILD)
SHRIMP (US, CANADA)
SWORDFISH (US)*
TUNA: BIGEYE, YELLOWFIN
(TROLL/POLE)
TUNA: CANNED SKIPJACK
AND ALBACORE*
YELLOWTAIL (US FARMED)
AVOID.
CAVIAR, STURGEON (IMPORTED)*
COD: ATLANTIC, IMPORTED PCF
FLOUNDERS, HALIBUT (ATLANTIC)
LOBSTER: SPINY (CARIBBEAN)
MAHI MAHI (IMPORTED)
MARLIN: BLUE*, STRIPED*
MONKFISH
ORANGE ROUGHY*
SALMON (FARMED, ATLANTIC)*
SHARKS*
SHRIMP (IMPORTED)
SNAPPER: RED
SWORDFISH (IMPORTED)*
TUNA: ALBACORE, BIGEYE,
YELLOWFIN (LONGLINE)*
TUNA: BLUEFIN*, TONGO
YELLOWTAIL: IMPORTED, FARMED
GOOD ALTERNATIVES.
AVOID.

turn the tide.

turn the tide.
TURN THE TIDE. BE AWARE.
eat less fish.

Sugar Cult

Designer: Ana Vieira, Nídia Dias

Client: Sugar Cult

Creating Date: 2010

Information: The project was created for College for the Communication Design II subject. This project expected not only the creation of the name and logo, but also of all inherent applications and content. The logo was created for an imaginary candy store, which we decided to do a gourmet store, with exclusive products.

Zürcher

Designer: Stas Sipovich
Photographer: Stas Sipovich
Client: Zuricher
Creating Date: 2009
Information: Brand identity, logo, character & packaging design for Swiss family chocolate producer and takeaway confectionery based in Zuricher.

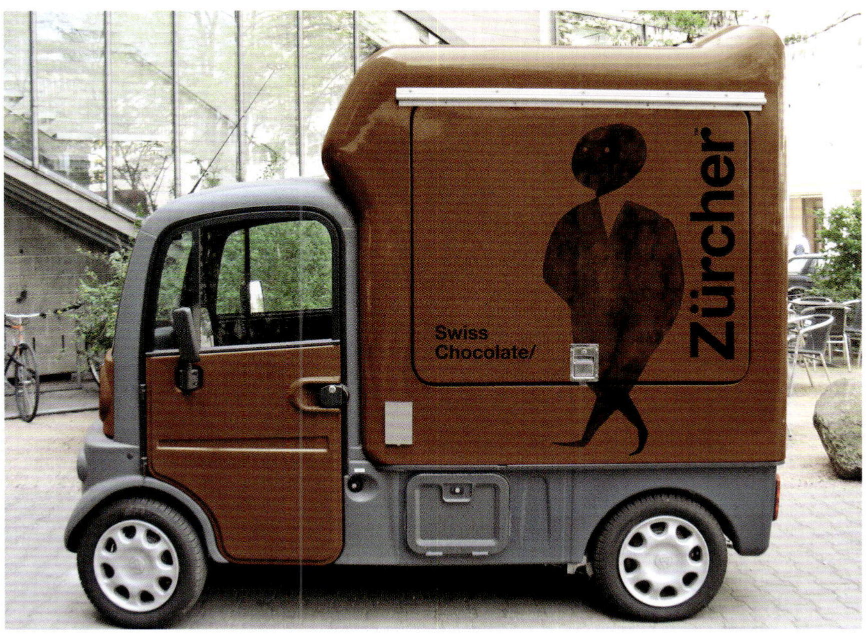

Morton & Peplow

Creative Director: David Azurdia, Ben Christie, Jamie Ellul

Designer: David Azurdia

Creating Date: 2007

Information: Morton & Peplow is a Munich delicatessen that specialises in British cuisine. The identity combines two icons of Britishness – the bowler hat and the domed silver service platter – to create a mark that evokes a sense of heritage and style. A candy colour palette and classic typography serve to continue this quintessentially British feel, tipping its hat to a lost era of elegant simplicity.

The Vegetable Bar

Design Agency: Magpie Studio

Creative Director: David Azurdia, Ben Christie, Jamie Ellul

Designer: David Azurdia

Creating Date: 2007

Information: Springing up each evening after the vegetable market closed, this impromptu venue was instantly known to locals as the Vegetable Bar. The identity captures its nightly metamorphosis with a vegetable/wine glass silhouette, and a subdued nocturnal colour palette.

Cupcake Identity

Design Agency: Mind Design
Creative Director: Holger Jacobs
Art Director: Craig Sinnamon
Client: Cupcake
Creating Date: 2010
Information: Identity for Cupcake, a spa and crèche for mothers with young babies. The challenge was to develop a logo that relates equally to mothers and children. The flexible logo made up from dots can either be used in a single colour or in multiple coloures to appeal to children. The Multi coloured dots appear in the interior design as well as in all printed material. Occasionally individual dots were replaced by small images, for example on the wall paper in the play area or on the inside cover of the main brochure. A candy colour palette and classic typography serve to continue this quintessentially British feel, tipping its hat to a lost era of elegant simplicity.

Opening soon
Opening soon
Opening soon
Opening soon

Gumbo Identity

Design Agency: Mind Design

Creative Director: Holger Jacobs

Client: Gumbo TV

Creating Date: 2010

Information: Identity for a children's animation artist. The letters of the logo change randomly and the website features an unusual navigation that opens all content within in a section at the same time.

Hive Identity

Design Agency: Mind Design

Designer: Marco Müller

Client: Gumbo TV

Creating Date: 2009

Information: Identity and design for a small chain of hair and beauty salons in London. As the salon is always busy like a bee hive, the logo relates to the shape of honey combs using warm yellow and orange colours. The individual letters are used in different combinations cepending on the application.

PARAMOUNT

PARAMOUNT

WINE LIST
BAR MENU
À LA CARTE
PARAMOUNT

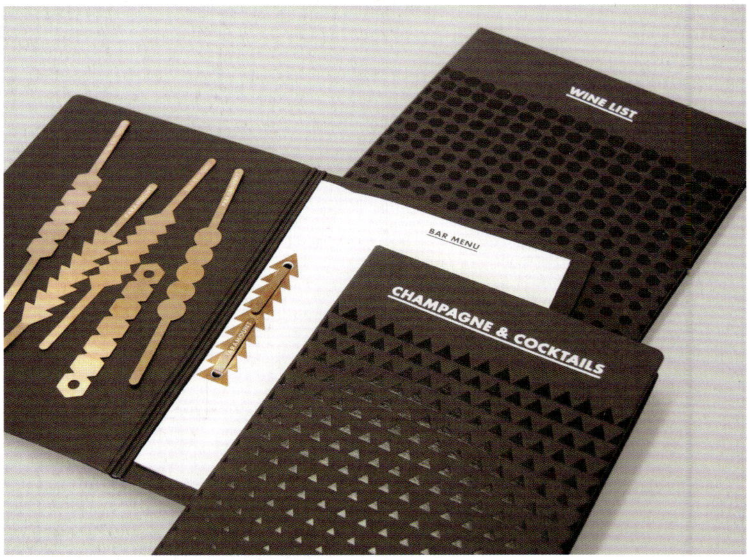
WINE LIST
BAR MENU
CHAMPAGNE & COCKTAILS

PARAMOUNT

PARAMOUNT
Centre Point
101–103 New Oxford Street
London WC1A 1DD
PHONE: +44 (0)20 7420 2900
FAX: +44 (0)20 7420 2919
EMAIL: info@paramount.uk.net
www.paramount.uk.net

Paramount Idenity

Design Agency: Mind Design

Designer: Johannes Höhmann

Creative Director: Holger Jacobs

Art Director: Craig Sinnamon

Client: Paramount

Creating Date: 2008

Information: Identity for Paramount, a members' club and event space situated on the top three floors of the 33-storey Centre Point building. The Paramount identity consists of a set of four graduation patterns which express an upwards movement. Each pattern is made from one of four simple shapes (hexagon, triangle, circle and stripe) that can be found in the building or the interior, repeated 33 times (for 33 floors). Different sections of the pattern have been used for different applications.

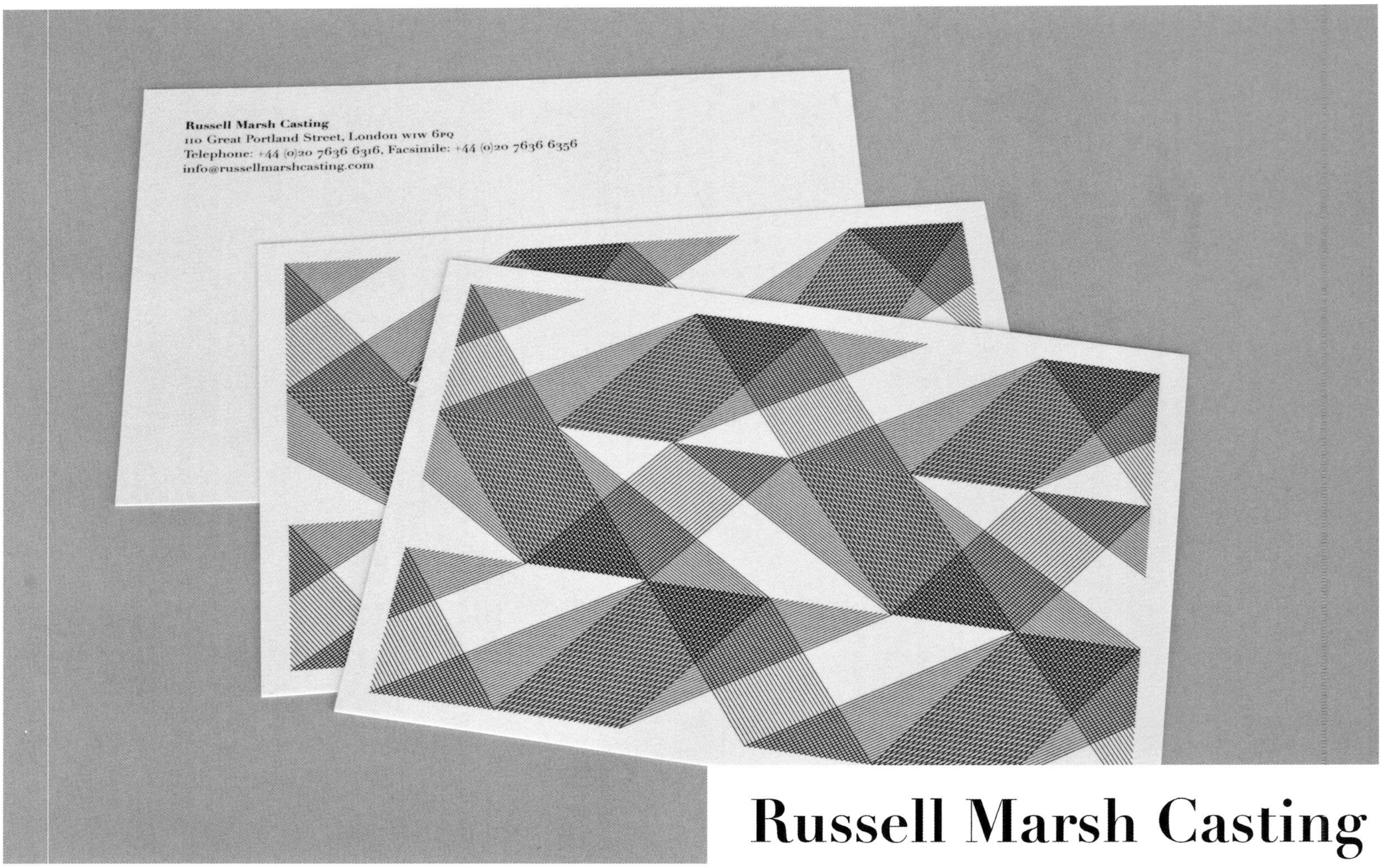

Russell Marsh Casting

Russell Marsh Casting Identity

Design Agency: Mind Design

Designer: Johannes Höhmann

Creative Director: Holger Jacobs

Art Director: Craig Sinnamon

Client: Russell Marsh Casting

Creating Date: 2007

Information: Russell Marsh casts models for fashion shows and photo shoots. Various line pattern related to the golden section were used on all printed material. The overlapping lines create different densities and connect at the edges of the format. The identity works without an actual logo, beside the line pattern it only uses minimal classic typography.

Znips Identity

Design Agency: Mind Design

Design: Johannes Höhmann

Creative Director: Holger Jacobs

Art Director: Craig Sinnamon

Client: Znips

Creating Date: 2009

Information: Identity for Znips, a hair and beauty salon in Central London. The logo is inspired by locks of hair and hand-cut lettering found in an 80's Punk fanzine. As part of the interior a piece of wall art was designed from chopped books resembling curled strands of hair and the curved shapes of the logo.

tea

t

blacktea — black tea

oolongtea — oolong tea

greentea — green tea

whitetea — white tea

infusiontea — infusion tea

supertea — super tea

Tea Identity

Design Agency: Mind Design

Designer: Magdalena Cuber

Creative Director: Holger Jacobs

Art Director: Craig Sinnamon

Client: Tea Limited

Creating Date: 2008

Information: Identity and overall design concept for a chain of tea shops, simply called "Tea".The idea of the logo is that the inner part of the letter "t" forms the tea leaf and changes colour according to the type of tea. The colour scheme is used to categorise similar type of teas and make the rather complex world of tea more accessible. The identity has been applied to packaging, menus and interior graphics. Occasionally the clean typographic design is contrasted by references to old-fashioned English tea culture such as tea cozies and doilies.

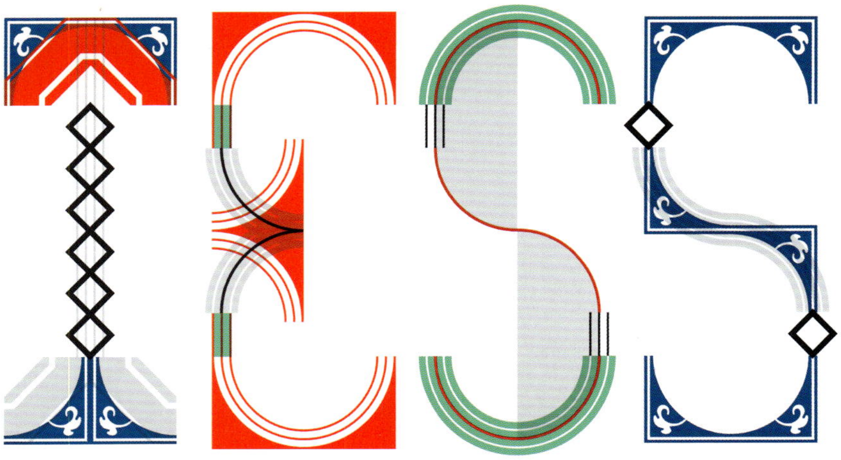

Tess Management Identity

Design Agency: Mind Design

Designer: Sara Streule / Johannes Höhmann

Creative Director: Holger Jacobs

Client: Tess Management

Creating Date: 2010

Information: Identity for a London based model agency. The identity uses several logo variations based on a modular system of Art Deco inspired elements. The same elements are being used as frames (which overlap images of the models) on various printed applications and on the website.

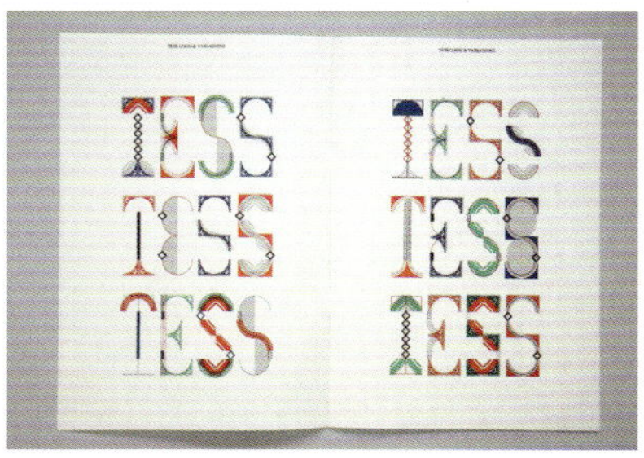

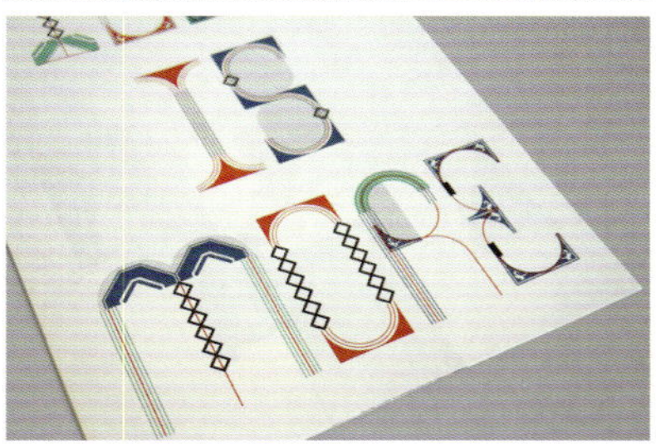

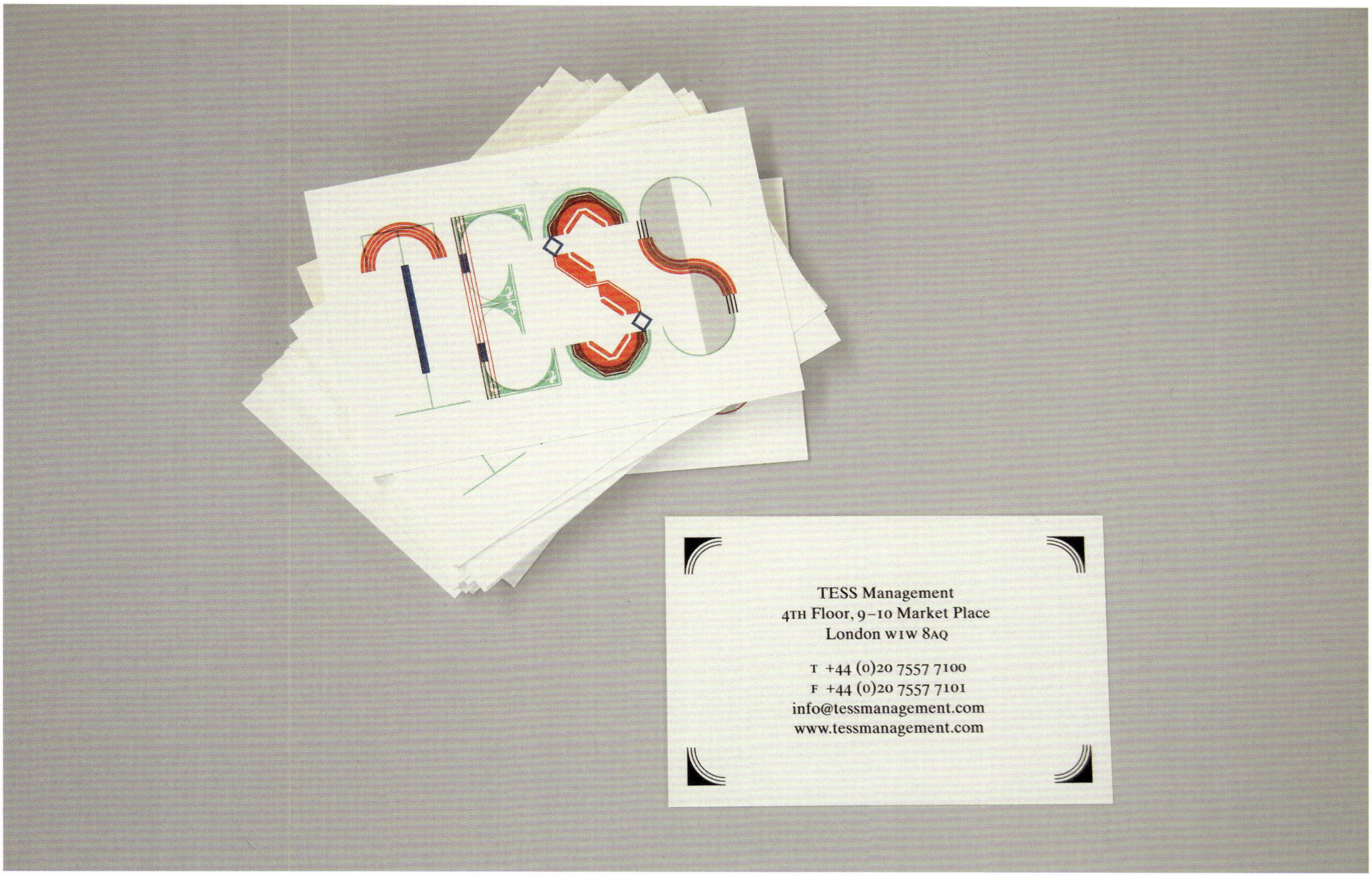
TESS
TESS Management
4TH Floor, 9–10 Market Place
London W1W 8AQ
T +44 (0)20 7557 7100
F +44 (0)20 7557 7101
info@tessmanagement.com
www.tessmanagement.com

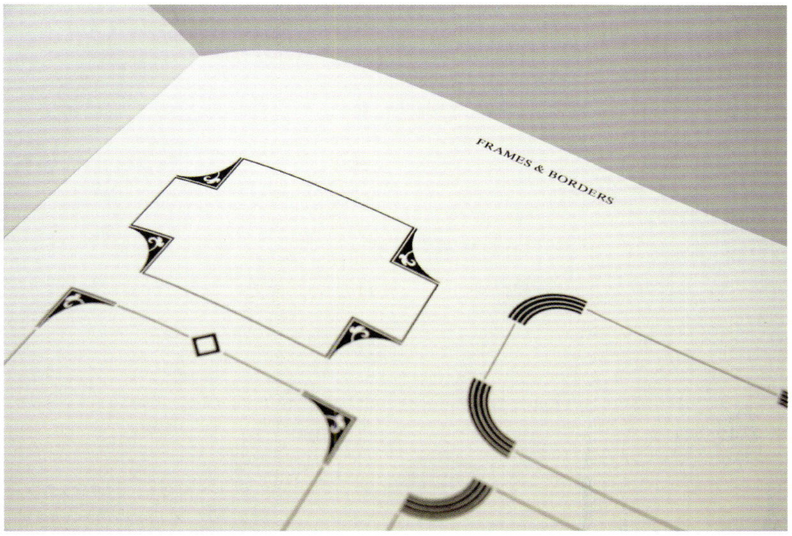
FRAMES & BORDERS

TESS
TESS Management
info@tessmanagement.com • www.tessmanagement.com

happy pills

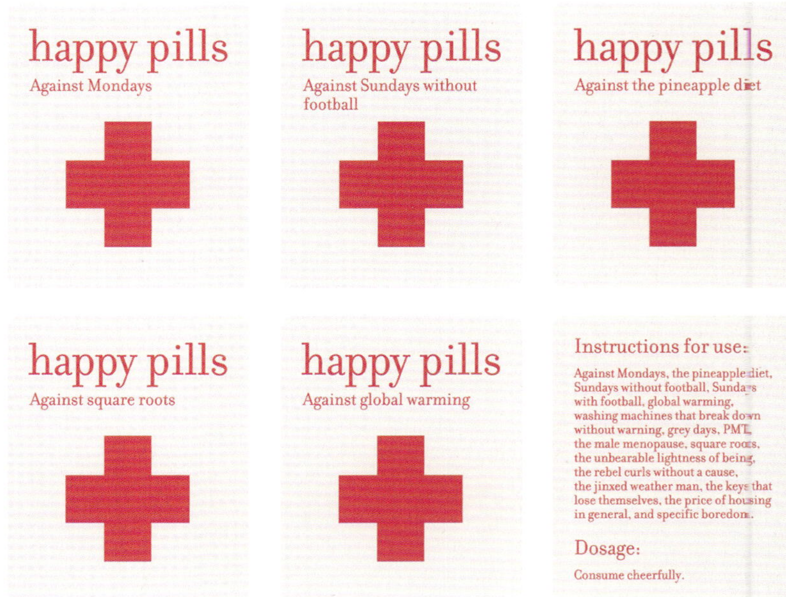
happy pills
Against Mondays
happy pills
Against Sundays without football
happy pills
Against the pineapple diet
happy pills
Against square roots
happy pills
Against global warming
Instructions for use:
Against Mondays, the pineapple diet, Sundays without football, Sundays with football, global warming, washing machines that break down without warning, grey days, PMT, the male menopause, square roots, the unbearable lightness of being, the rebel curls without a cause, the jinxed weather man, the keys that lose themselves, the price of housing in general, and specific boredom.
Dosage:
Consume cheerfully.

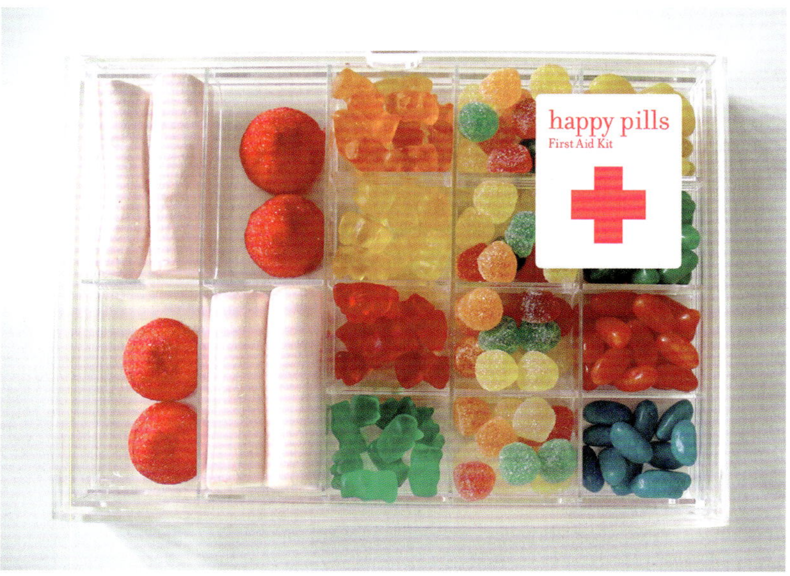
happy pills
First Aid Kit

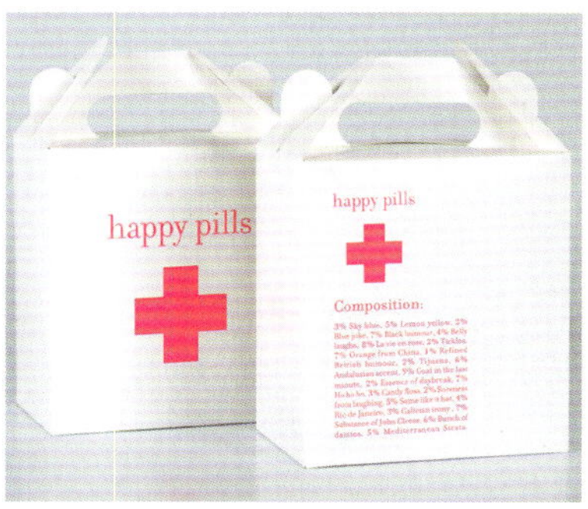
happy pills
happy pills
Composition:

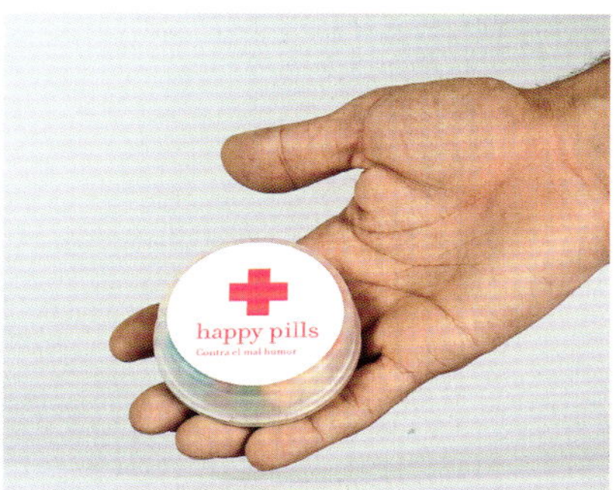
happy pills

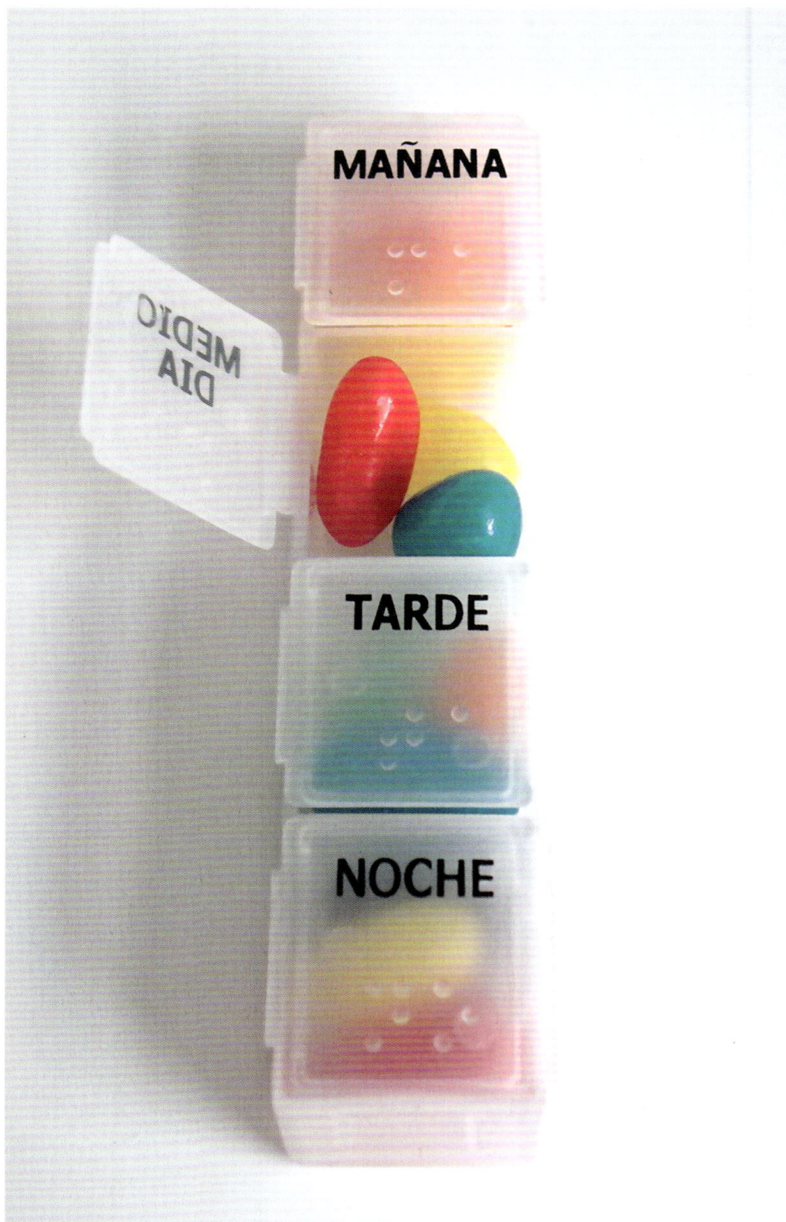
MAÑANA
MEDIO DIA
TARDE
NOCHE

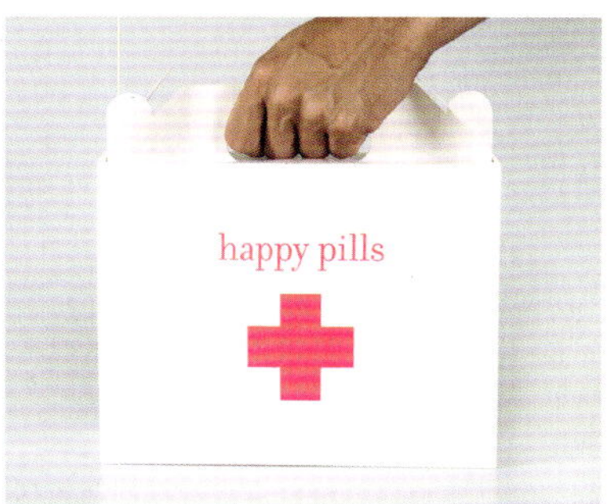
happy pills

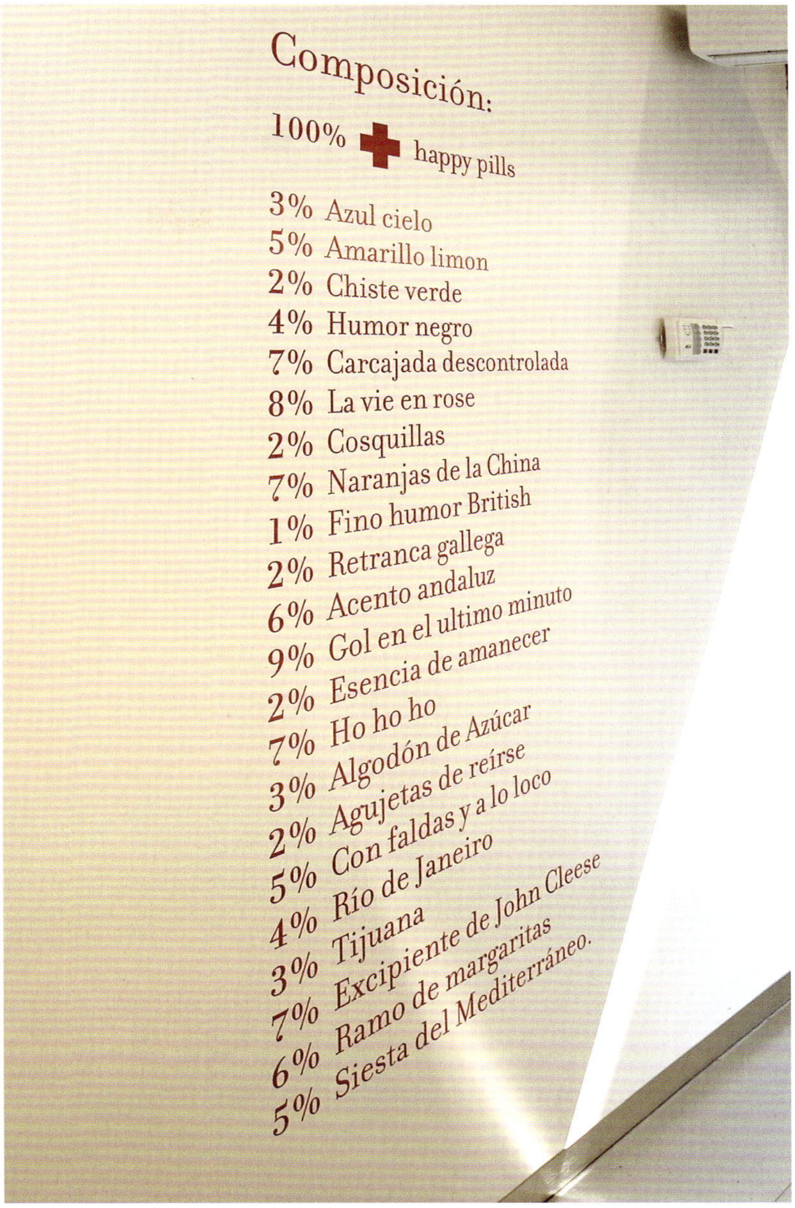

Happy Pills Identity

Design Agency: m-m design studio

Client: Happy Pills

Creating Date: 2007

Information: A candy store in Barcelona called Happy Pills. If this isn't innovative design, then the designer doesn't know what is. It might be his favourite design concept of the year.

I+Drink

I+Drink Identity

Design Agency: m-m design studio

Client: I +Drink

Creating Date: 2009

Information: This company is dedicated to the world of cocktails, but from a modern and innovate approach, where the R+D and quality would be the engine of the project. From here emerges the naming/concept I+Drink (I+D in Spanish means R+D "Research and Development") which is not only added to the concept of drinks, but to somany other connotations that help to explain the soul of the brand: I+Love, I+Wow!, I+E-mc2, I+Poison, I+Santiago de Cuba, I+Sinatra, I+Manhattan, I+Yes!, I+Drink on tour (for catering), etc. They maintain in Oviedo (north of Spain) a local that serces as laboratory and showroom dedicated to investigate and develop new proposals. The designers have applied the concept to all levels bearing in mind their place in the project: mobile bar, modular seats, lamps, dishes, waiters, façade, etc. The designers wanted to distinguish the bar, that is conceived in a way that it shows implicitly the relation that I+Drink has with the catering world. The bar is built as separate and mobile modules, each of them with a different function (the beer tap, bottle station, warehouse, dishwasher, etc). This way the modules can be used as a in house fixed bar or as a moving bar for possible events. The modules where designed inspired by "flight case" (containers of tools for music concerts) and graphic signs were added indicating the references for each use. The sign on the façade was adapted so that it could be used (also) as outside bar and so keep the façade as simple as possible.

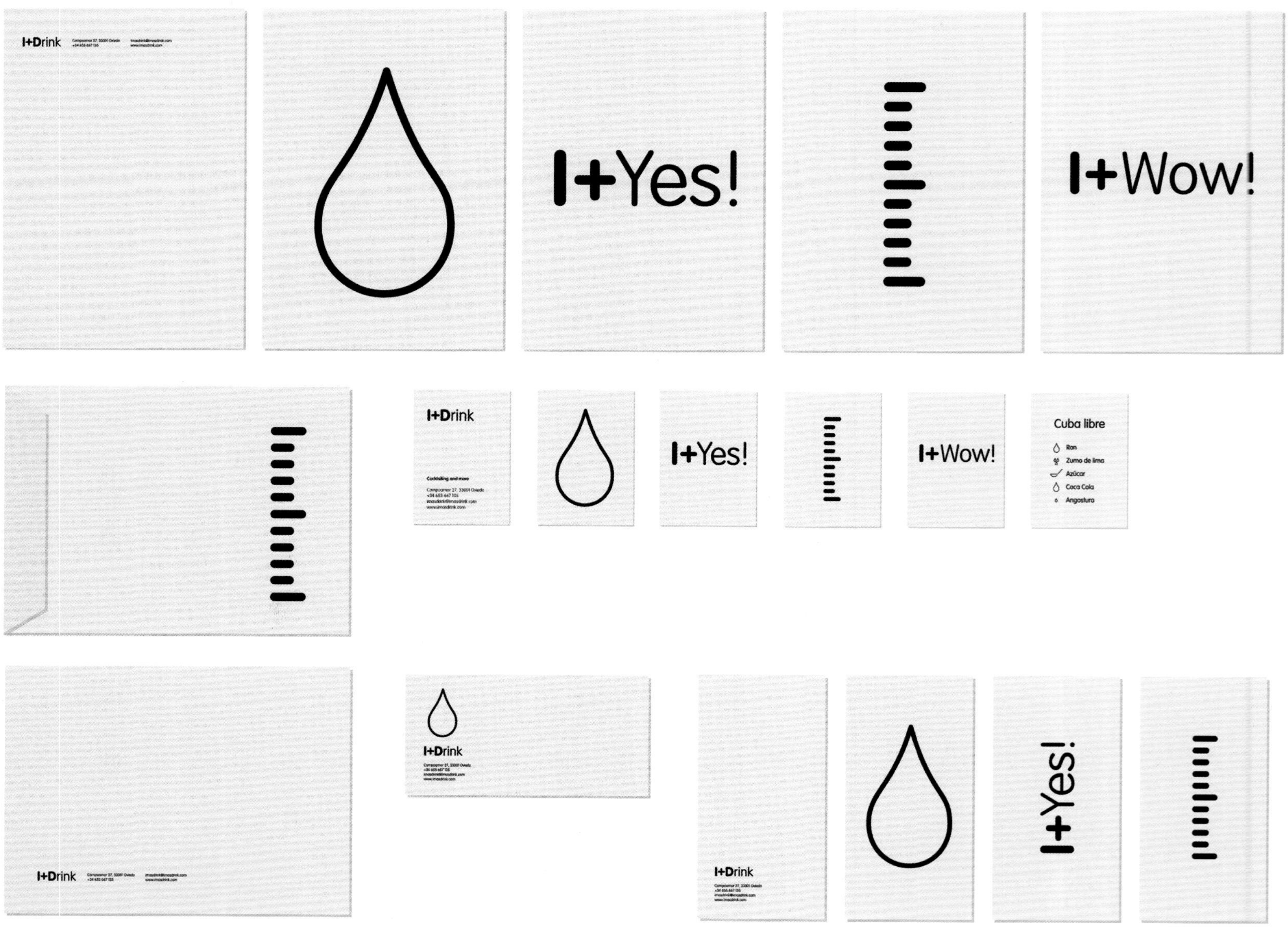

I+Drink

I+Drink

4/4

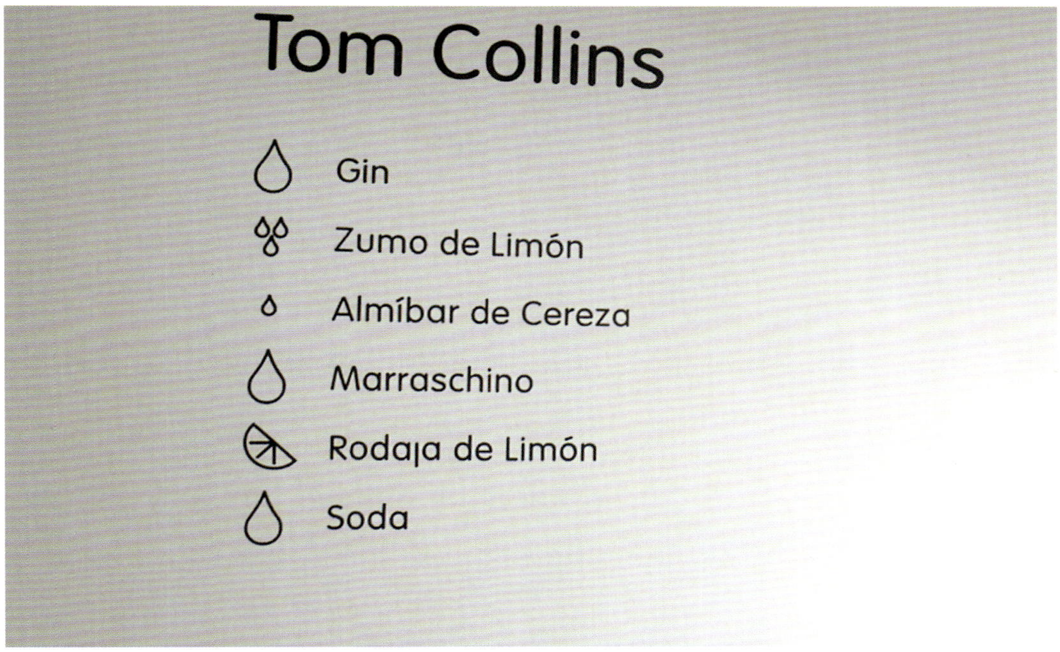
Tom Collins
Gin
Zumo de Limón
Almíbar de Cereza
Marraschino
Rodaja de Limón
Soda

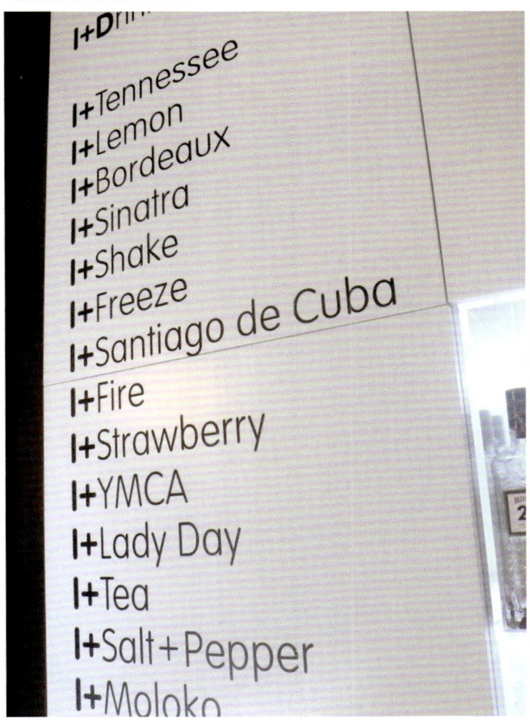
I+Tennessee
I+Lemon
I+Bordeaux
I+Sinatra
I+Shake
I+Freeze
I+Santiago de Cuba
I+Fire
I+Strawberry
I+YMCA
I+Lady Day
I+Tea
I+Salt+Pepper

I+D

I+Wow!

JULES ET [redacted] MOI

Jules et moi Identity

Design Agency: m-m design studio

Client: Jules et moi

Creating Date: 2009

Information: Masculine underwear. The naming in the first phase was to be "Jules et Jim", as François Truffaut's film of the year 62, but because of some disadvantages at the registration of the brand, it was decided to change it to "Jules et moi." We felt like to reflect this change of direction in the logo, literally erasing "Jim" to change the "moi." Not that anyone but us would understand this nod, but sometimes you do not know why these things give depth to the brand and make them seem more "real." The proposal, if approved and produced, has not yet been comercialised.

lollipop

Lollipop Identity

Design Agency: m-m design studio

Client: Lollipop

Creating Date: 2009

Information: Lollipop distributes Dutch brands of baby clothes. These brands are defined by being modern, functional and far away of more classic blue and pink clothes. With a name like Lollipop it was impossible not to work with this image. m-m design represented it in a very simplified way, just a stick and a circle, just like a child would do it. The result is very pop, very Lollipop.

lollipop

lollipop

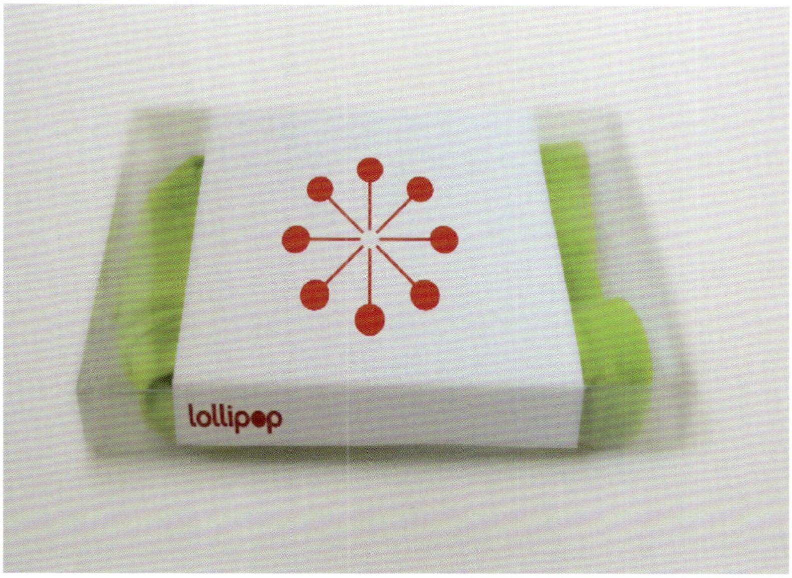
lollipop

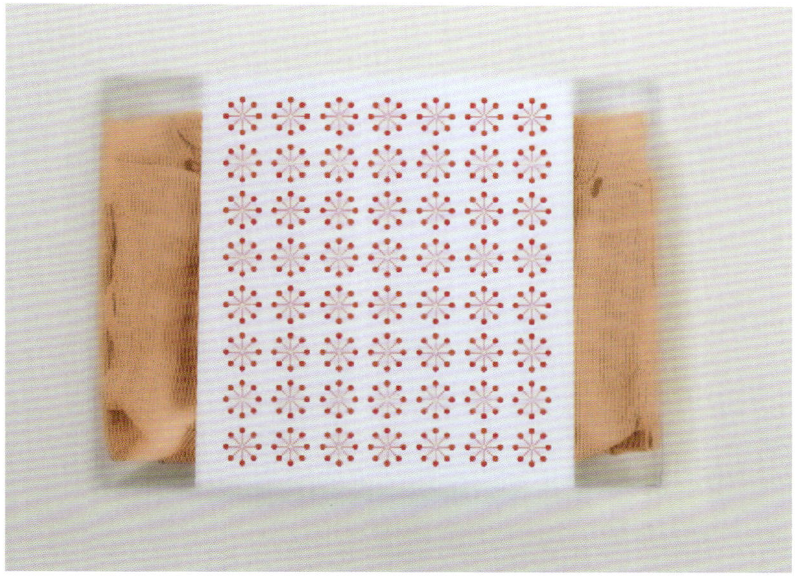

lollipop
www.lollipopagency.com

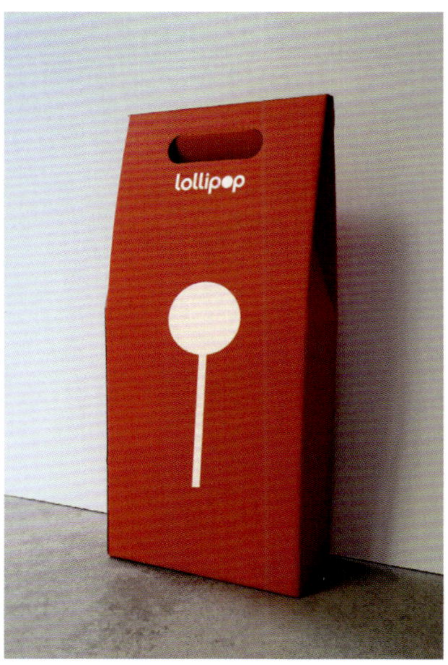
lollipop

lollipop

POK Identity

Design Agency: m-m design studio

Client: Lollipop

Creating Date: 2010

Information: With POK you can share and spread mobile phone contents such as pictures, videos, blogs, contacts, etc. You can visit and contact other profiles, that means that POK is a service that allows to create an extense net of individuals that are in contact and share contents. The proposal was to create a brand identity that represents this community that is constantly changing, like a living being, growing, transforming, moving, developing. With this concept in mind, m-m design didn't create a unique logotype. The identity is in constant movement, and changes in every application.

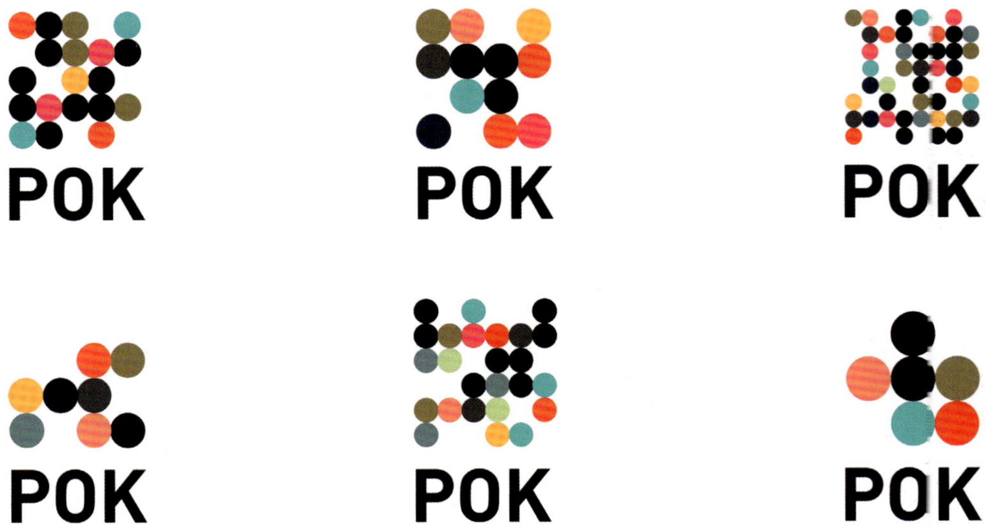

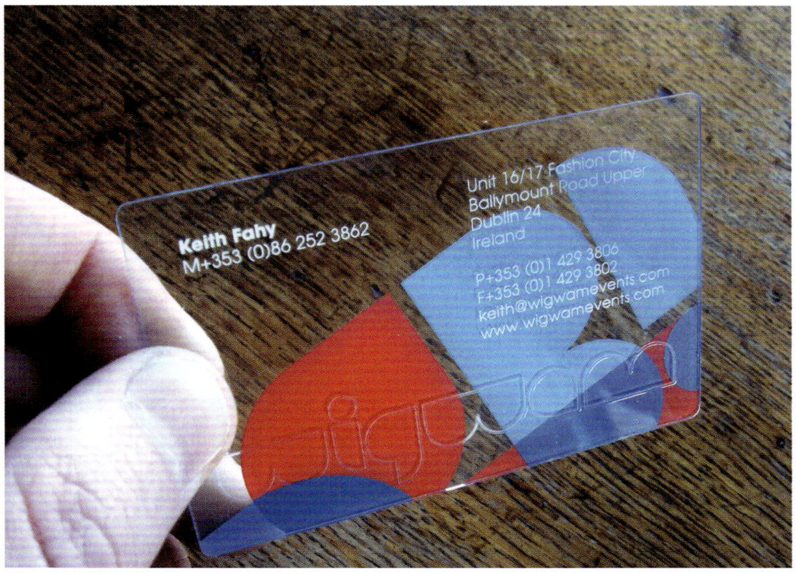
Keith Fahy
M+353 (0)86 252 3862
Unit 16/17 Fashion City
Ballymount Road Upper
Dublin 24
Ireland
P+353 (0)1 429 3806
F+353 (0)1 429 3802
keith@wigwamevents.com
www.wigwamevents.com

Möoi Identity

Design Agency: SeventhDesign™
Creative Director: María José Rojas
Designer: Bruno Siriani
Client: Grupo Multifood
Creating Date: 2010
Information: Möoi is part of a brand new concept in Buenos Aires: the contemporaneous food. This wave has been merged in this project with the modern art & design to build a nice space, comfortable and very impressive utilising a great amount of different shapes, textures and colours.

MÖOI

MÖOI
MÖOI

MÖOI
MÖOI
MÖOI
MÖOI

MÖOI

MÖOI
MÖOI

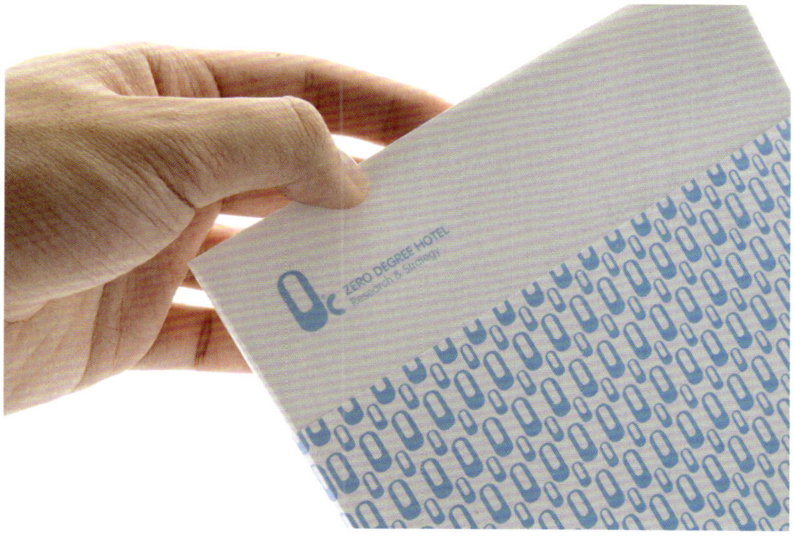

Zero Degree Hotel Identity

Design Agency: Studiowill

Client: Zero degree hotel

Creating Date: 2007

Information: Studiowill developed a Corporate Identity, sub brand and applications for a small hotel chain in Niseko Japan, catering predominantly to western tourists who loves to ski. The name of the hotel is called Zero Degree Hotel.

SEPTIMA
BODEGA

Bodega Septima Identity

Design Agency: SeventhDesign™

Creative Director: Bruno Siriani

Client: Levi Group

Creating Date: 2010

Information: Septima is a young winery in Argentina, property of the Codorniu Group that has more than 400 years of expertise. Modern style, quality and knowledge should be basics of this redesign.

In advance of a new line, the studio worked to expand the reach of "quality" in new brand image and packaging forms that speak to a shift in position: from a common wine brand to a daily pleasure but also an extravagance. The resulting refreshing reinforced Septima's market leadership position by infusing the brand with fresh spirit and modern appeal.

Kids Cafe Piccolo Identity

Design Agency: VONSUNG Design
Creative Director: Joseph Sung
Client: KIDS CAFÉ PICCOLO
Creating Date: 2009
Information: KIDS CAFÉ PICCOLO was designed to offer a fairy tale feeling for children with an adult-like atmosphere for their parents to enjoy. The branding design agency responsible for the overall branding design of the complex.

KIDS
CAFE 피콜로
PICCOLO

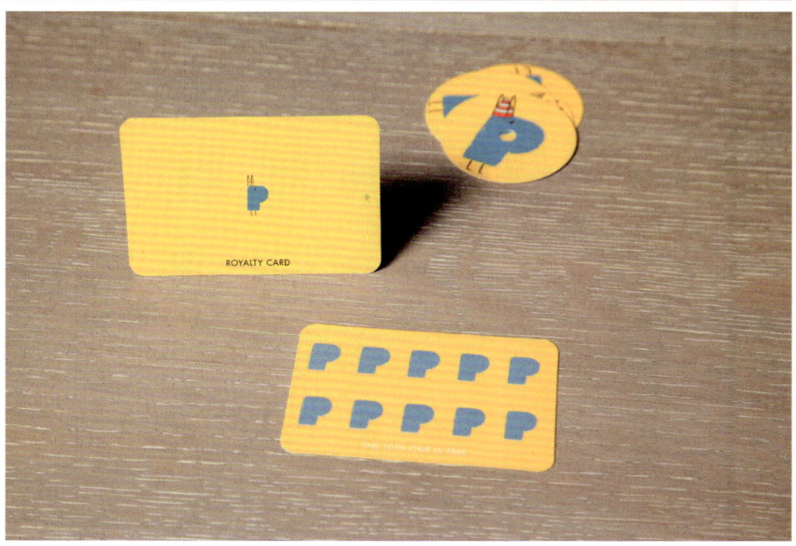

KIDS CAFE PICCOLO

KIDS CAFE PICCOLO
서울시 광진구 구의동 212-3 CS Plaza 2층
T 02-2201-3252 F 02-2201-3253
PICCOLO
PICCOLO

KIDS CAFE PICCOLO
SWEETS
DRINKS
MEALS

La Colmena Identity

Design Agency: Raquel Quevedo

Creative Director: Raquel Quevedo

Creating Date: 2010

Information: Concept, identity and packaging design for the confectionery La Colmena, inspired in old vintage sweet and bees.

Suite 88 Identity

Creative Director: Louis Gagnon

Designer: René Clément

Creating Date: 2008

Information: Suite 88 is an exclusive gourmet chocolate boutique located in Montreal. The designers were asked to develop Suite 88's branding programme. First, they created a simple, elegant logo, which was easy to integrate in all presentations: from bags, to boxes...to the way chocolates are displayed in windows and even how the dessert plates are decorated. After winning many national and international design awards for the excellence of its logo and its entire identity programme, Suite 88 won a major City of Montreal award for the ensemble of the boutique's design. Suite 88's success has been so outstanding they are considering opening more stores.

Marabans. Coffee and Tea Identity

Design Agency: Series nemo

Designer: Own Team

Client: Distribución Cafés Finos

Creating Date: 2010

Information: The new corporate identity of Marabans is really simple. That same simplicity is applied in a complex way in its extensive product range creating a chromatic and photographic universe own. Marabans evokes close, wished and Mediterranean places, and invites us to enjoy unforgettable moments in its company... DON'T WALK ALONE.

Melt Identity

Designer: Jesse Kirsch

Client: Melt

Creating Date: 2009

Information: Melt, a gourmet chocolate shop, plays with the characteristics of melted chocolate with its logo and packaging in a fun and sophisticated way. The bar's patterns look as if they were illustrated with warm, liquid chocolate while the tins have the look of being dipped. Even the truffle box has shiny chocolate finger prints as if it was just given to you by the chocolatier. The packaging serves not to outdo the actual chocolate, but instead mimics the product serving to reenforce it.

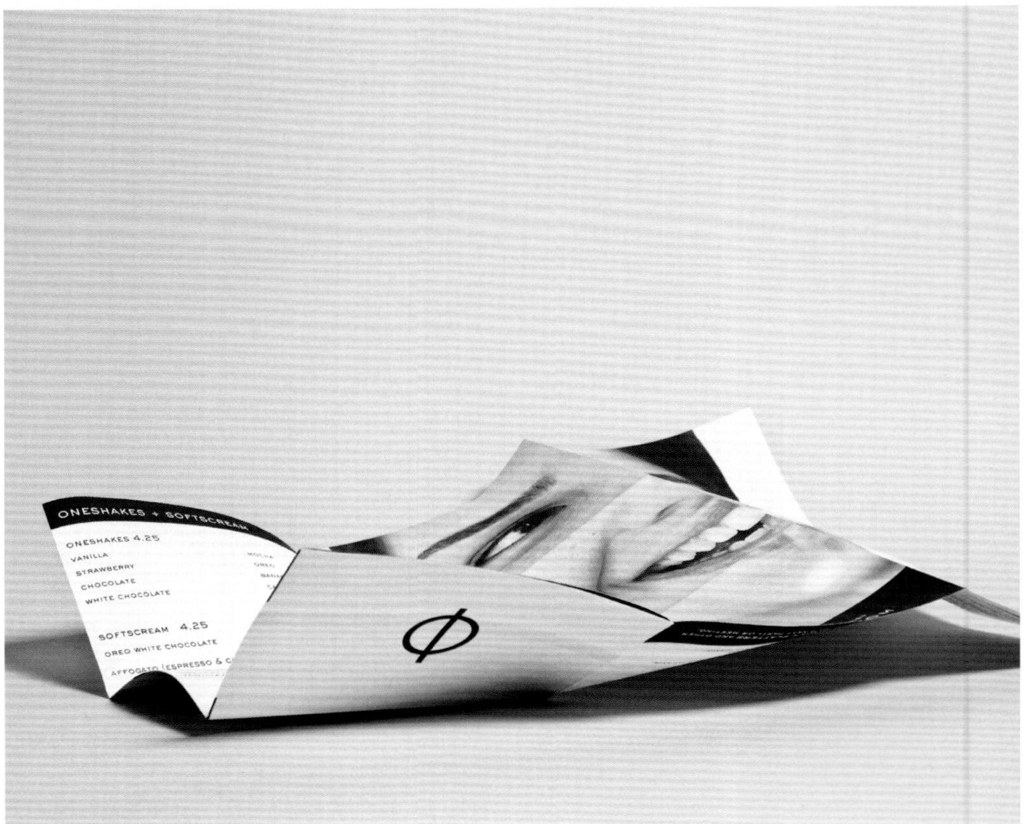

Oneburger Restaurant Identity

Design Agency: Lemon Yellow

Client: Oneburger Restaurant

Creating Date: 2010

Information: The identity was developed with the intention of communicating a purist's approach to food, one that would not be intimidating to the layman. It's effective and functional branding has come to represent transparency in the food process, a minimalist amount of intervention between the customer and his burger.

Pro Arte

Design Agency: 3group
Designer: Ryszard Bienert
Client: Fundacja Pro Arte
Creating Date: 2008
Information: The print work as well as the logo were designed around the contrast between black and white. The logo is flexible, so that on some materials like on the letterhead, the designers have played with it, using large areas of white closed off by areas of black logo with cutouts. The materials have been created for artistic foundation, which has allowed them to underline the value of the game between black and white.

Dan Alexander & Co. Identity

Design Agency: Dan Alexander & Co.

Client: KINETIS

Creating Date: 2008

Information: Identity through Design means harnessing the designers' artistic creativeness in order to gain business advantage for their clients. They analyse and decompose brands into their core visual particles. This focus allows them to map out labels upon a wide spectrum of creativity and thus attribute each and every brand its specific gravity.

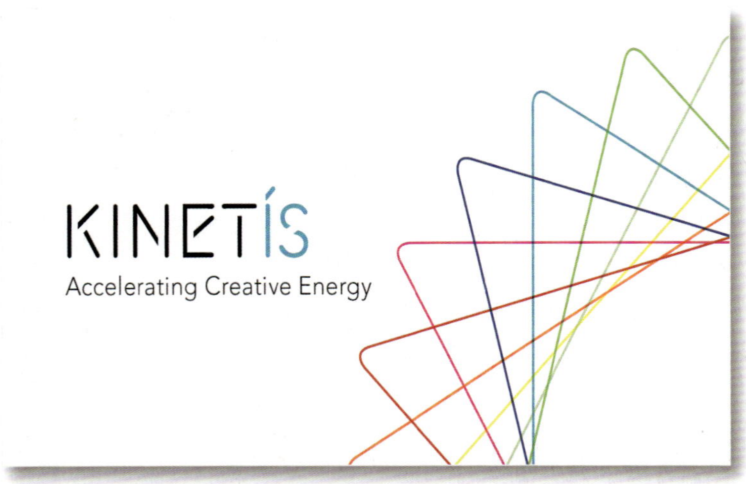

Luckyfish Identity

Design Agency: Studio Hinrichs

Designer: Kit Hinrichs & Laura Scott

Client: Luckyfish

Creating Date: 2008

Information: A visual translation of the name, the Luckyfish logo highlights one of eight fish in red, the colour for good luck in Japanese culture, and references the restaurant's conveyor belt service. The identity is used comprehensively throughout the entire restaurant's graphics, extending to signage, the website, menus and dinnerware as well as T-shirts, baseball caps and other ancillary items.

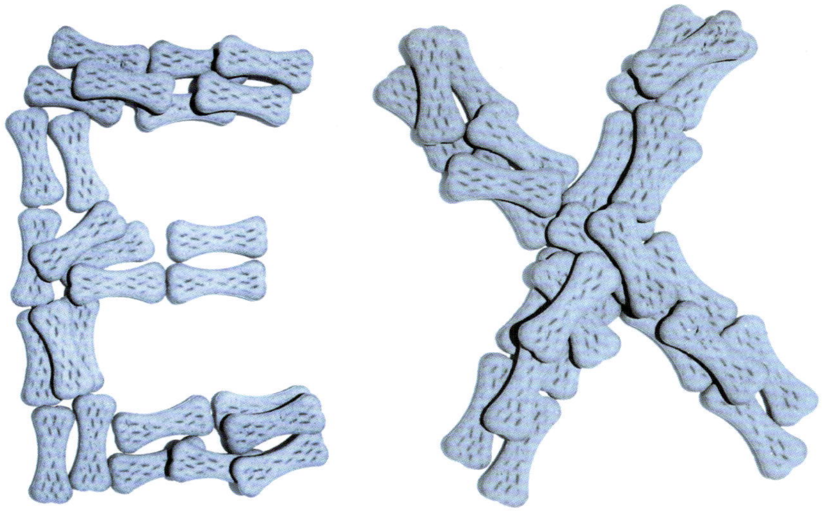

EXPOAANIFEIRA
Porto, 17 Junho 2008
Excelentissimo(a) Sr./Sra.
EXPOAANIFEIRA
CATS&DOGS
Att. Exmo. (a) Sr. (a)
Director(a) da Cats&Dogs
Rua Nossa Senhora das Flores N 231
Ramalde
4100 - 364 Porto

Aanifeira Identity

Design Agency: Sergio Alves

Client: Aanifeira

Creating Date: 2008

Information: Project developed for an exhibition for an organisation called "Aanifeira". The concept was designed for children and young people. Collaboration with Eurico Sá Fernandes

CAMP Identity

Creative Director: Louis Gagnon

Designer: Homer Mendoza

Client: Camp Restaurant Bar

Creating Date: 2009

Information: Located in the heart of Crescent Street, the CAMP Restaurant Bar offers local customers and tourists alike Al Fresco daytime dining as well as festive evenings inside once the shades are drawn. Paprika was commissioned to come up with a pure, clean design to contrast with the festive trendy atmosphere of the area, one that would do justice to the fresh, seasonal menu. The programme is simple and fun, creating a laid-back environment.

Domison Identity

Creative Director: Louis Gagnon

Art Director: René Clément

Designer: René Clément

Client : Domison

Creating Date: 2009

Information: Domison is a furniture brand whose philosophy is to give access to good design for everyone. The designers treat the leaf and the name like graphical elements, creating patterns, playing with the logo; they make it move, change its angle, repeat it, etc. The designers play with juxtaposition, transparency, overlapping and duplication of elements.

Lucky Seven Trophy

Design Agency: MusaWorkLab

Designer: MusaWorkLab

Client: IWC Schaffhausen ,Luís Figo Foundation

Creating Date: 2010

Information: The identity was inspired on the football graphics to make an emblem with the number 7 (the Figo number and the lucky number) and also the ball with the lucky clover. The invitation for the event was inspired on the identity and the Luis Figo image.

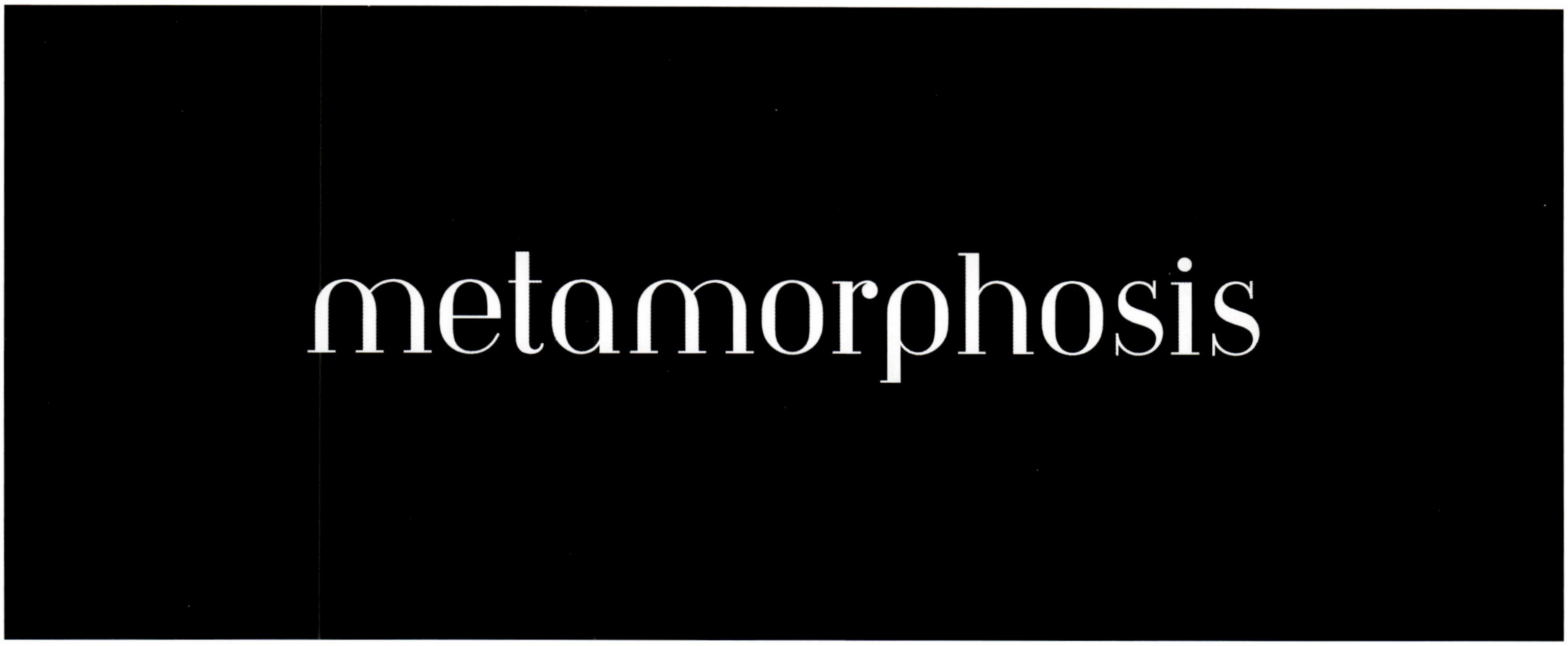

Metamorphosis Identity

Design Agency: Zhishi design

Client: Metamorphosis

Creating Date: 2010

Information: Logo & identity for the Metamorphosis yoga school.

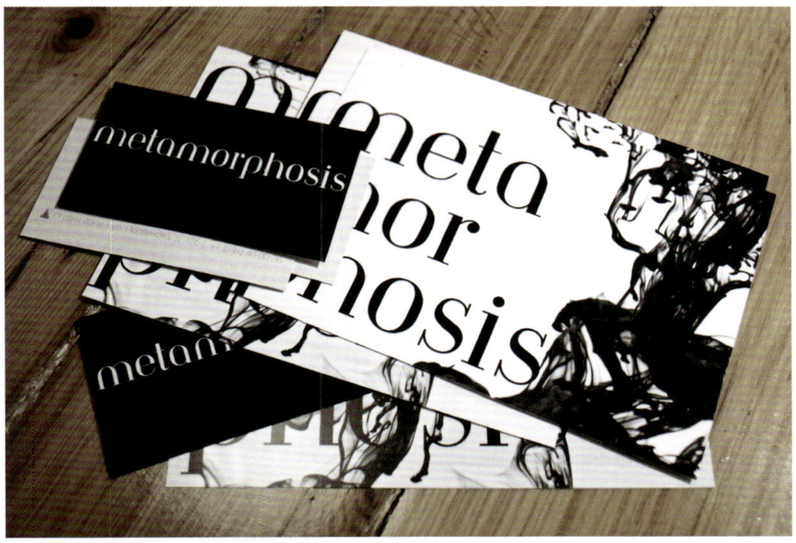

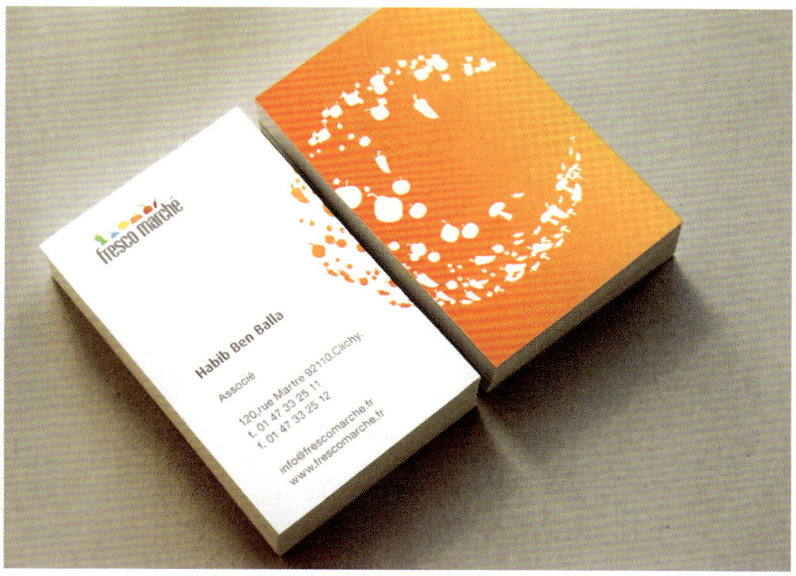

Fresco Marché Identity

Design Agency: SeventhDesign™

Designer: Bruno Siriani

Client: IWC Schaffhausen, Luís Figo Foundation

Information: This work helps facilitate communication between client stakeholders, resulting in adaptable systems that define visual communication across an organisation.

Dj Taktel & Comodo's Control Remoto

Design Agency: Menta

Creative Directors and designers: Raúl Climent, Xavi Calvo & Elisa Gómez

Client: Coffy records

Creating Date: 2010

Information: Packaging and poster design for Coffy Records. Dj Taktel and Comodo, sampler and musical cut and paste masters, paying graphic tribute to Saul Bass in their new album "Control Remoto".

Trool Identity

Design Agency: Studio Kmzero

Client: Trool

Creating Date: 2010

Information: To frame the necessary concepts regarding safe surfing a world of colourful little characters has been created. Divided in families, the little Trool Monters embody through their kinship to the main tribes, different ways of exploring and living the web. Behind the simple, appealing interface, a complex project on naming, mood design and web development is under study – to bring the online blog to the status of leading Italian web portal for the youngest.

trool
prova
racconta
impara

trool.it
tutti i ragazzi ora on line!

trool.it
tutti i ragazzi ora on line!

huttons

Huttons Identity

Design Agency: Superfried studio

Client: Huttons

Creating Date: 2007

Information: Huttons is a retail chain covering a wide range of products from scented candles and women's clothes to high-end furniture. They required a complete re-brand covering all aspects including signage, point of sale and marketing materials. This was a challenging brief as despite 80% of customers being female it was important that the brand did not alienate men. To create that fine balance an abstract icon of a flower was developed in a very subtle pink. In contrast the primary colour selected was a much stronger and masculine dark brown. Finally to create further distinction a bespoke font was created.

Cappele, Luxurious Welsh Rural Accommodation

Design Agency: Kutchibok

Designer: Alwyn Thomas, Siôn Dafydd

Client: Cappele

Creating Date: 2010

Information: Luxurious Welsh rural accommodation offers lifestyle accessories and locally sourced organic meat and bespoke artisan products. It was important for the brand to reflect the deeply rooted historical and cultural elements of this traditional yet luxurious Welsh farmhouse as well as impart a sense of top class luxury. Classic, uncompromising quality had to be reflected in the branding, so Kutchibok decided to use a rich yet understated, organic colour palette for the marketing brochures and labels; a sophisticated and elegant serif font for the text combined with the purity of the blind embossing of the Cappele logo mark.

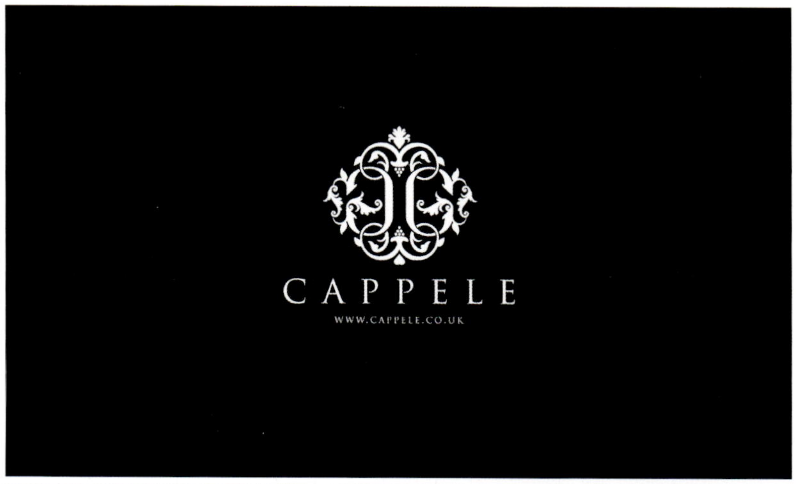

Hebbes Identity

Design Agency: Trapped in Suburbia

Client: Museum Gouda

Creating Date: 2009

Information: The "Gotcha!" project, or "Hebbes!" in Dutch, Museum Gouda is one of the few museums in the world to take the first steps towards liberating their historic heritage collections into the 3D scan medium for all to view. Walking into the space you see a big 3D (hologram) screen. In front of the screen you see a touchscreen display and a small cube. On the display you can select an art object and with the cube you can control the art object on the 3D screen. We designed the identity and the exhibition.

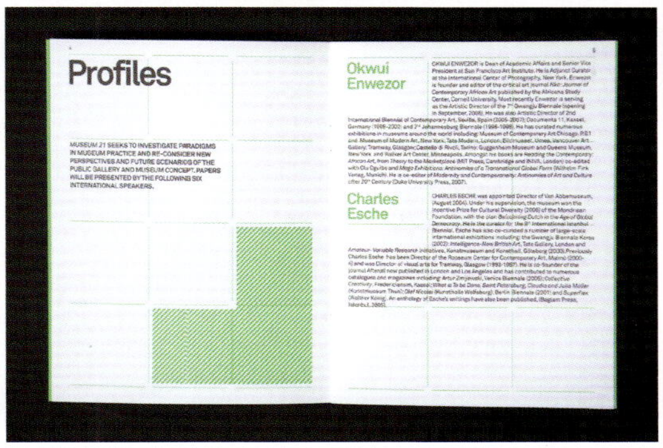

Museum 21 Identity

Designer: Jim Delaney

Client: Irish Museum of Modern Art International Symposium

Creating Date: 2008

Information: Development of identity & promotional material. The purpose of the symposium was to address the role of gallery and museum space in the 21st century, this was reflected in the identity by picking out of the word "use" within the "museum 21" logo.

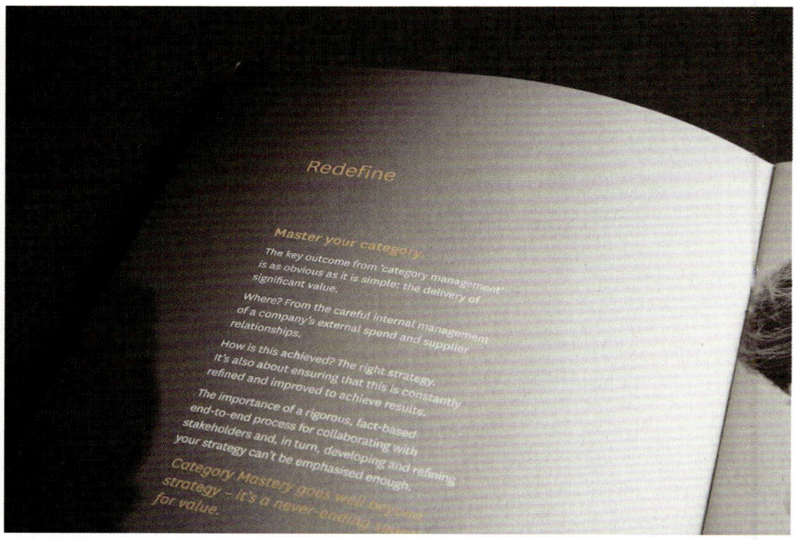

The Source Procurement Corporate Identity

Design Agency: TANK

Creative Director: Jim Antonopoulos

Designer: Chris Butcher, Zoe Coombe

Client: The Source Procurement

Creating Date: 2010

Information: A brand mark was designed which linked back to the Faculty masterbrand both in style and substance, and photography was used to capture the innovation that exists when great business minds get together.

THE SOURCE
With Compliments

Tania Seary
Founding Chairman
502 Albert Street
East Melbourne VIC 3002
T +61 3 9650 6665
F +61 3 9654 2777
M +61 409 185 207
E tania.seary@thesourceprocurement.com.au
www.thesourceprocurement.com.au
THE SOURCE

Lettera22
una ricerca di Emanuele Piccardo su Adriano Olivetti

Lettera 22

Designer: Dan Alexsander

Client: Lettera 22

Dreating Date: 2010

Information: This was a work for "plug_ in" publisher. The graphics for the DVD "lettera 22", a documentary about Adriano Olivetti. First, we created 200 copies, in 7" format. Then 50x70 posters, flyers, folders, pins. For the second edition the circulation was higher; the packaging changes into a poster/newspaper and contains the DVD. The monogram composition with the two "2", reminds the ink ribbon of the legendary typewriter Lettera 22, by Olivetti.

Bankinter Identity

Design Agency: Saffron Brand Consultants
Creative Director: Saffron
Designer: Design Team Saffron
Client: Bankinter
Creating Date: 2006
Information: Bankinter is the leading Spanish bank in innovative technology. It's a thinking bank that attracts thinking clients. But its brand had become a bit cold and remote. It was no longer appealing to its natural customer base – mainly younger people. How could Bankinter reinvent itself and stay in the game? Sophisticated, intelligent, informed even opinionated and outspoken, Bankinter's personality emerges in the way it communicates it is authoritative, thoughtful and direct. Everything about the visual style including the specially designed typeface emphasises this.

bankinter.

bankinter.
Por qué contratar en Bankinter un Depósito y un BonoClip explicado en doce puntos:
12%
BonoClip Garantizado
Usted
es rentable
es rentable

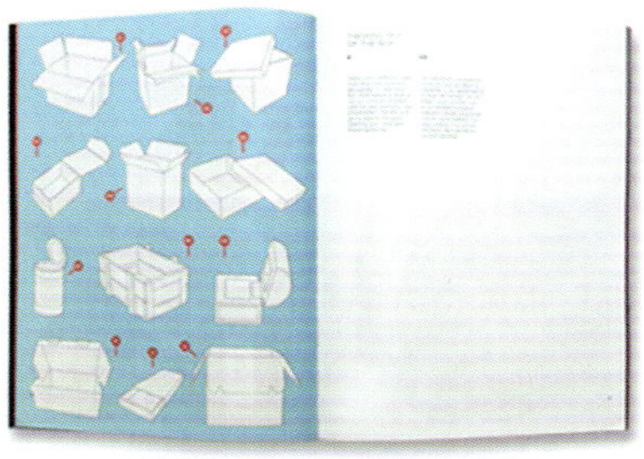

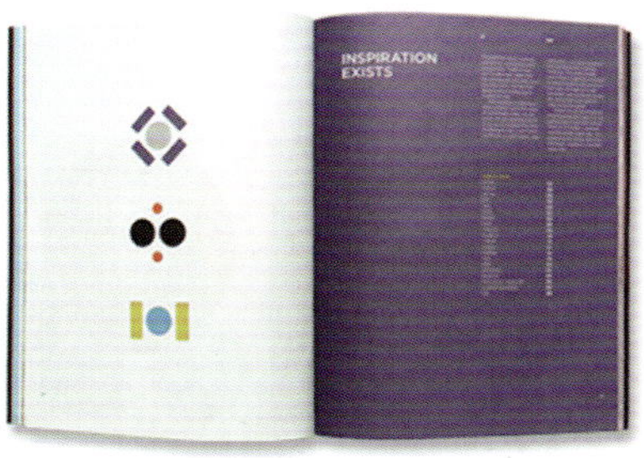

Dynamobel Identity

Design Agency: Saffron Brand

Creative director: Saffron

Designer: Design Team Saffron

Client: Dynamobel

Creating Date: 2006

Information: The concept that has guided the redesign of Dynamobel's brand identity has been the idea of lateral thinking, on which the company's ethos is deeply grounded. Dynamobel, seeks to offer solutions to architects and interiors professionals that do not compromise for function.

dynamobel
www.dynamobel.com

dynamobel
PRODUCTOS
FERIAS / EVENTOS
PROYECTOS

QF Hotel Corporate Design

Design Agency: Amen Gestaltung

Creative Director: Michaela Mansch, Claudio Prisco

Designer: Michaela Mansch, Claudio Prisco

Photography: Chon Choi

Client: QF Hotel

Creating Date: 2010

Information: AMEN Gestaltung was commissioned to develop an integrated concept of corporate design, image folder, guidance system and web design. Continous simplicity signifies the basic concept of the network QF HOTEL consisting of corporate design, website, image folder and guidance system playing with particular materials and colours and stringent compliance corresponding to the interior concept of the hotel.

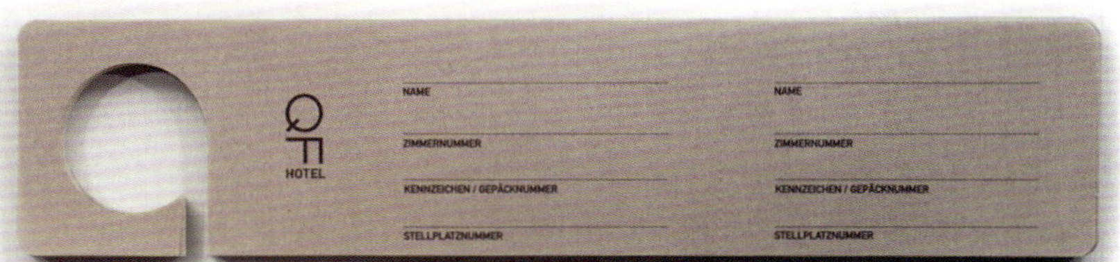

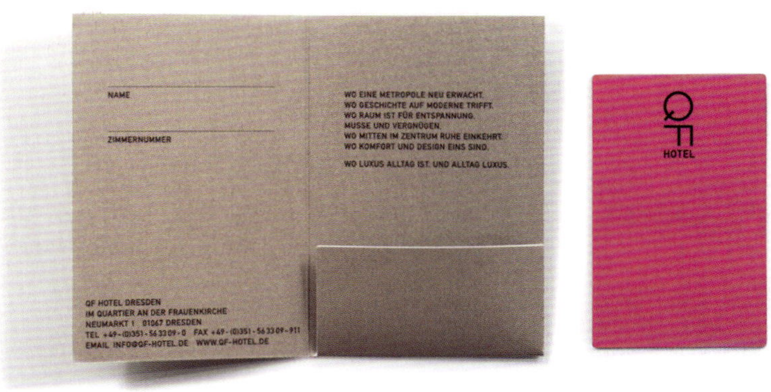

DAS QF HOTEL BEFINDET SICH IM ZENTRUM DRESDENS DIREKT AM NEUMARKT NEBEN DER FRAUENKIRCHE.

DIE ZIMMERKATEGORIEN CLASSIC, SUPERIOR UND DELUXE REPRÄSENTIEREN KOMFORTABLE EINZEL- UND DOPPELZIMMER MIT DER ZEITLOS ELEGANTEN EINRICHTUNG AUS DEM STUDIO LORENZO BELLINI IN ROM. DIE MODERNEN SUITEN BIETEN EINZIGARTIGE AUSBLICKE ÜBER DIE HISTORISCHE ALTSTADT. HOCHWERTIGES MOBILIAR, MINIBAR, ZIMMERSAFE, FLAT SCREEN TV UND DIE VOLLKLIMATISIERUNG ALLER RÄUME SIND EINE SELBSTVERSTÄNDLICHKEIT. DARÜBER HINAUS VERFÜGT JEDES ZIMMER ÜBER EINEN GERÄUMIGEN SCHREIBTISCH MIT INTEGRIERTEN MEDIENANSCHLÜSSEN. DIE BADEZIMMER SIND IN ITALIENISCHEM NATURSTEIN GEHALTEN.

DAS QUARTIER AN DER FRAUENKIRCHE GIBT MIT SEINEN INITIALEN QF AUCH DEM HOTEL SEINEN NAMEN. UNTER EINEM DACH BEFINDEN SICH HIER ZAHLREICHE EINKAUFS- UND FREIZEITANGEBOTE VON DER LUXUSBOUTIQUE BIS ZUM SCHÖNHEITSSALON. EINE GROSSE AUSWAHL AN RESTAURANTS UND CAFÉS LIEGT IN UNMITTELBARER NACHBARSCHAFT DES HOTELS, Z.B. ANNAM IMPERIAL (ASIATISCH), PIAZZA NOVA (MEDITERRAN), NEUMARKT 1 (LEICHTE MODERNE KÜCHE), KAYS (VEGETARISCH) ODER ONTARIO (KANADISCH).

WO EINE METROPOLE NEU ERWACHT.
WO GESCHICHTE AUF MODERNE TRIFFT.
WO RAUM IST FÜR ENTSPANNUNG, MUSSE UND VERGNÜGEN.
WO MITTEN IM ZENTRUM RUHE EINKEHRT.
WO KOMFORT UND DESIGN EINS SIND.

WO LUXUS ALLTAG IST, UND ALLTAG LUXUS.

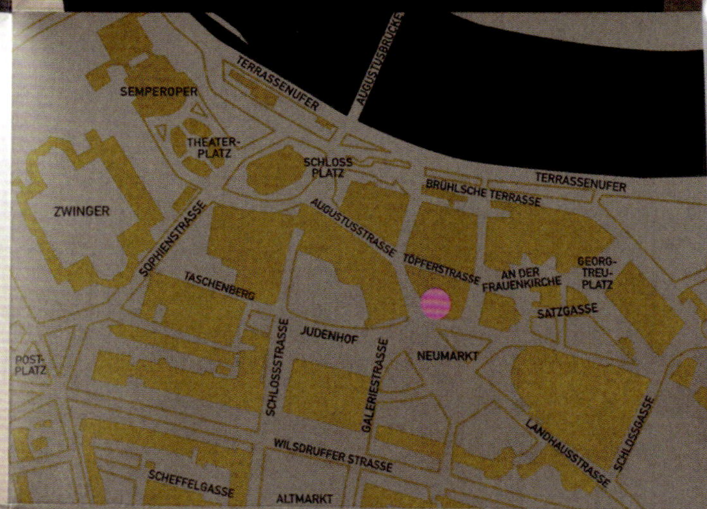

QF HOTEL DRESDEN
IM QUARTIER AN DER FRAUENKIRCHE
NEUMARKT 1 01067 DRESDEN
TEL +49-(0)351-563309-0 FAX +49-(0)351-563309-911
EMAIL INFO@QF-HOTEL.DE WWW.QF-HOTEL.DE

QF
HOTEL

© World Health Organization 2008 / Designed by F A B R I C A (Art: V. Gudenus, Photo: P. Martinello)
720 CHILDREN DIE FROM ROAD TRAFFIC CRASHES EVERY DAY.
KEEP KIDS SAFE.
Seat-belts, helmets, car seats, bicycle and pedestrian lanes, daytime running lights, speed limits, drinking and driving laws, and graduated driver licensing prevent road traffic injuries.
World Health Organization
unicef
www.who.int/violence_injury_prevention/child
www.unicef.org/health/index_childinjury.html

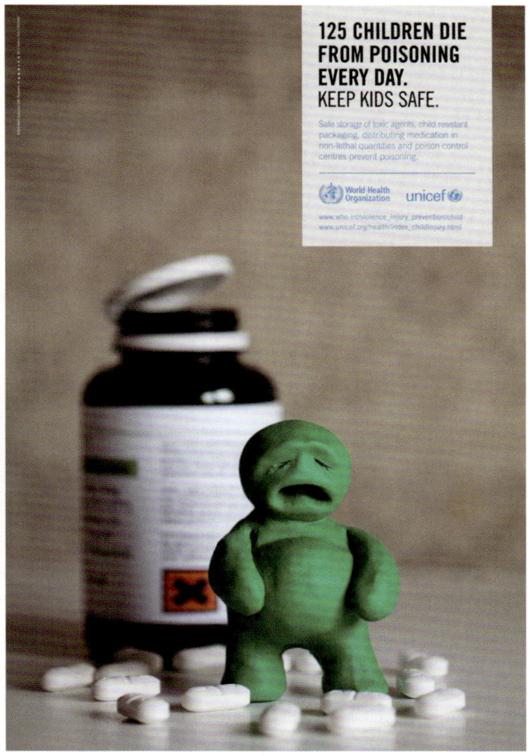

Child Injury Prevention Campaign

Design Agency: FABRICA
Art Director: Valerie Gudenus
Creative Director: Omar Vulpinari
Photography: Piero Martinello
Dreating Date: 2008
Information: The launch of the World Report on Child Injury Prevention took place on December 10 in Vietnam-Hanoi. UNWHO and UNICEF have commissioned Fabrica's Visual Communication department, directed by Omar Vulpinari to conceive a global advocacy and awareness raising campaign.

In order to use a universal visual language related to children, Austrian graphic designer Valerie Gudenus created putty characters engaged in the five dangerous situations. While concise informational texts convey the startling facts, the result is visually impacting, memorable and convincing.

Climate Change Hurts

Design Agency: FABRICA

Art Director: Alexandre Saumier Demers

Photography: Alexandre Saumier Demers

Creative Director: Omar Vulpinari

Creating Date: 2009

World No Tobacco Day Campaign

Design Agency: FABRICA

Art Director: Gabriele Riva,Namyoung An

Creative Director: Omar Vulpinari

Photography: Sebastiano Scattolin,Piero Martinello

Information: Fabrica designed the series of three posters for this initiative. Each poster surrealistically communicates the pictorial warnings' main goal: to not just tell the truth, but show it.

Road Safety Campaign

Design Agency: FABRICA

Art Director: Yianni Hill

Creative Director: Omar Vulpinari

Photography: Yianni Hill / Reed Young

Creating Date: 2007

Information: This campaign was commissioned by UNWHO for the First United Nations Global World Road Safety Week 2007. The campaign includes five posters and public service announcements addressing "young road users" which are the most frequent victims of road accidents. The aim of the operation is to raise awareness and promote action amongst the general global public around the five factors of greatest impact in road injuries regarding young road users: helmets, seatbelts, drinking and driving, speeding, and visibility.

Too late to fasten your seat-belt
Wearing a seat-belt reduces the risk of being ejected from a vehicle and suffering serious or fatal injury by between 40% - 65%.
Be part of the solution: wear a seat-belt.
ROAD SAFETY IS NO ACCIDENT
www.who.int/roadsafety

Too late to stop drinking
Consuming alcohol before driving increases the risk of a crash as well as the likelihood that death or serious injury will result. Passing a drink-driving law and enforcing it can reduce the number of road deaths by 20%.
Be part of the solution: never drink and drive.
ROAD SAFETY IS NO ACCIDENT
www.who.int/roadsafety

Too late to be seen
Pedestrians and cyclists can be difficult to see on the roads, which increases their risk of road traffic injuries. Wearing lightly-coloured or reflective clothing makes them much more visible and can help avoid collisions.
Be part of the solution: be seen on the road.
ROAD SAFETY IS NO ACCIDENT
www.who.int/roadsafety

Too late to slow down
Speed kills all types of road users – drivers, pedestrians and cyclists. A 5% cut in average speed can reduce the number of fatal crashes by as much as 30%.
Be part of the solution: don't speed.
ROAD SAFETY IS NO ACCIDENT
www.who.int/roadsafety

BOEKENWEEK
hoofdsponsor
organisatie
Stichting Collectieve
Propaganda van het
Nederlandse Boek
Februari 2009, Stichting CPNB, Amsterdam, 09BW32 Concept en vormgeving: De Designpolitie, Fotografie: Gerrit Serné, Model: Gabber
11 T/M 21 MAART 2009

BO
11 T/

Boekenweek

Design Agency: De Designpolitie

Creating Date: 2009

Information: The CPNB (Collective Promotion for the Dutch Book) commissioned De Designpolitie to do a poster for the annual Bookweek. This year's central theme is "animals in literature". In a series of four posters the designers portrayed a dog with a severe identity crisis who is turning to literature for help.

FRASCATI
FABU
LOUS
FRAS
CATI
FIRST WEEK FRASCATI
WO 17 T/M ZA 20 SEPTEMBER
WWW.THEATERFRASCATI.NL

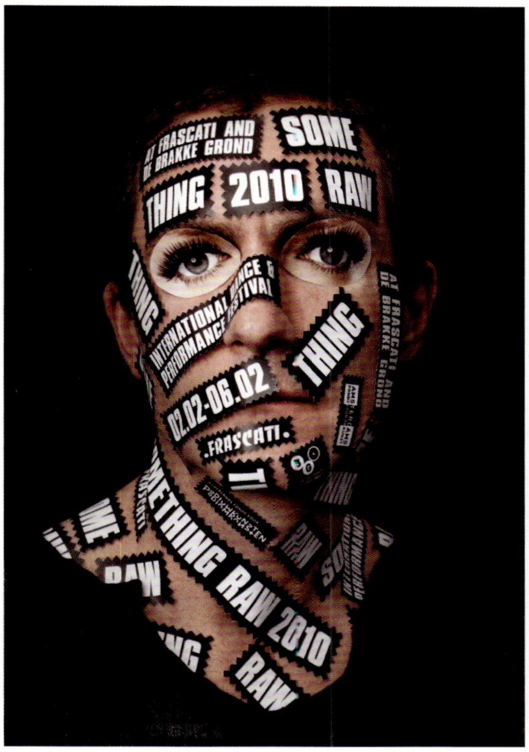

Something Raw

Design Agency: De Designpolitie

Creating Date: 2010

Information: Something Raw is an international dance and performance festival organised by Frascati and De Brakke Grond. For the campaign De Designpolitie dressed two dancers with the basic information.

Frascati Theatre

Design Agency: De Designpolitie

Creating Date: 2008

Information: Frascati is a theatre in the centre of Amsterdam. You can see great plays by established theatre makersthere and at the same time it is home to young and upcoming artists. Their work in progress is shown on a seperate location.The new identity was launched at the beginning of the cultural season.

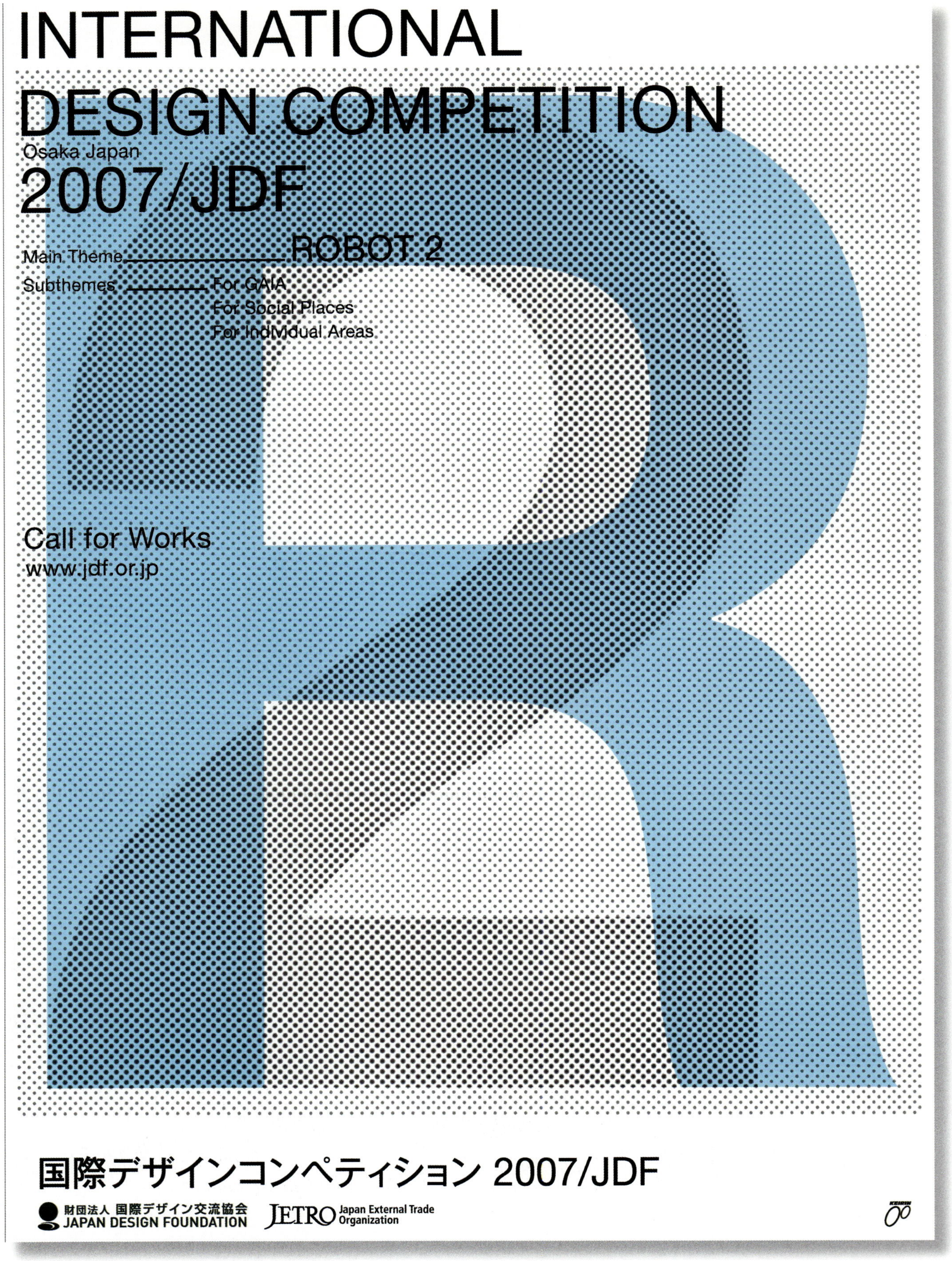

International Design Competition 2007

Design Agency: Shinnoske Design

Designer: Shinnoske Sugisaki

Client: Japan Design Foundation

Creating Date: 2007

Information: Poster for call for entry of an international design competition which main theme "Robot 2". Using initial R and 2 as a symbol, key colour of blue expresses sub themes environment of the planet.

The Border

Design Agency: Shinnoske Design

Designer: Shinnoske Sugisaki

Client: JAGDA TOKYO

Creating Date: 2007

Information: Poster for a gallery JAGDA TOKYO run by JAGDA, the most authoritative graphic designers association in Japan. A collaborative exhibition titled "The Border".

Rethank

Design Agency: ADearFriend

Designer: Chris Ro

Photography: Nojisu

Client: Rhode Island School of Design

Creating Date: 2009

Information: A project exploring materiality, texture and finding new experiences in the everyday. This series of posters attempts to re-examine the often disappearing message of recycling or rethanking materials that may support another lifespan. Taking the forgotten, discarded and often misplaced and using them to re-examine a message. The project explores amplifying the beauty of these often forgotten materials and aims to use this heightened awareness to bring forward the possibilities in recycling these and re-thanking them.

Weathervane Music

Art Direction: Mark Pernice
Designer: Mark Pernice
Photography: Mark Pernice
Creating Date: 2009
Information: Weathervane Music Organisation limited-edition poster for their launch and first fundraising event. Designed from organised musical instruments and studio gear.

WEATHERVANE MUSIC LAUNCH PARTY 6/25, 9PM AT KUNG FU NECKTIE 1250 N. FRONT STREET
VIEWING & LISTENING PARTY FOLLOWED BY THE ARMCHAIRS AND PAPERTRIGGER

B.C. CAMPLIGHT
DANIELSON
EAST HUNDRED
SUNSET
THURSDAY NOV 12TH 9PM
JOHNNY BRENDAS
FIRST ANNUAL FUNDRAISER CONCERT
WEATHERVANE MUSIC

Puma / Carrousel

Design Agency: 3group

Designer: Ryszard Bienert

Client: Andrzej Dobosz

Creating Date: 2009

Information: The posters were produced for the exhibition of works by Andrzej Dobosz.

Sofa

Design Agency: 3group

Designer: Ryszard Bienert

Client: Piotr Blamowski

Creating Date: 2008

Information: The poster was produced for the exhibition of work by Piotr Blamowski. The subject of the exhibition is a baroc styled sofa, created from bronze, with rich ornamentation (organic and mytholigcal motives). Through the use of typeface, the designers have made an effort to reflect the shapes and the copius decorations. The colour of the poster has significance, reflecting the colour of the material used to cover the sofa.

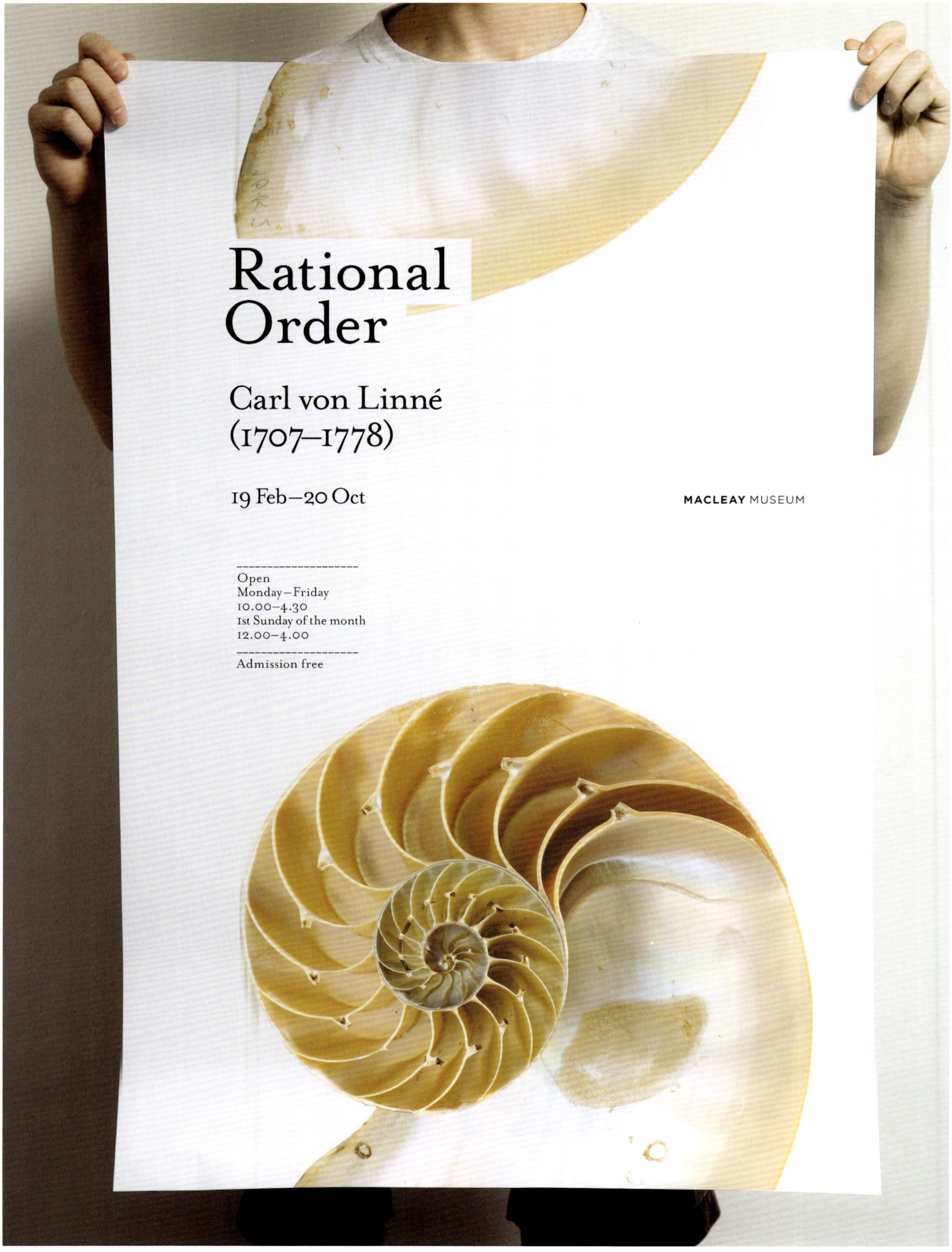
Rational Order
Carl von Linné (1707–1778)
19 Feb–20 Oct
MACLEAY MUSEUM
Open
Monday–Friday
10.00–4.30
1st Sunday of the month
12.00–4.00
Admission free

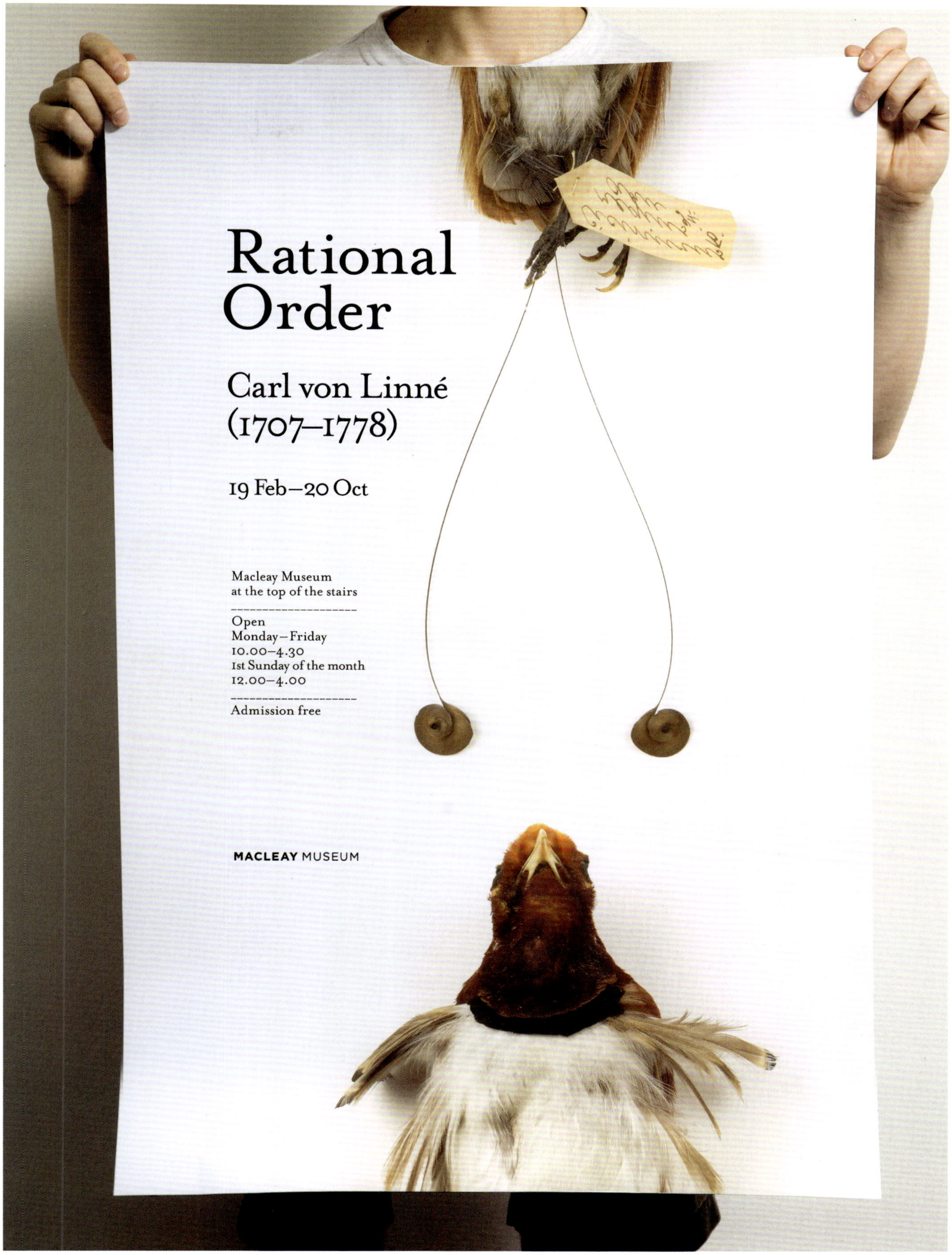

Linnaeus Posters

Design Agency: Naughtyfish Design Studio

Client: Macleay museum

Creating Date: 2006

Information: These posters were created to advertise the Linneaus exhibition at the Macleay museum at the University of Sydney. This exhibition celebrated the life and work of Swedish scientist Carl von Linné on the 300th anniversary of his birth. Carl von Linné (Linnaeus) was responsible for laying the foundations for the modern scheme of Bionomial nomenclature, and is also considered one of the fathers of modern ecology. The imagery came from the objects used in the exhibition.

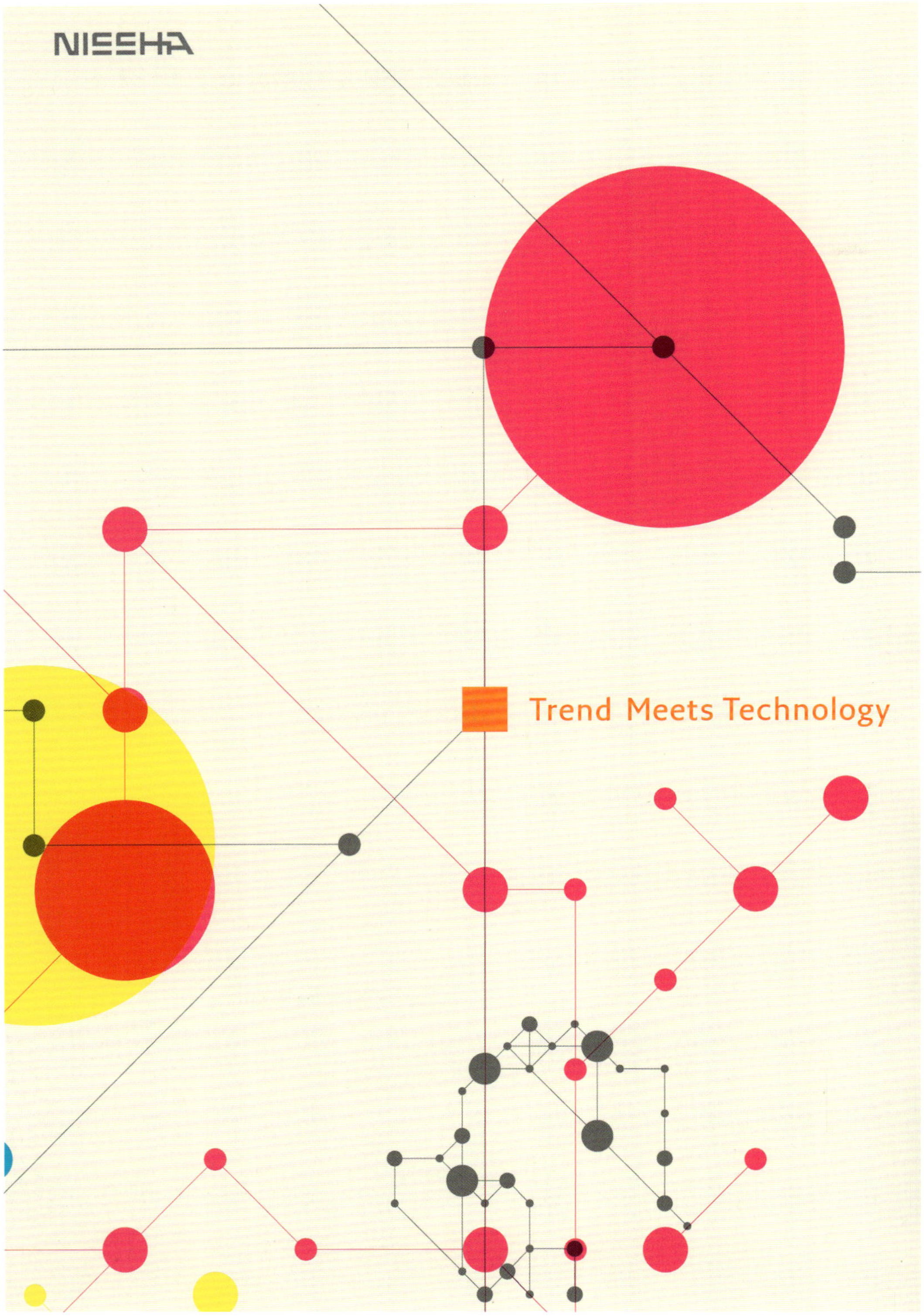

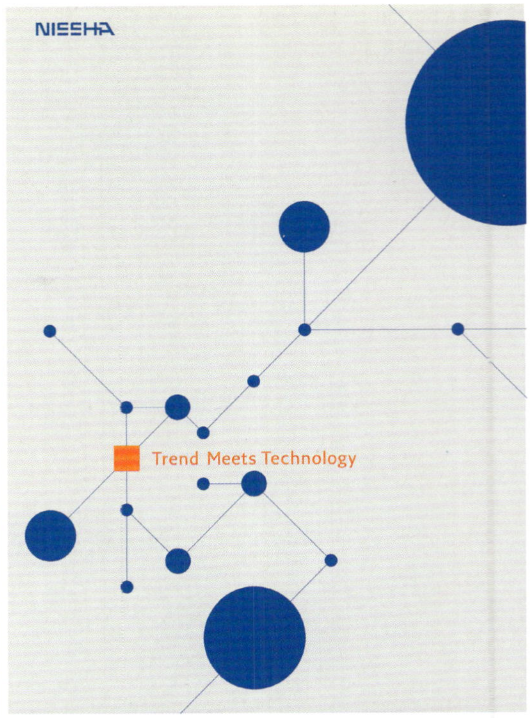

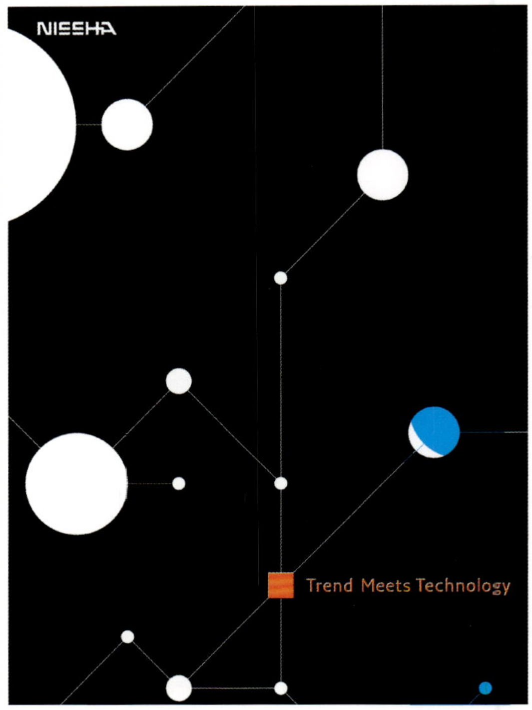

Nissha Brand Poster

Design Agency: Shinnoske Design

Designer: Shinnoske Sugisaki, Shinsuke Suzuki

Client: Nissha Printing Work

Creating Date: 2007

Information: Posters representing the company's brand symbol. The brand symbol is a visualisation of the brand statement "Trend Meets Technology". Trend is represented by circles and symbolises finding the needs of the market and their customers. Technology is represented by the square and symbolises the approach behind their products and services.

Northe Sea Jazz Festival

Design Agency: Samsayonara

Client: Rotterdam

Creating Date: 2008

Information: Poster for the North Sea Jazz Festival in Rotterdam

Cracow Literature Days

Design Agency: Edgar B k

Creative director: Edgar B k

Client: Villa Decius

Creating Date: 2009

9.10.2008
17.00 - 18.00 Willa Decjusza Inauguracja
18.00 - 19.30 Willa Decjusza Homines Urbani, premiera antologii "Ludzie, miasta"
21.00 - 23.00 Klub Lokator Kawiarniane stoliki pisarzy, wieczór literacki
10.10.2008
10.00 - 12.00 Instytut Goethego HALMA, literackie stypendia w Europie, seminarium
10.00 - 16.00 Instytut Goethego Multimedialna czytelnia Homines Urbani
18.00 - 20.00 Bunkier Sztuki Słowa, obrazy, dźwięki: performance
21.00 - 23.00 Klub Piękny Pies One man show, wieczór literacki
11.10.2008
10.00 - 13.00 Willa Decjusza Literatura i miasto, debata
14.00 - 16.00 Willa Decjusza Co nowego w polskiej kulturze, wykład
20.00 - 22.00 Willa Decjusza Willa Babel, wieczór literacki
IV
Krakowskie Dni
Literatury
homines@urbani.com
termin: 9-11 października 2008
IV
Kra
wsk
atu

Made in Reflex

Designer: Florent Carlier

Creating Date: 2009

Information: Thoses two are the first ones. Florent Carlier combined black and white pictures and typographic work. The first poster symbolises his working desk in Paris (the inside), and the second is a street of Paris where he sometimes finds inspiration (the outside). The name Reflex is the agency he is working for now.

Lecture Series Posters

Designer: Danish Lecture

Creating Date: 2009

Information: Posters announcing lecture series in Aarhus and Copenhagen.

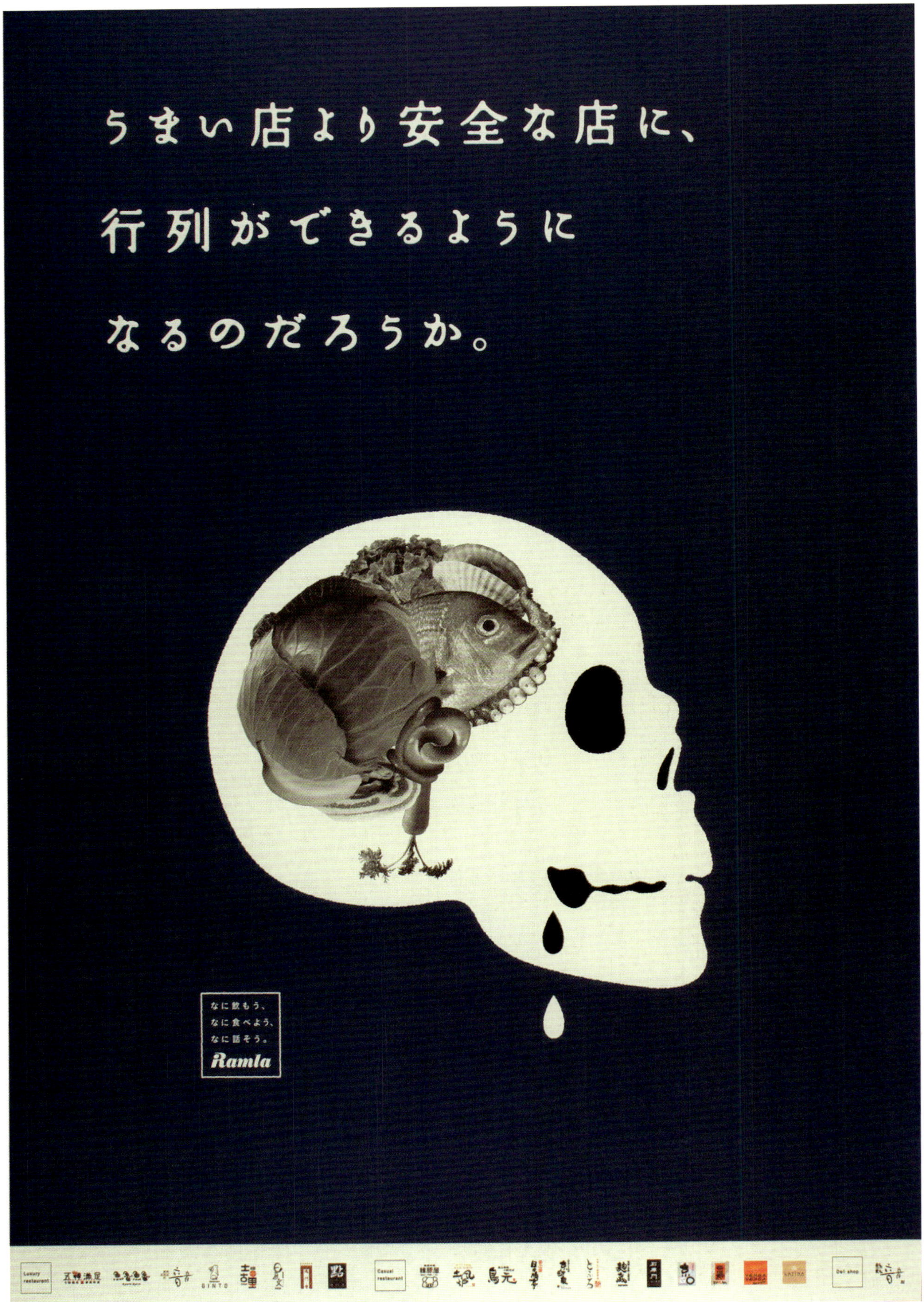

Ramla Posters

Design Agency: E. Co., Ltd.

Designer: Kenichi Matsumoto

Client: Ramla

Creating Date: 2007

Infermation: Posters for recruitment of new employees.

別れ話に
使える店は
いい店だ。
Ramla

手づくり風の
「風」ってなに？
Ramla

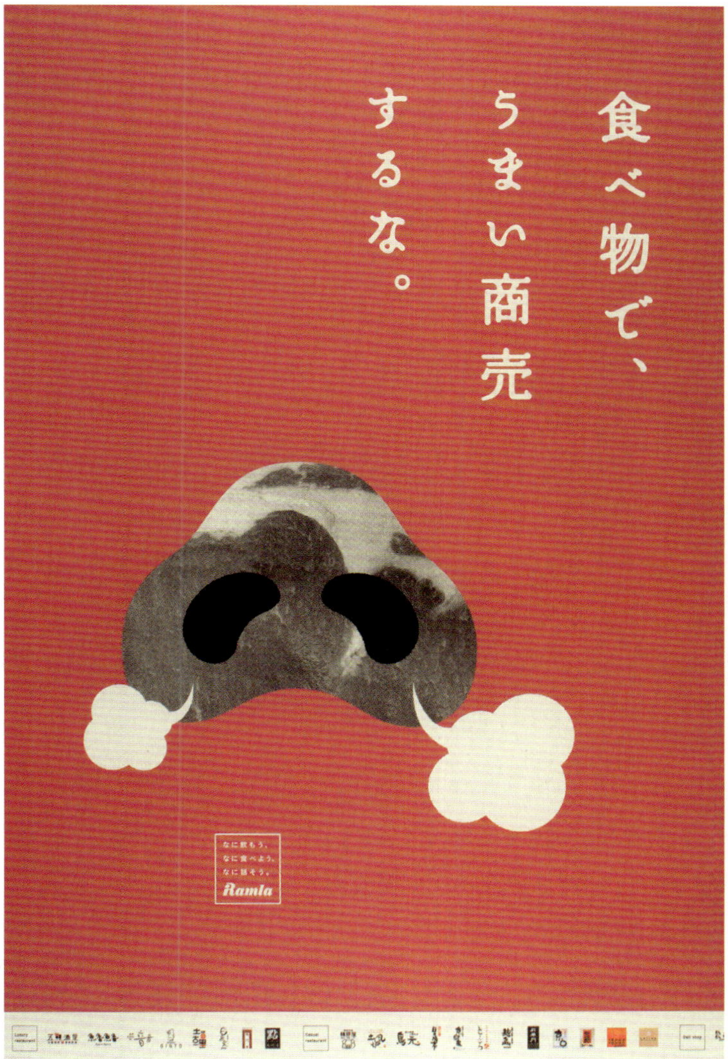
食べ物で、
うまい商売
するな。
Ramla

酒場がなかったら、
生まれてこなかった
人もいる。
Ramla

HitotsuBashi Univ. Photo Club Exhibition Poster

Design Agency: E. Co., Ltd.

Designer: Kenichi Matsumoto

Creating Date: 2006

Information: Utilising the "one" in the name of the university became a typographic element in the works, and also represented each participant in the exhibition.

My life process
Lines show direction, processing and trace. while you drive a car or walk the This is the space where you can draw make your own of graphic symbols and lines. I represented man's life path by extended interpretation of this lines and symbols when I watched leading actor's memory travel in the movie 'Peppermint Candy'. This is the space where you can draw and recollect your life at the same time. Abstract line and graphic icons that are given to you manifest your changed emotion and memory in the past. Each icon can be represented as your own visual language. Freely try to make your own story.
04
7
life is love...
love is life...

The Possibility of Each-Phoneme System of Hanguel

Designer: Hyoun Youl Joe

Creating Date: 2006

Information: A poster for Hanguel typography system

9
9
6
7

Photomonth in Krakow

Design Agency: Edgar B k
Creative Director: Edgar B k
Client: Foundation of Visual Arts
Creating Date: 2010

Bom Dia

Design Agency: Sergio Alves

Client: Self promotion

Creating Date: 2009

Information: In this initial project, the idea was to create a visual conflict, which would cause an impact. The design brings together contemporary and classic forms.

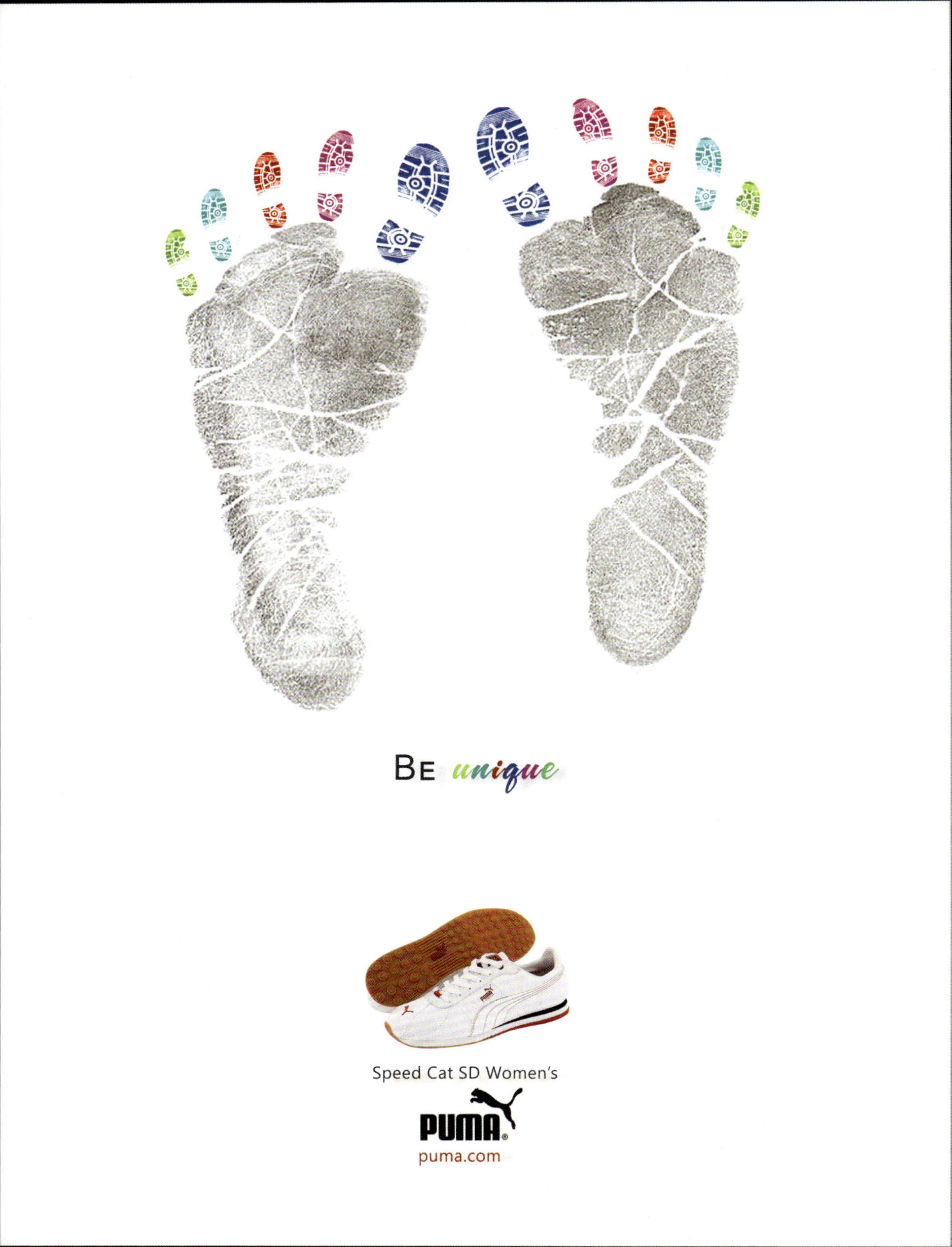

Puma

Design Agency: Creative Spice Up

Creative Director: Olga Cuzuioc

Designer: Olga Cuzuioc

Photography: Olga Cuzuioc

Creating Date: 2010

Information: The designers tried to make the ad easy to navigate and emphasise the special/new feature Puma was bringing to the table. Their "ad

Be unique
Mystere Fade SD Women's
PUMA
puma.com

Pickwick
Herbal Tea
Cherry Berry Twist
pickwick.com
A sip of sensation
Pickwick

Food & Wine

Design Agency: Creative Spice Up
Creative director: Olga Cuzuioc
Designer: Olga Cuzuioc
Photography: Olga Cuzuioc
Client: Columbus
Creating Date: 2010

Pickwick Tea

Design Agency: Creative Spice Up
Creative Director: Olga Cuzuioc
Designer: Olga Cuzuioc
Photography: Olga Cuzuioc
Creating Date: 2009
Information: The brief was challenging the designers to create an ad series that would promote their new tea flavours. The goal was to make the brand look very special and fresh. The designers tried to come up with an idea that would catch their viewers attention but would still emphasise the great flavours that Pickwick tea had to offer. The soft yet colourful visual invited consumers to buy their great product and experience the unique atmosphere created by their new flavors.

High Lights

Designer: Sergio Alves

Client: EAPA (Arvore Art School)

Creating Date: 2009

Information: Concept of a graphic image for the exhibition of projects for 2006-2009 for the art school – "Escola Artistica e Profissional Árvore". The typography was made with screws, in the way to represent the construction of a person in that school.

Bullie Bear

Design: Sergio Alves

Client: TNE

Creating Date: 2010

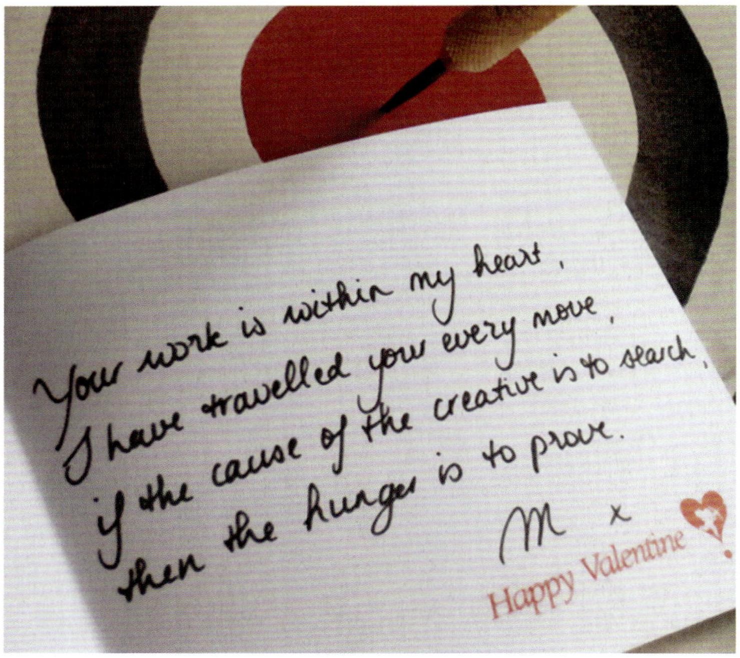

Valentine's Poster

Art Direction: Monique Kneepkens

Designer: Monique Kneepkens

Photography: Florian Groehn

Retouching: Justin Overell

Creating Date: 2009

Information: The idea was to, at this Valentine's Day, aim for the heart of those studios/agencies I love the most. Those creative directors received a parcel on Valentine's Day, containing a little Valentine's card, a dart and a double sided A3 poster. The poster showed a guy on one side, a girl on the other side. Both show a target painted on their chest. If one puts the poster up, and uses the dart, one could really aim for the heart.

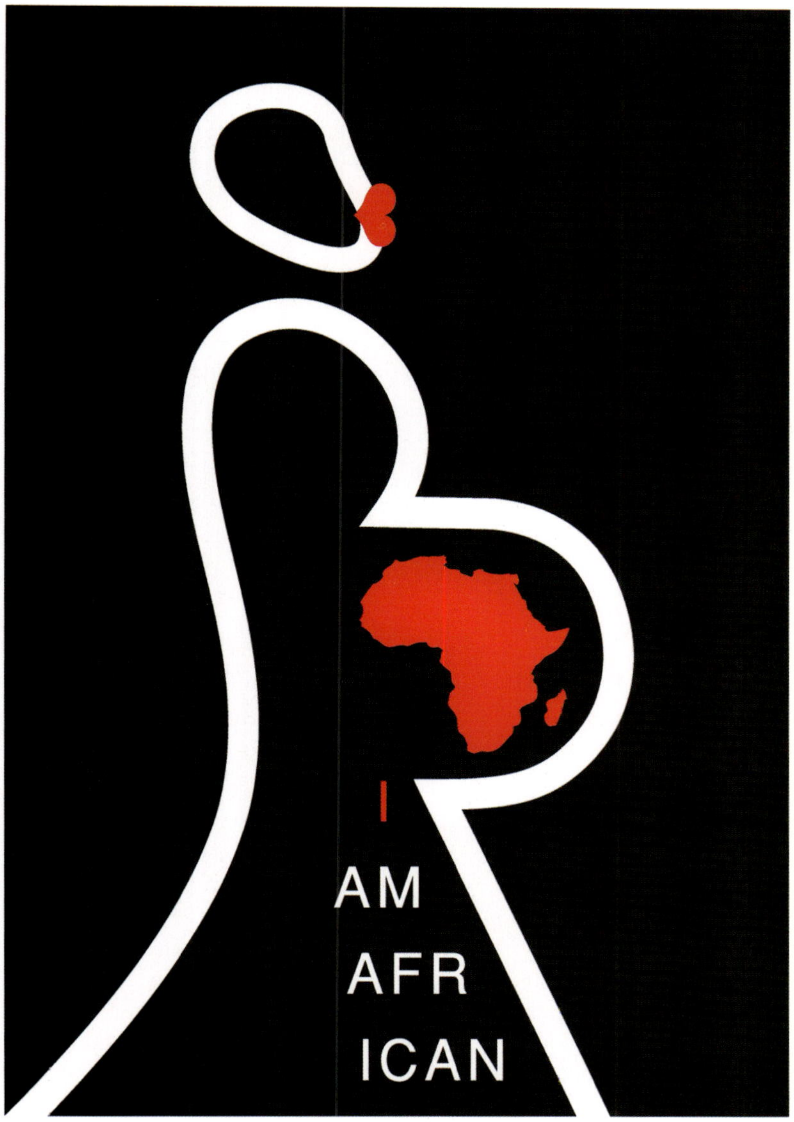

Peter Vasvari Poster

Designer : Peter Vasvari

Creating Date: 2009

GET
LOST
IN
THE
WOODS
THIS
SUMMER
Ford Fiesta
MOONLIGHT
CINEMA

Moonlight Cinema 2009/10 Posters

Design Agency: Naughtyfish Design Studio

Client: Moonlight Cinema

Creating Date: 2009

Information: Moonlight is Australia's largest national outdoor cinema chain and takes place in national parks around the country. The studio saw a parallel between the fantastical journeys that Moonlight takes its patrons on in the woods and popular children's fairy tales. A series of illustrations was created and used across the identity. Patrons could collect the series of postcards. The distinctive illustration style, flat colour & moon element was a common thread across the material.

Rubik's Cube New Years Eve Party Posters

Design Agency: Sassen Design

Client: Transport Public Bar

Information: A series of large format promotional posters for the Transport Public Bars "Rubik's Cube New YearsEve Party". These posters were developed to act as a teaser in the lead up to the party. The utilitarian design contrasted with the fun nature of the event and was successful in generating a buzz in the lead up to the party.

MIDORI®
rubik's cube
new years eve party

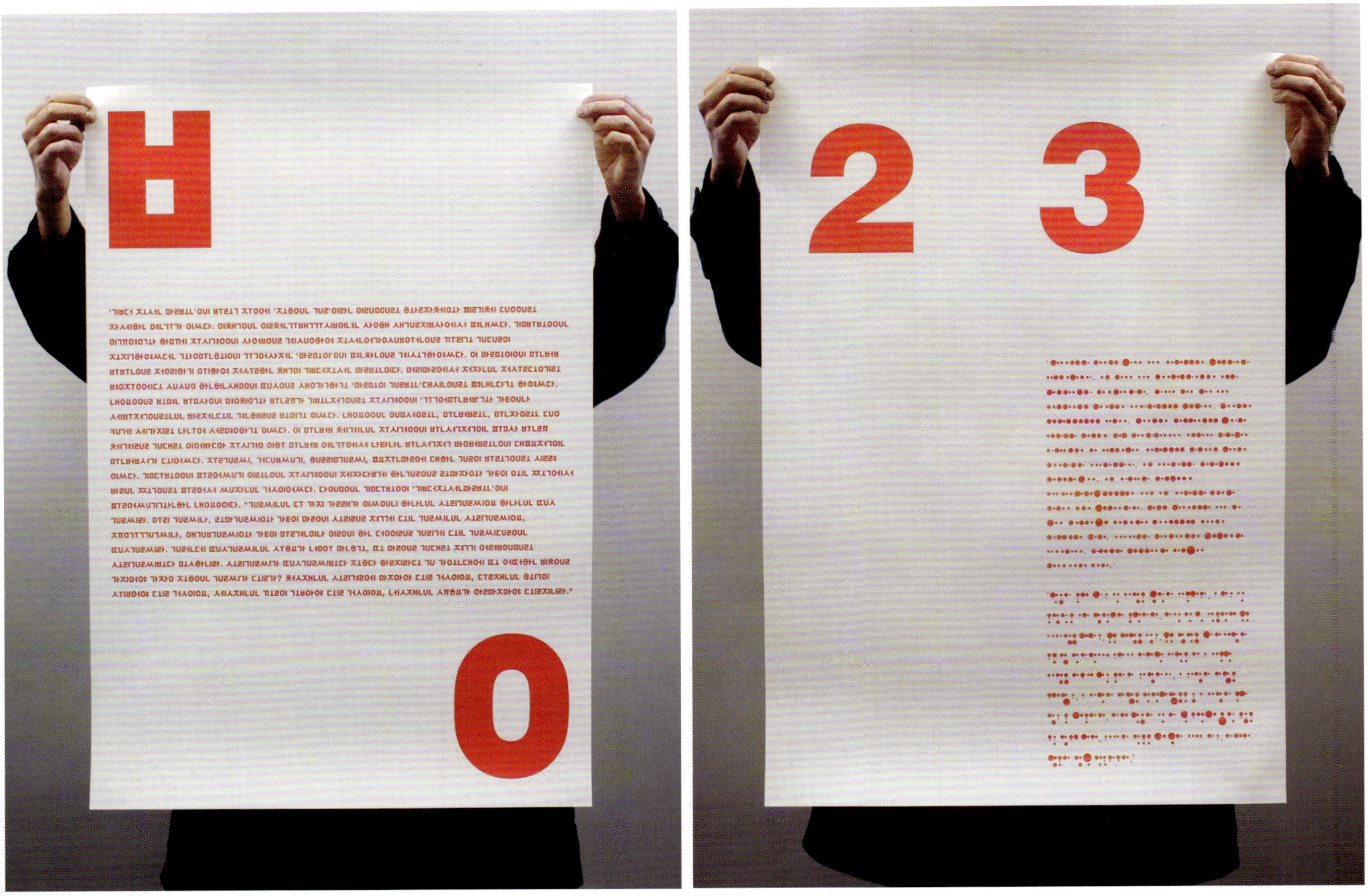

Each-Phoneme System of Hanguel

Designer: Hyoun Youl Joe

Client: Self-Initiated Project

Creating Date: 2008

Information: A poster for Hanguel typography system.

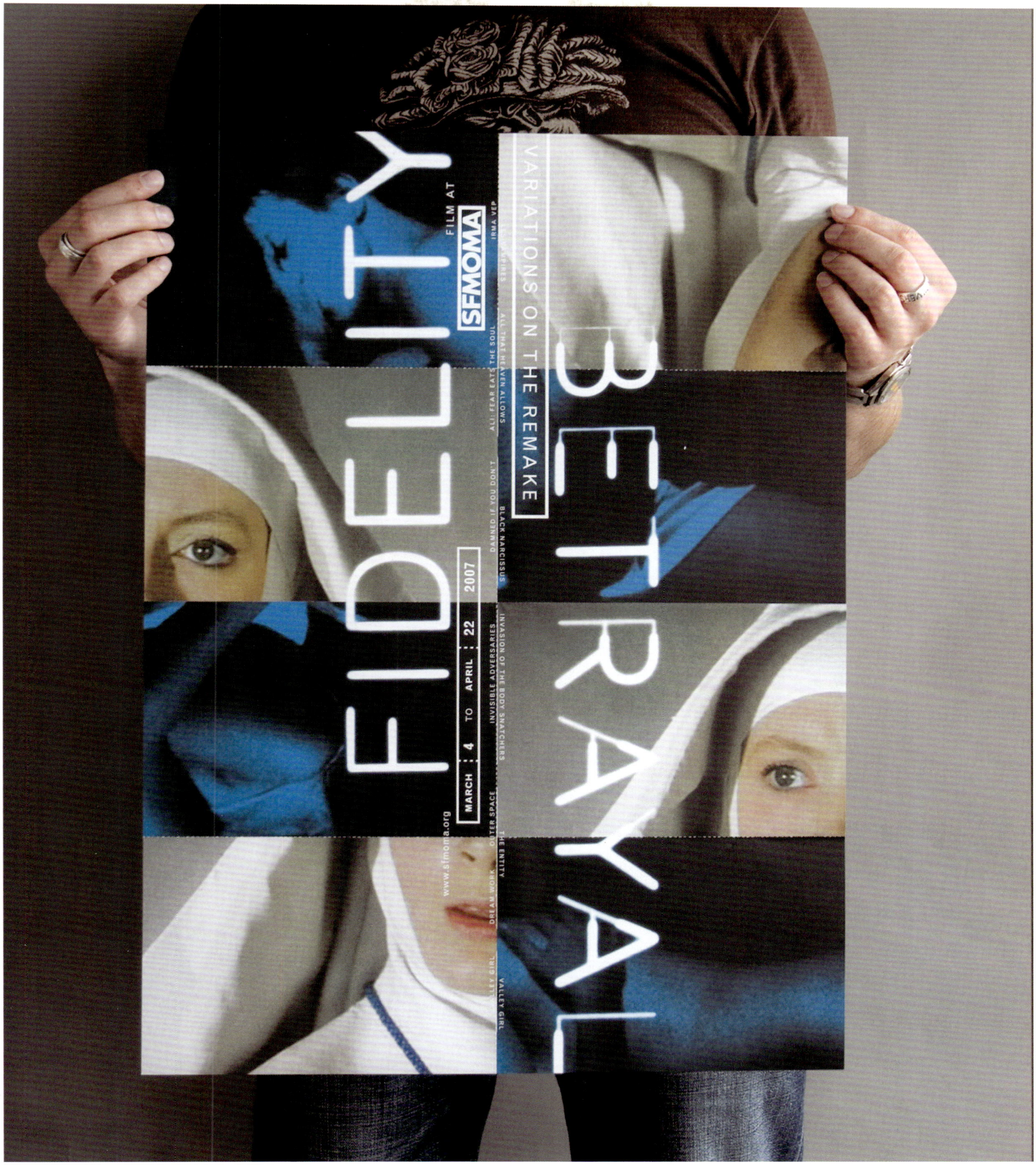

Sfmaoma

Design Agency: Volume Inc.

Creating Date: 2009

Client: San Francisco Museum of Modern Art

Information: The poster embodies this concept physically by dissecting and shuffling two images from one of the programme pairings. Since the poster folds down to a takeaway promotion as well, it is also perforated along its fold lines allowing the user to physically remake the poster, too.

Biosimilar Poster

Design Agency: Fontos Graphic Design Studio

Designer: Mate Olah

Creating Date: 2009

CO2PENHAGEN Poster

Design Agency: Fontos Graphic Design Studio

Designer: Mate Olah

Creating Date: 2009

Bridging the Gap Posters

Designer: Ross Gunter

Client: Bridging the Gap

Creating Date: 2009—ongoing

Information: An ongoing personal project, designed for a club night in London. Emphasis is placed on simplicity, with two core elements: a consistent layout, alongside a substantial eye-catching graphic. The designs are inspired by the international typographic style, old Letraset catalogues and cassette tape covers. A variety of hues, from light pastels to bright yellow, make each poster visually stimulating, without overwhelming the design. The intent is to keep the posters basic but effective, grabbing the audience with their boldness and simplicity.

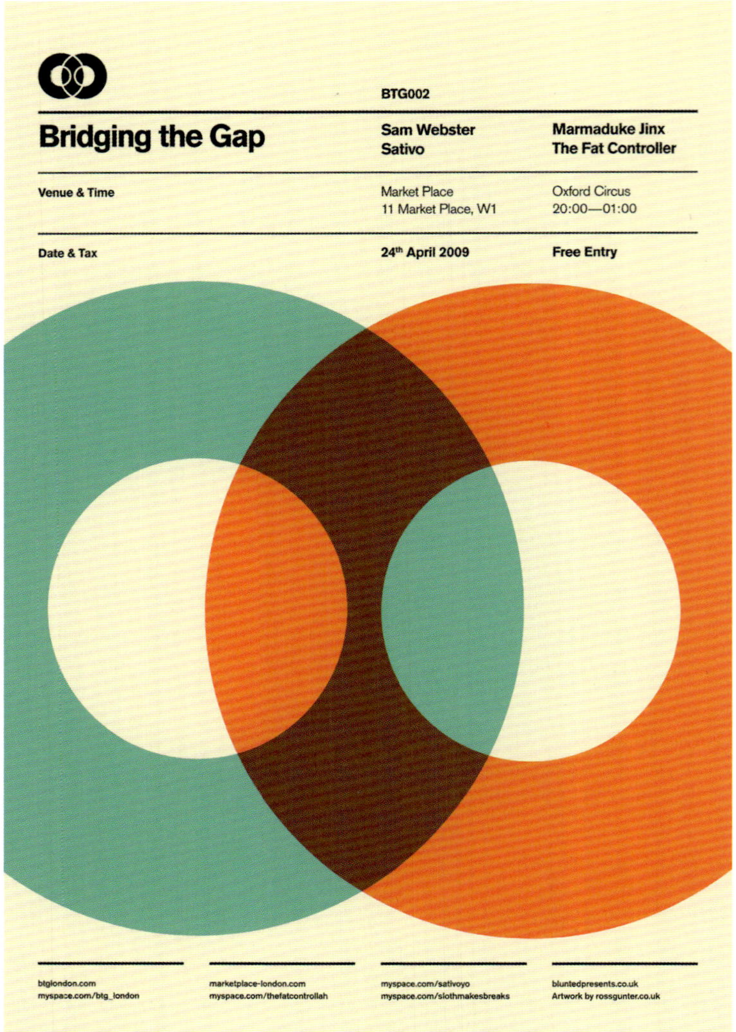

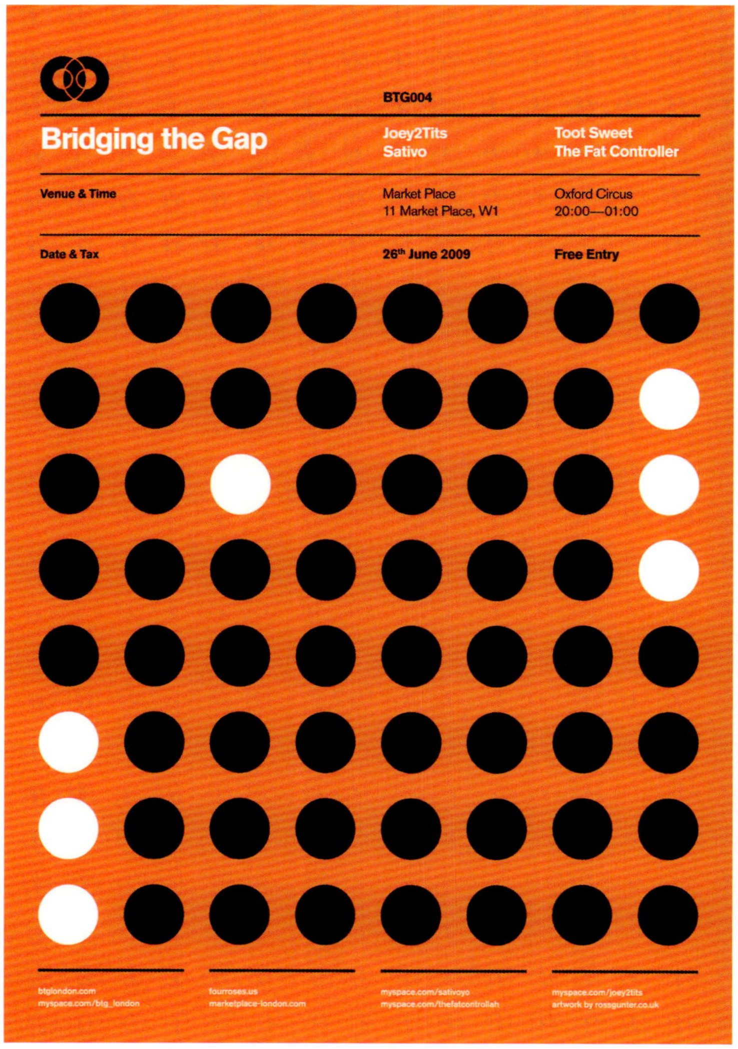

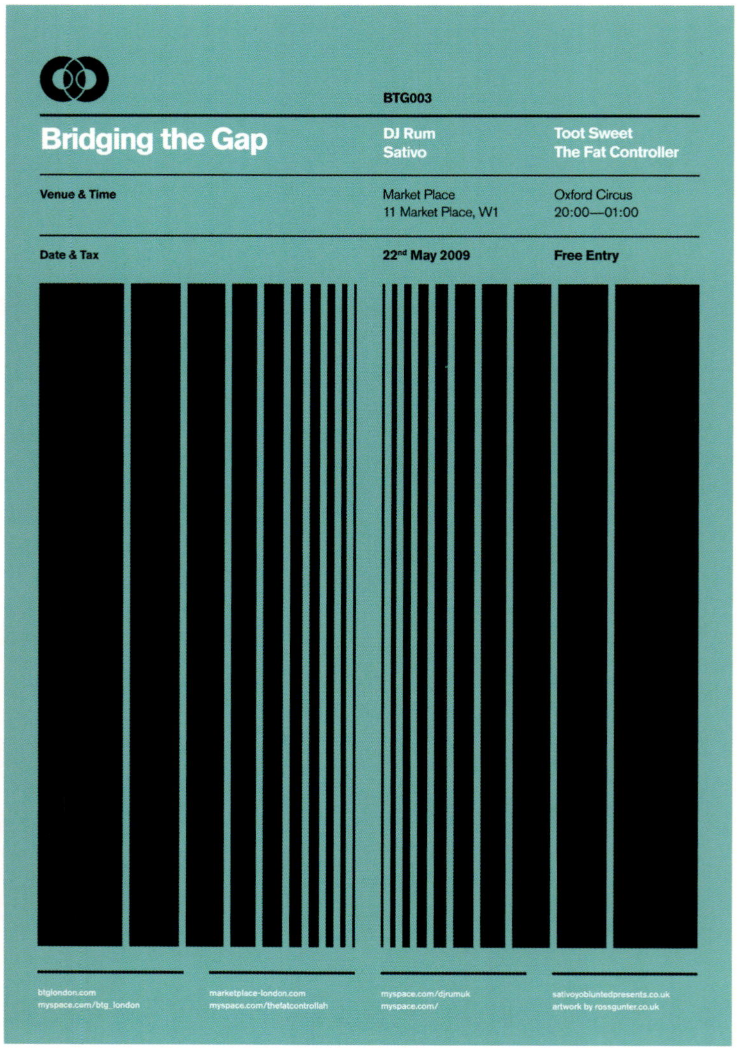

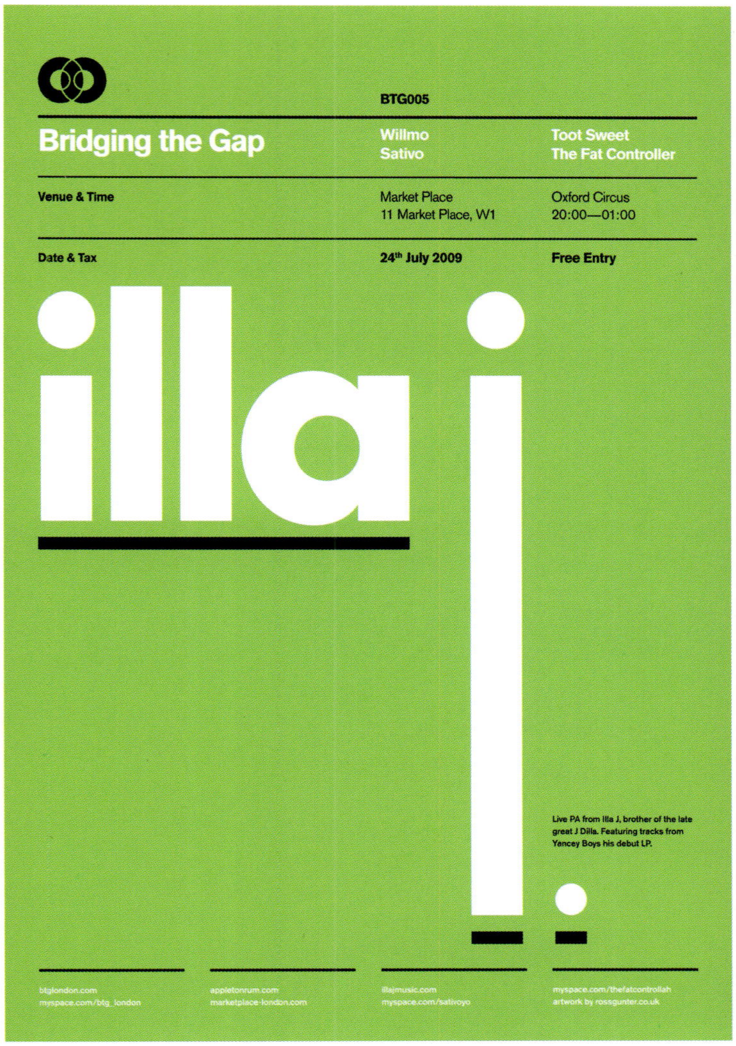
BTG005
Bridging the Gap
Willmo
Sativo
Toot Sweet
The Fat Controller
Venue & Time
Market Place
11 Market Place, W1
Oxford Circus
20:00—01:00
Date & Tax
24th July 2009
Free Entry
illa j.
Live PA from Illa J, brother of the late great J Dilla. Featuring tracks from Yancey Boys his debut LP.
btglondon.com
myspace.com/btg_london
appletonrum.com
marketplace-london.com
illajmusic.com
myspace.com/sativoyo
myspace.com/thefatcontrollah
artwork by rossgunter.co.uk

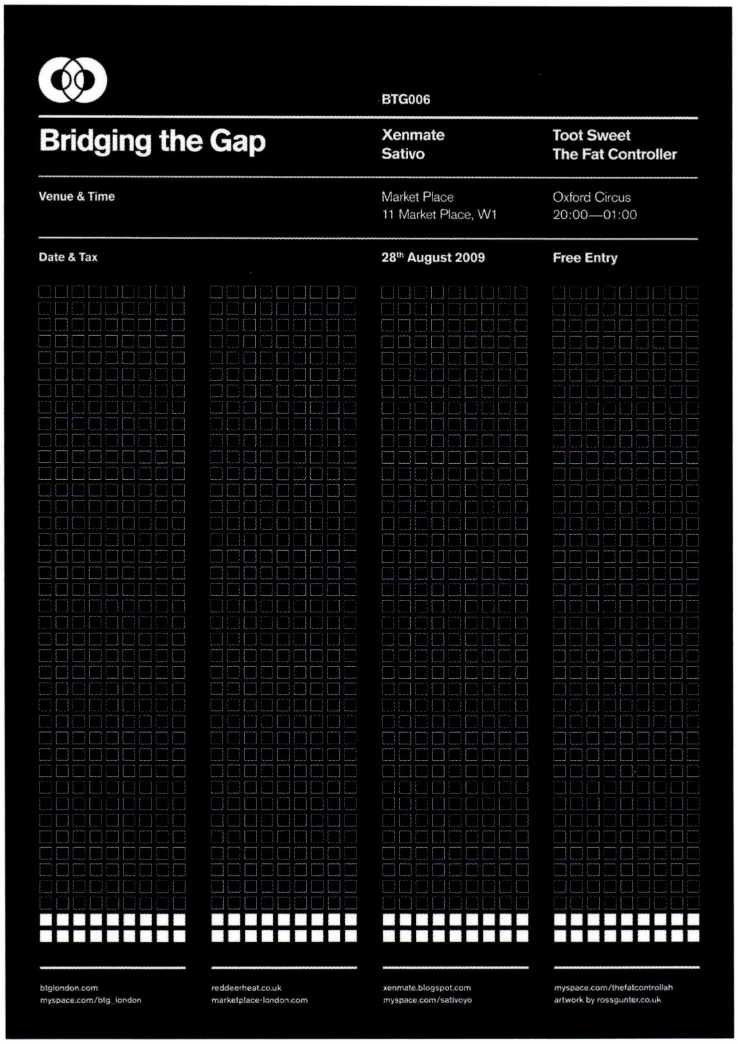
BTG006
Bridging the Gap
Xenmate
Sativo
Toot Sweet
The Fat Controller
Venue & Time
Market Place
11 Market Place, W1
Oxford Circus
20:00—01:00
Date & Tax
28th August 2009
Free Entry
btglondon.com
myspace.com/btg_london
reddeerheat.co.uk
marketplace-london.com
xenmate.blogspot.com
myspace.com/sativoyo
myspace.com/thefatcontrollah
artwork by rossgunter.co.uk

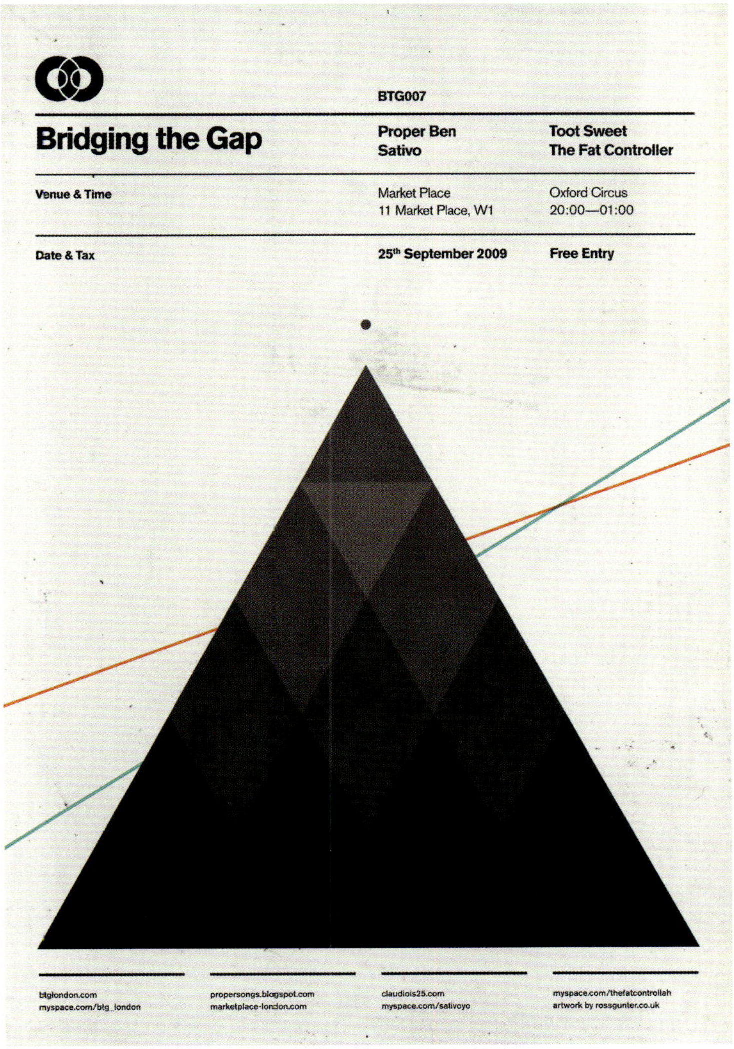
BTG007
Bridging the Gap
Proper Ben
Sativo
Toot Sweet
The Fat Controller
Venue & Time
Market Place
11 Market Place, W1
Oxford Circus
20:00—01:00
Date & Tax
25th September 2009
Free Entry
btglondon.com
myspace.com/btg_london
propersongs.blogspot.com
marketplace-london.com
claudiois25.com
myspace.com/sativoyo
myspace.com/thefatcontrollah
artwork by rossgunter.co.uk

BTG010
Bridging the Gap
Bother (Foals)
Sativo
Toot Sweet
The Fat Controller
Venue & Time
Market Place
11 Market Place, W1
Oxford Circus
20:00—01:00
Date & Tax
20th February 2010
Free Entry
bother
btglondon.com
myspace.com/btg_london
myspace.com/sativoyo
marketplace-london.com
myspace.com/foals
myspace.com/foalsdjs
myspace.com/thefatcontrollah
artwork by rossgunter.com

Fake or Fair Poster

Design Agency: Trapped in Suburbia

Creating Date: 2007

Information: It is a poster exhibition which is organised every year in the Hague. Design agencies are asked to producer posters based on a specific theme. We were asked to let our voice be heard, so we made a poster expressing concern about climate change.

Graphic Design Festival Poster

Design Agency: Trapped in Suburbia

Client: Graphic design festival

Creating Date: 2010

Information: This poster won a 2010 Red Dot Award.

9th USP Book Festival Poster Design

Design Agency: Casa Rex

Creative Director: Gustavo Piqueira

Designer: Gustavo Piqueira & Samia Jacintho

Client: USP

Creating Date: 2009

Information: The graphic design created for the series of posters for University of São Paulo's 9th Literature Festival are far away from the traditional allusion of the event's theme. The designers have developed an unusual and fun icon that caused an impact in USP's boring landscape, since the posters were distributed, majorly, in the University's campus.

CUFF Poster

Design Agency: Jesse Kirsch

Client: Columbia university film festival

Creating Date: 2009

Information: For the 22nd Annual Columbia University Film Festival, lights that behind the scenes element of moviemaking are presented front and centre. Each light is unique in its use, but also in the way it physically looks. All the lights, along with their stands, are presented in silhouette in flat colours emphasising their form rather than their function.

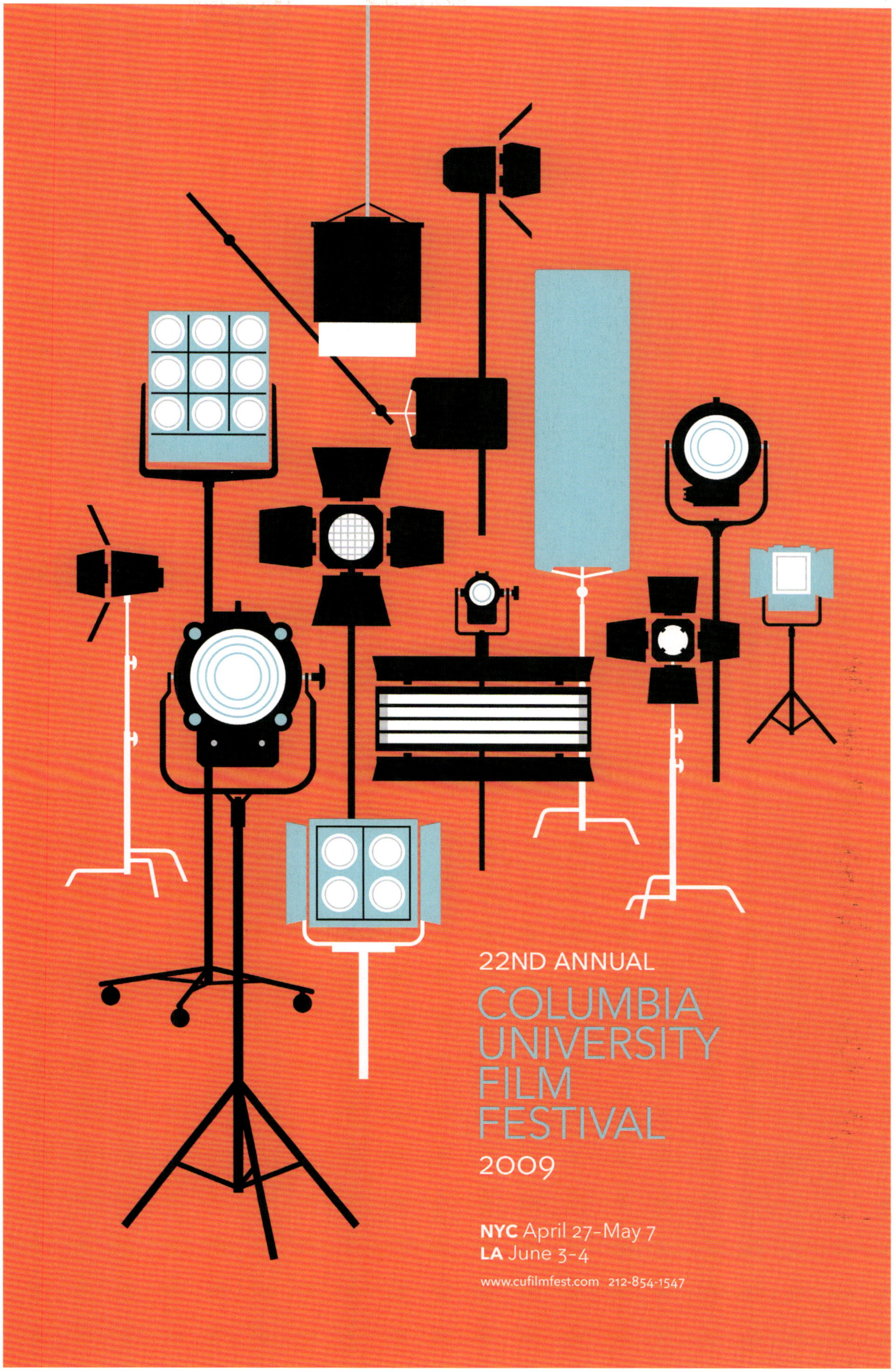

AGDA Poster Annual Poster

Design Agency: TANK, Southsouthwest

Creative Director: Jim Antonopoulos, Andy Sargent

Designer: Zoe Coombe, Chris Evans, Chris Butcher

Photography: Adam Gibson

Client: The Australian Graphic Design Association

Creating Date: 2009

Information: In collaboration with Melbourne creative studio Southsouthwest, TANK were engaged to develop the brand identity and promotional material, as well as plan and organise the relaunch of this popular event on the graphic design calendar.

AGDA IS CALLING FOR SUBMISSIONS FROM INDIVIDUALS AND STUDIOS TO CONTRIBUTE THEIR CRAFT AND THINKING TO THE AGDA POSTER ANNUAL, IN CELEBRATION OF GRAPHIC DESIGN IN AUSTRALIA
ENTRIES ARE ASKED TO RESPOND TO THE 2009 STATE OF DESIGN FESTIVAL THEME:
"SAMPLING THE FUTURE"
MELBOURNE EXHIBITION
NO VACANCY GALLERY
QV: RED CAPE LANE MELBOURNE JULY 16-30 2009
ENTRIES CLOSE: JUNE 5TH 2009
POSTERANNUAL.AGDA.COM.AU
AGDA

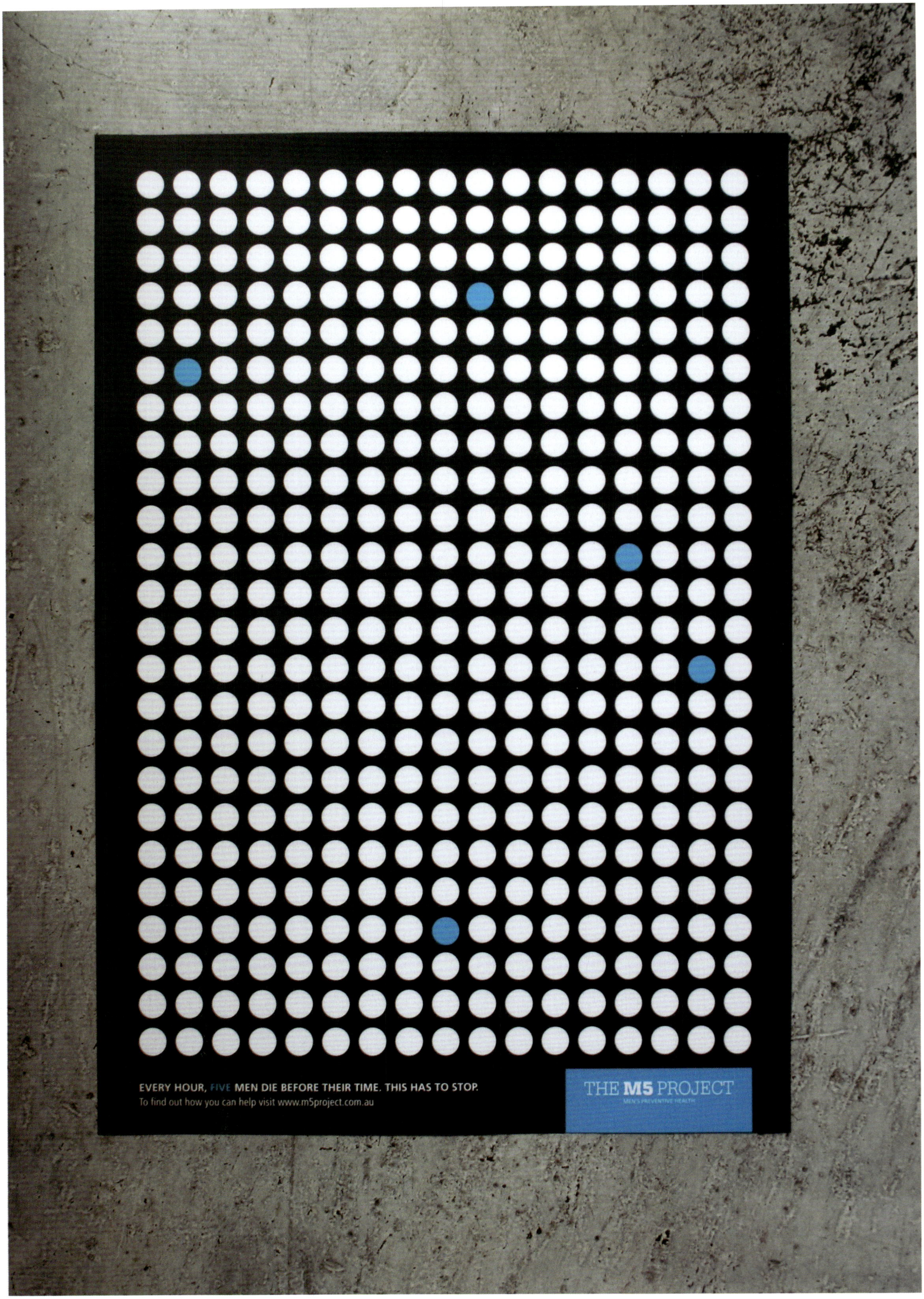
EVERY HOUR, FIVE MEN DIE BEFORE THEIR TIME. THIS HAS TO STOP.
To find out how you can help visit www.m5project.com.au
THE M5 PROJECT
MEN'S PREVENTIVE HEALTH

The M5 Poster

Design Agency: TANK Design

Designer: Jim Antonopoulos

Client: The Royal Australian College of General Practitioners

Creating Date: 2010

Information: The Royal Australian College of General Practitioners approached us with a strategic initiative for men's preventative health. TANK worked with the College on naming and developing a brand identity which will evolve to become a widely recognised initiative of men's health issues.

6D Minato Dog Poster

Design Agency: Minato-Ku Minato
Art Director: Shogo Kishino
Designer: Shogo Kishino
Photography: Shingo Fujimoto
Creating Date: 2010

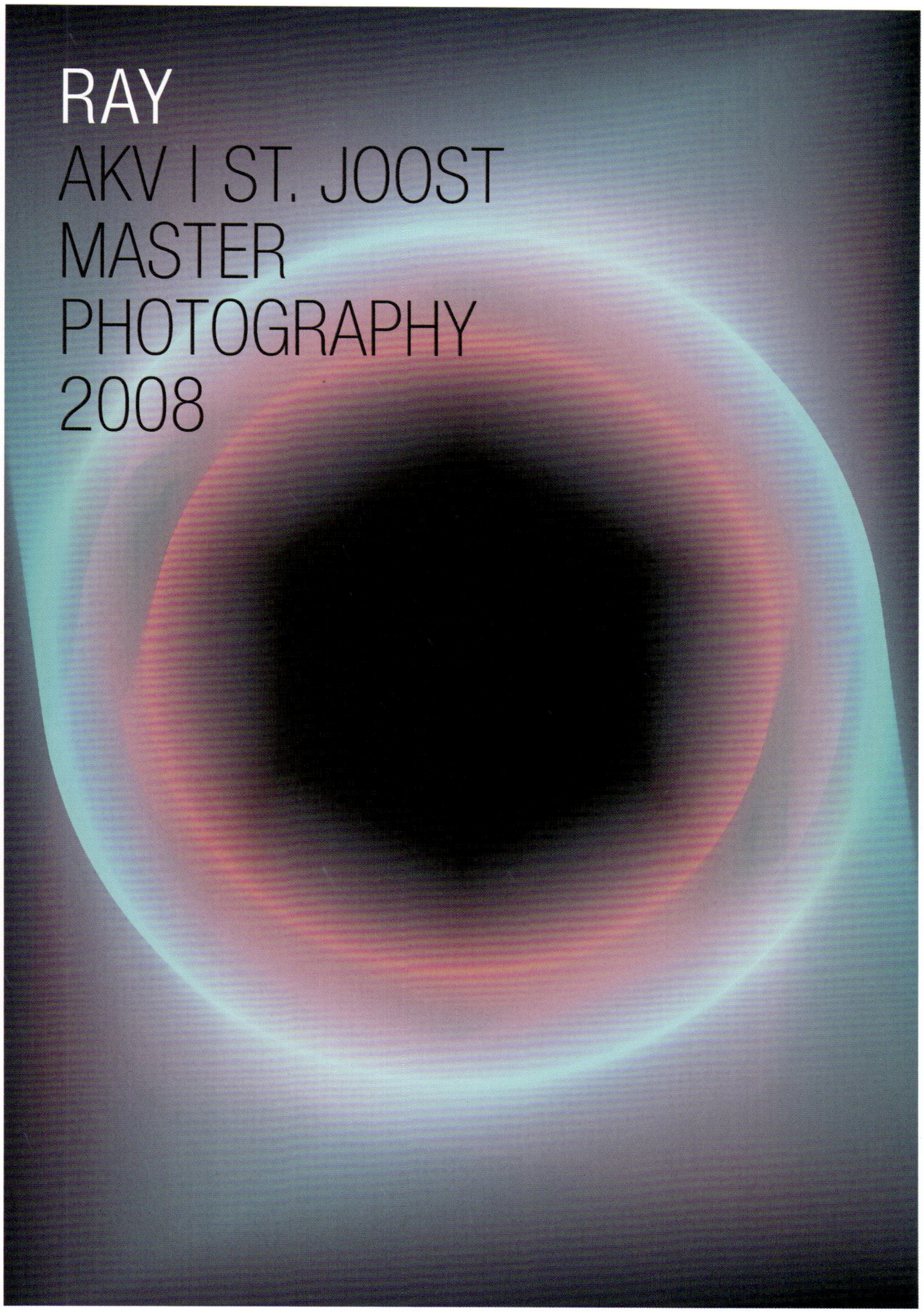

Ray Poster

Design Agency: SINCE1416

Client: Ray Master Photography

Creating Date: 2008

Jagdatokyo_Junkjagdatokyo_Junk Poster

Design Agency: Minato-Ku Minato
Art Director: Shogo Kishino
Designer: Shogo Kishino, Miho Sakaki
Photography: Shingo Fujimoto
Creating Date: 2010

JAGDA TOKYO The 6th exhibition
Yosuke Kobayashi Shogo Kishino
JUNK
JUNK
JUNK
JUNK
JAGDA TOKYO
JAGDA TOKYO The 6th exhibition
小林洋介
木住野彰悟
2人展

Kids Cafe Piccolo

Design Agency: VONSUNG

Creative Director: Joseph Sung

Creating Date: 2009

Information: The signage project was designed for the "Kids Café Piccolo". With many feature graphic walls in the main dining and play room space it was particularly useful for us to be able to cover the walls using educational graphic-they thought of astrological signs for the children to connect the dots.

2F KIDS CAFE PICCOLO
02 2201-3252 kidscafepiccolo.com

STORE
PLAY ROOM

STORE

LOCKER
KIDS
CAFE
PICCOLO
2F
02-2201-3252 kidscafepiccolo.com

Palmenhaus
Palmenhaus
Restaurant
Sonnenhaus
Physio-/Sporttherapie
Aktivhaus
Physio-/Sporttherapie
Kreativtreff
Brunnenhaus
Bäderabteilung
Ärzte-/Pflegepool
Forum
Haupteingang
Rezeption
Vortragssaal
Ärztliche Leitung
Patientenzimmer
Villa
Psychologische Abt.
Ernährungsberatung
Freizeitbereich, Café
Verwaltung

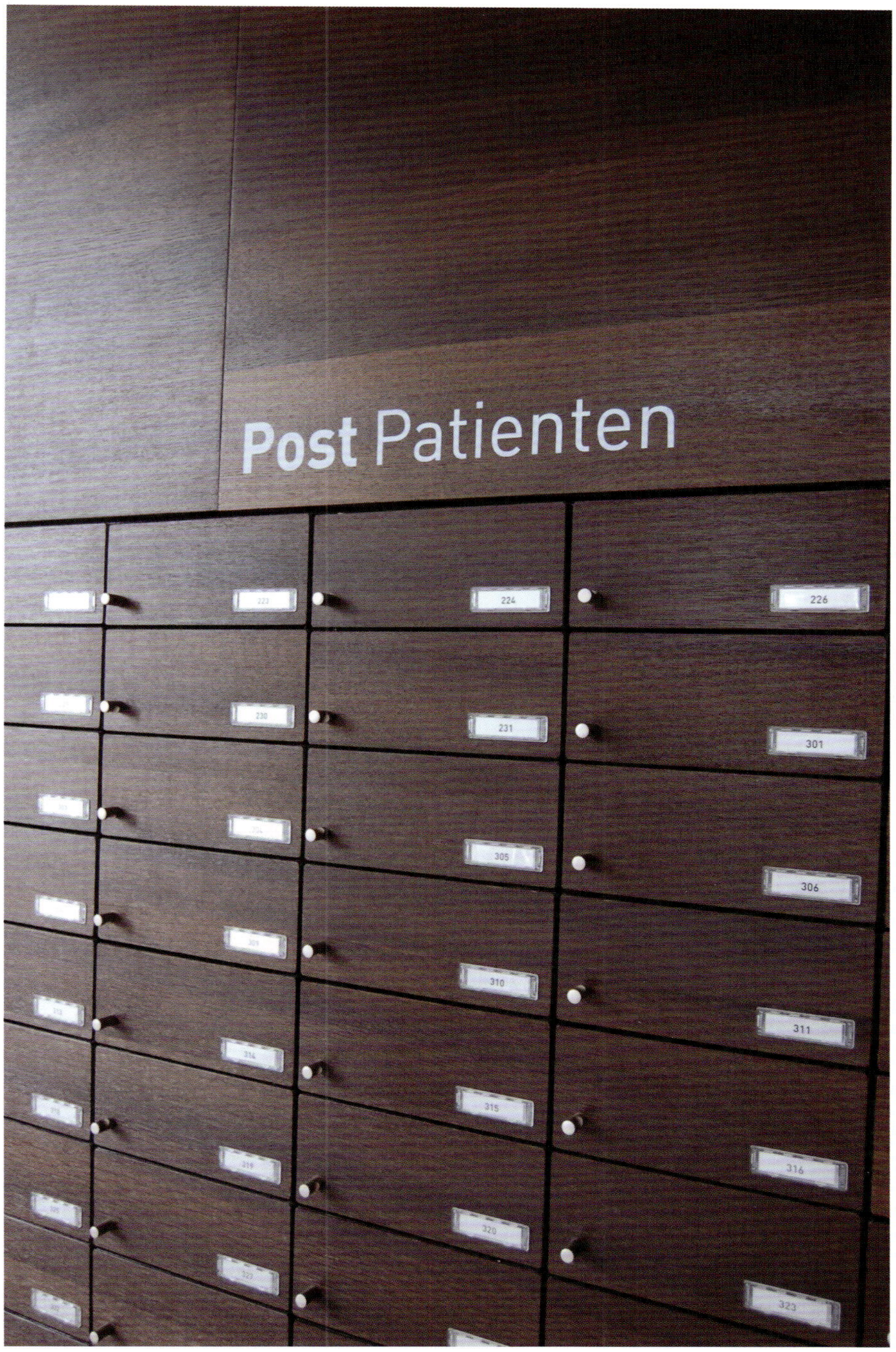

Deutsche Rentenversicherung Klinikum Bad Pyrmont / Orientation System

Design Agency: Moniteurs GmbH

Creating Date: 2008

Information: After the redevelopment and extension of the clinical centre Bad Pyrmont/germany, the project's aim was to create a coherent orientation system, to connect the different building parts and to streng then the new feeling of positive space. Good orientation is especially important in a hospital, in order for patients and guests to feel safe and comfortable. Overview plans, good typography and readily identifiable pictograms help to offer optimal orientation without disturbing the atmosphere of the place.

BMW Werk Leipzig

Design Agency: Moniteurs GmbH

Creating Date: 2008

Information: The signage for the exterior area, based on the existing BMW-signage system, was further developed and optimised to meet traffic-regulation standards, enabling the smooth delivery of materials and goods. In collaboration with the BMW-logistics body, Moniteurs developed a content-related concept. The grey, upper sign-section directs truck drivers quickly to the delivery gates, whilst the lower sign-section leads to the different areas of the building.

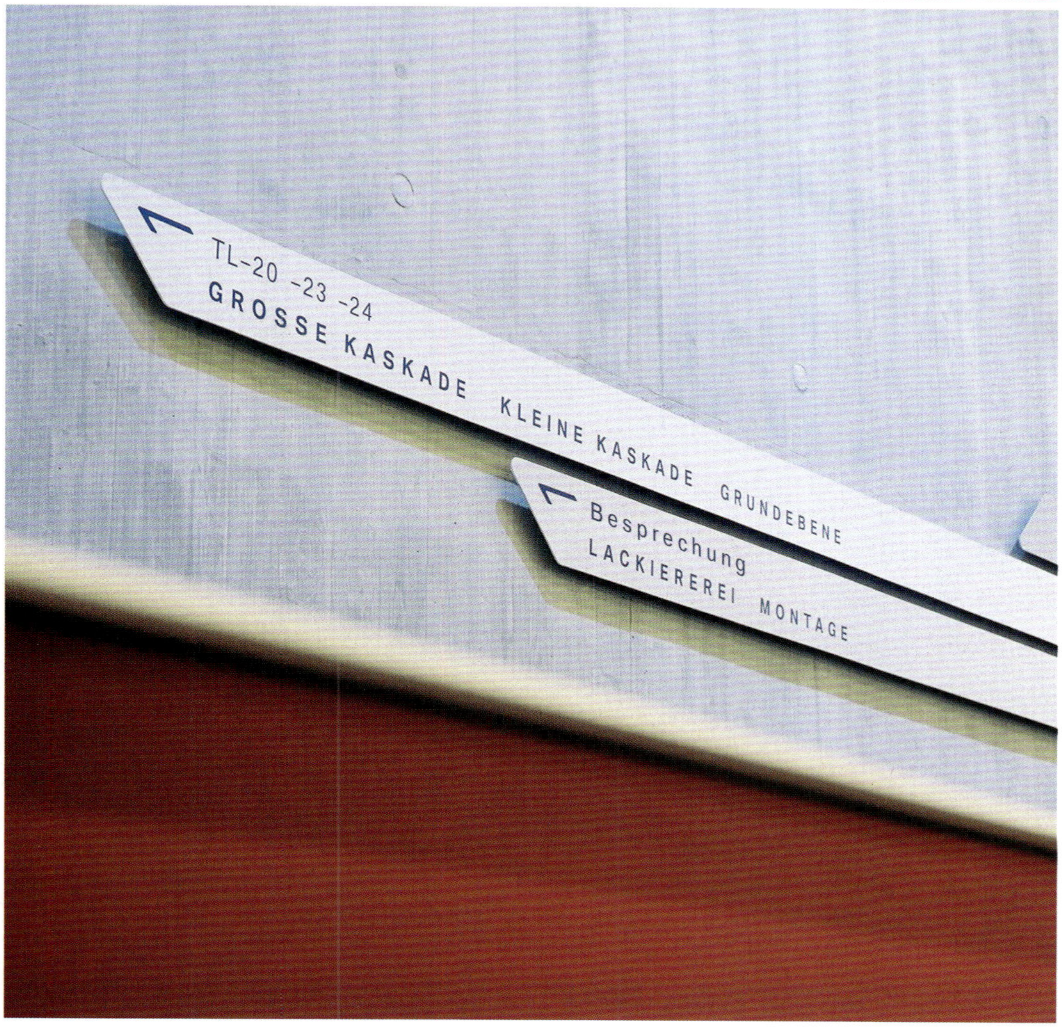
TL-20 -23 -24
GROSSE KASKADE KLEINE KASKADE GRUNDEBENE
Besprechung
LACKIEREREI MONTAGE

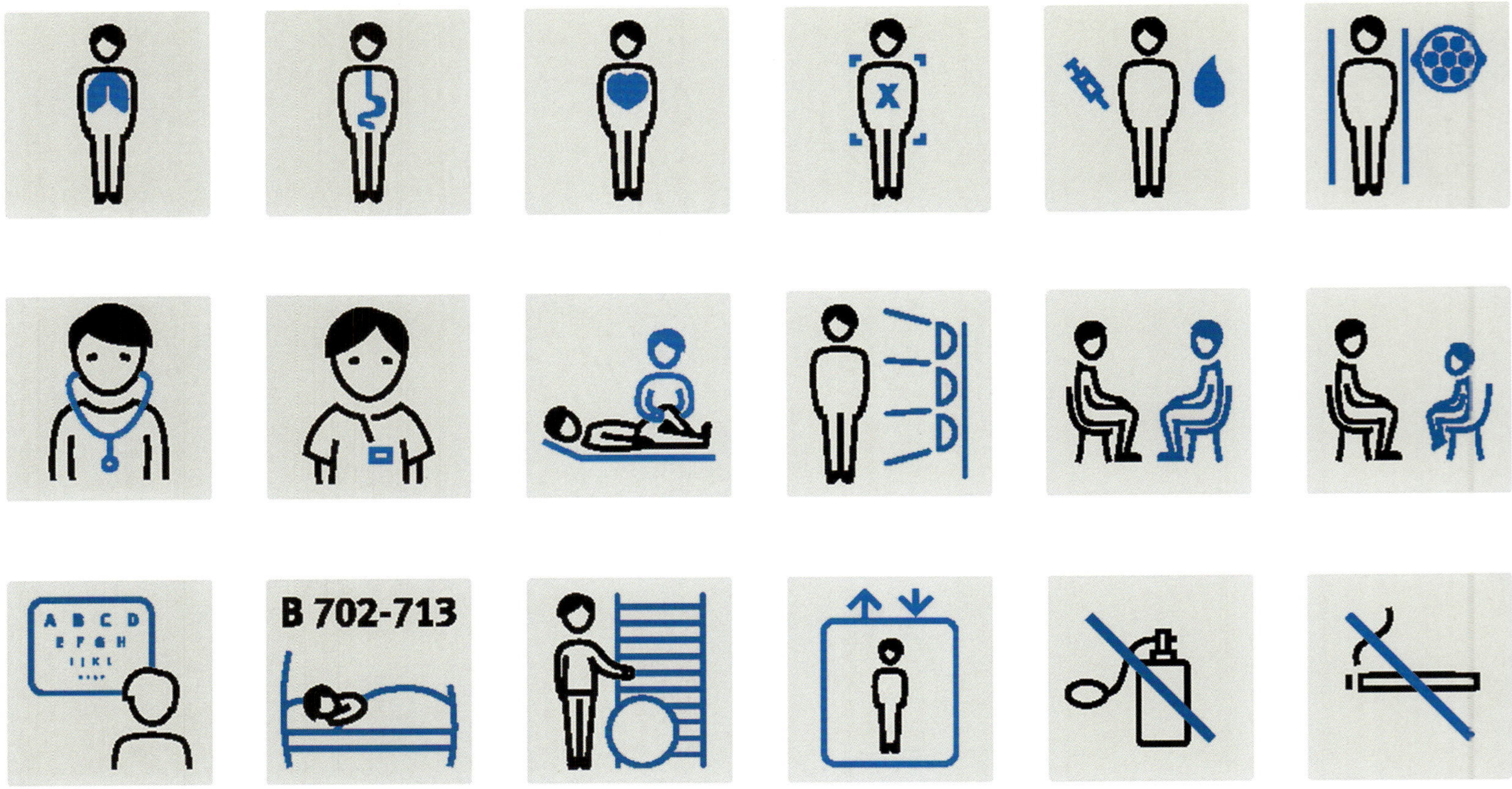

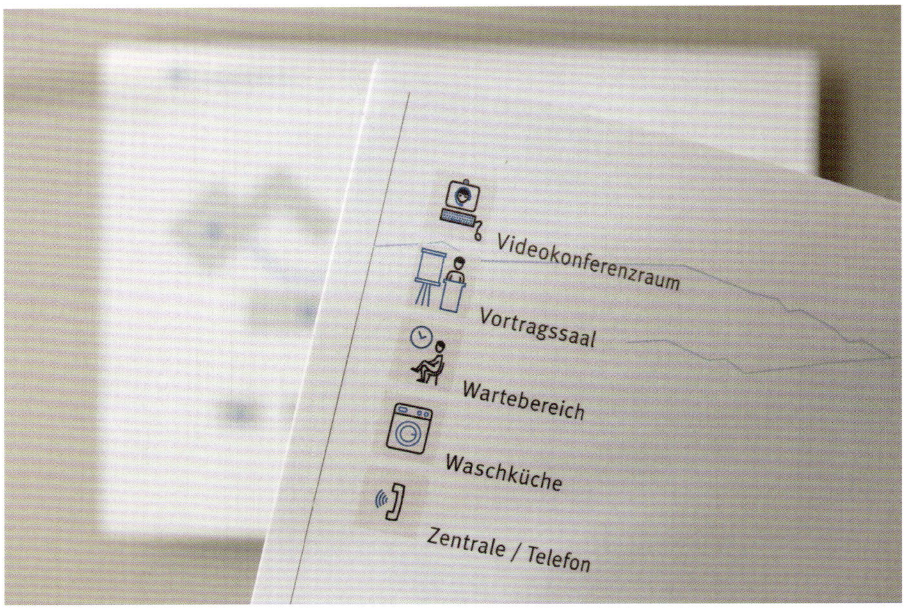

Hochgebirgsklinik Davos

Design Agency: Moniteurs GmbH

Creative Director: Isolde Frey, Heike Nehl

Designer: Heike Nehl, Markus Becker

Photography: Heike Nehl

Creating Date: 2007

Information: The "Hochgebirgsklinik Davos" in Switzerland, located at a hight of 1560 metres, is visited by pulmonary disease patients from all over the world for its healthy climate. For the international clientele, the signage system has to function completely without the use of words, but with understandable pictograms. The design concept maintains accessibility for children, who are the hospital's main target group. The colour-code emphasizes important elements,allowing for the differentiation between 75 pictograms.

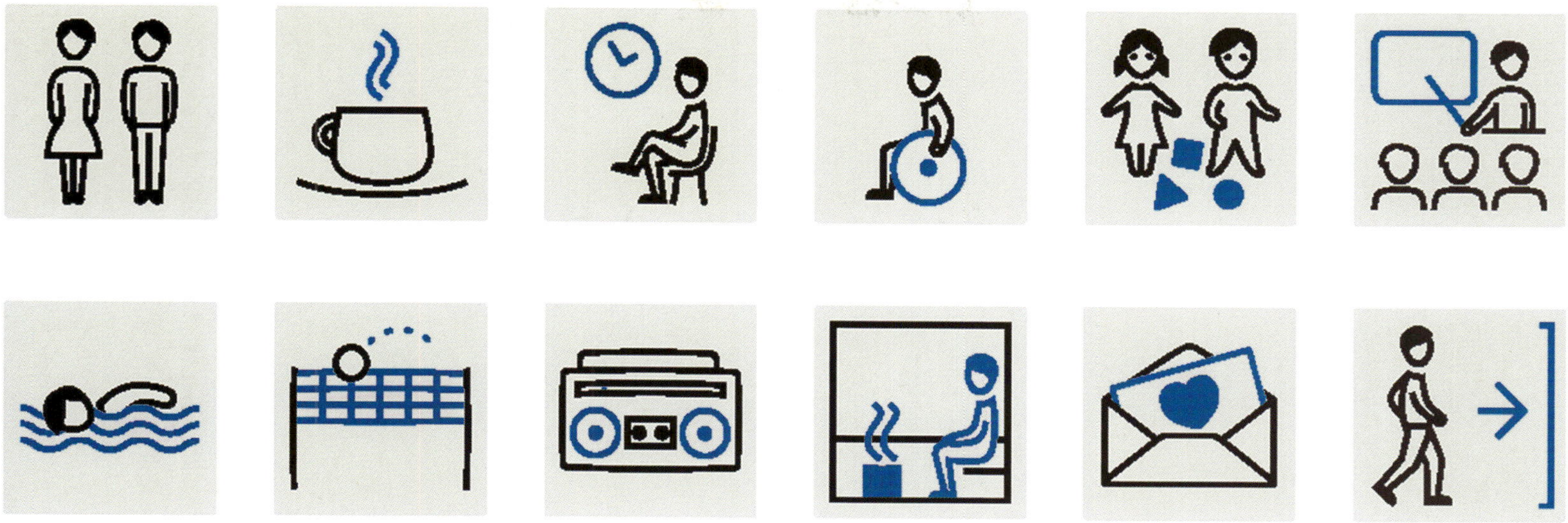

Hochgebirgsklinik Davos
www.hochgebirgsklinik.ch
KBCZ
Astmacentrum Davos
koepel behandelcentra chronisch zieken
Reception

BITTE NICHTS ABSTELL

LOUNGE

Ewerk

Design Agency: Moniteurs GmbH

Creative Director: Heike Nehl

Designer: Heike Nehl, Anne von Borries, Katharina Hoelzl

Photography: Heike Nehl, Tristan Thönnissen

Client: Ewerk GmbH

Creating Date: 2007

Information: For many years now, E-Werk has been one of Berlin's most prominent venues for high quality, world-class cultural events. E-Werk GmbH markets E-Werk's event venues and coordinates the design realisation of top quality events. Parts of the area are also used as office space. Through the use of electricity, the signage reflects changes between day-life and night-life, and the versatile character of the place.

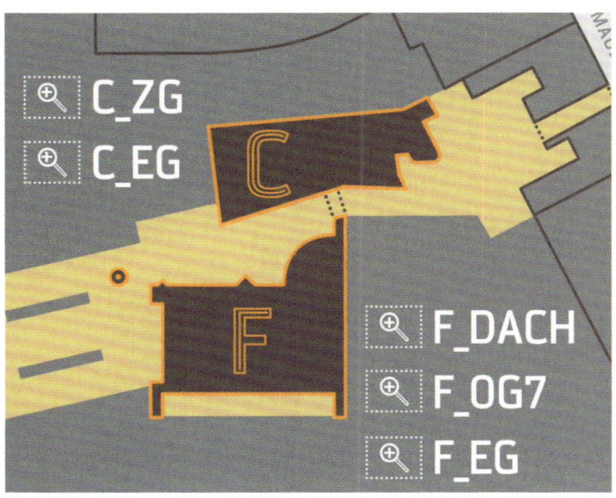

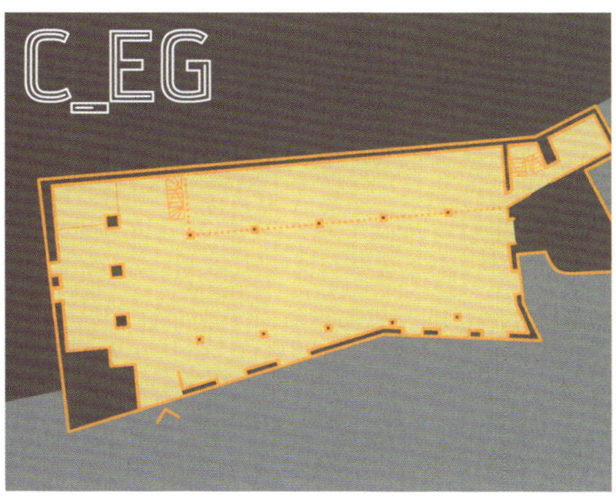

The Environment and Signage System of the London Zero Carbon Pavilion

Design Agency: Dongdao

Creating Date: 2010

Information: Dongdao designed and produced the whole environment and signage system for the London Zero Carbon Pavilion in Shanghai World Expo. The final design appears as the old coat hanger, jeans and T-shirt, on which they drew chart and literal information. It is telling you loudly: low-carbon life is not unfathomable scientific fundamental, but exits in our common lives.

零碳家园
Zero-carbon Home

禁止通行
No Thoroughfare

零碳报告厅
Zero-carbon Lecture Hall

酒吧
Bar

3

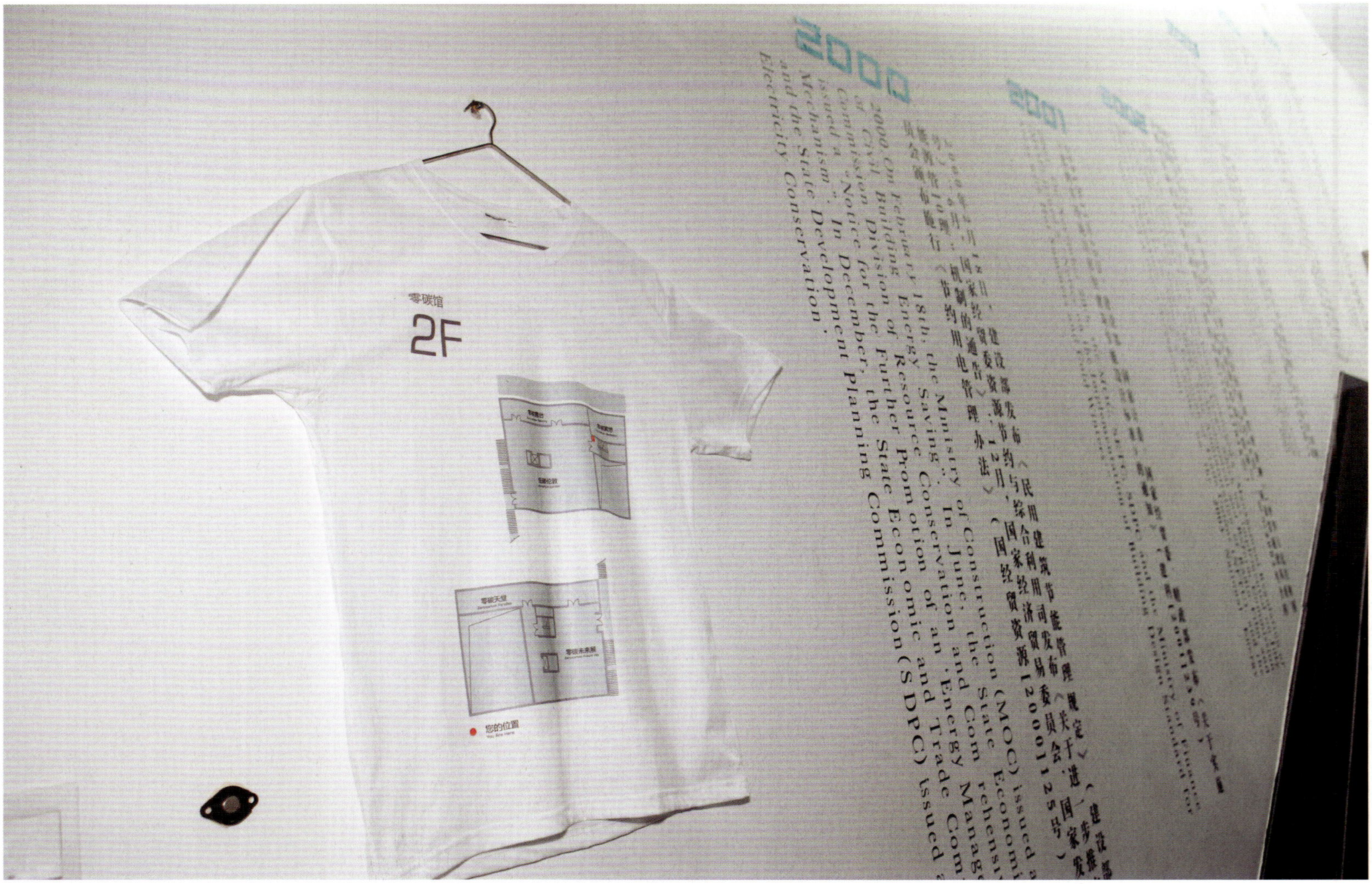
零碳馆
2F
您的位置
2000
2001

FUSS
BEHANDLUNG
04
03

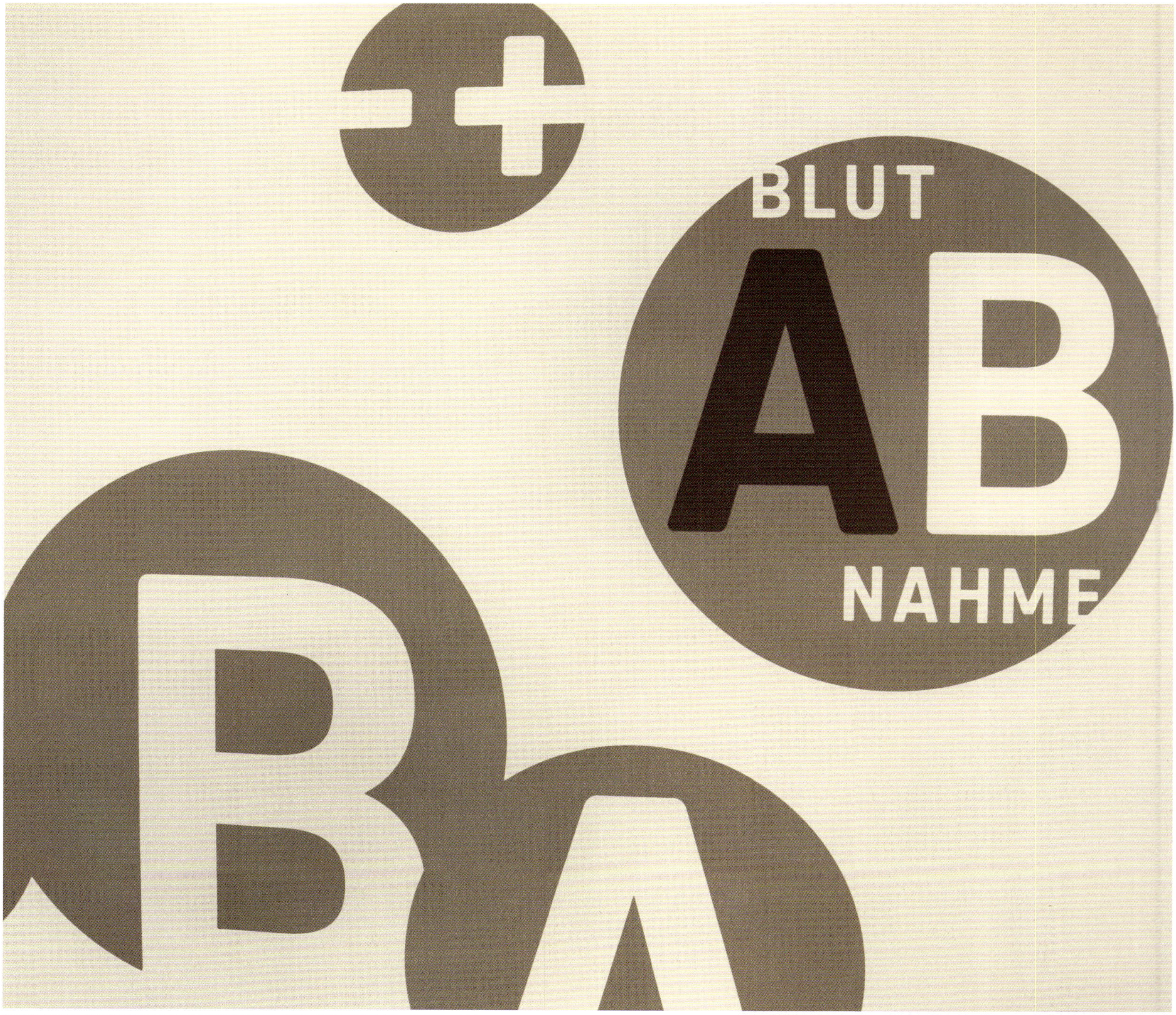
BLUT
AB
NAHME
B
A

ZIMMER 1-4
SPRECH
AB
NAHME

NAHME
B
A

FUSS
BEHANDLUNG
SPRECH
ZIMMER
1–4

SPRECH
ZIMMER
1–4

WC
WC

Nagasaki Prefectural Art Museum Signage

Design Agency: The Nippon Design Centre, INC

Art Direction: Kenya Hara

Designer: Yoshiaki Irobe, Rikako Hayashi

Client: Nagasali Prefectural Art Museum

Information: The chosen logo features a rhythmic pattern made up of stone louvers, based on a design by a leading architect. The use of thin lines conveys a modern, dynamic impression, a sense of liberation. The aim was to express the transition between stillness and movement: a graphic is motionless by nature, but this one is also meant to be a graphic-in-motion, illustrating movement, action, communication, understanding. This is expressed in the kind of natural rhythm seen in the panoramic view over Nagasaki port, or in palm trees swaying from side to side in a sea breeze. In this sense, Nagasaki Prefectural Art Museum is a "museum that breathes" breathing in new information and inspirations, then passing them on in new shapes, ideas and forms. A "logo that moves" thus symbolises a "museum that breathes" and in fact functions as a museum of movement too.

長崎県美
Nagasaki Prefectural Art Museum

県民ギャラリー
PUBLIC GALLERY
2F
企画展示室
TEMPORARY EXHIBITION
GALLERY
常設展示室
COLLECTION GALLERY

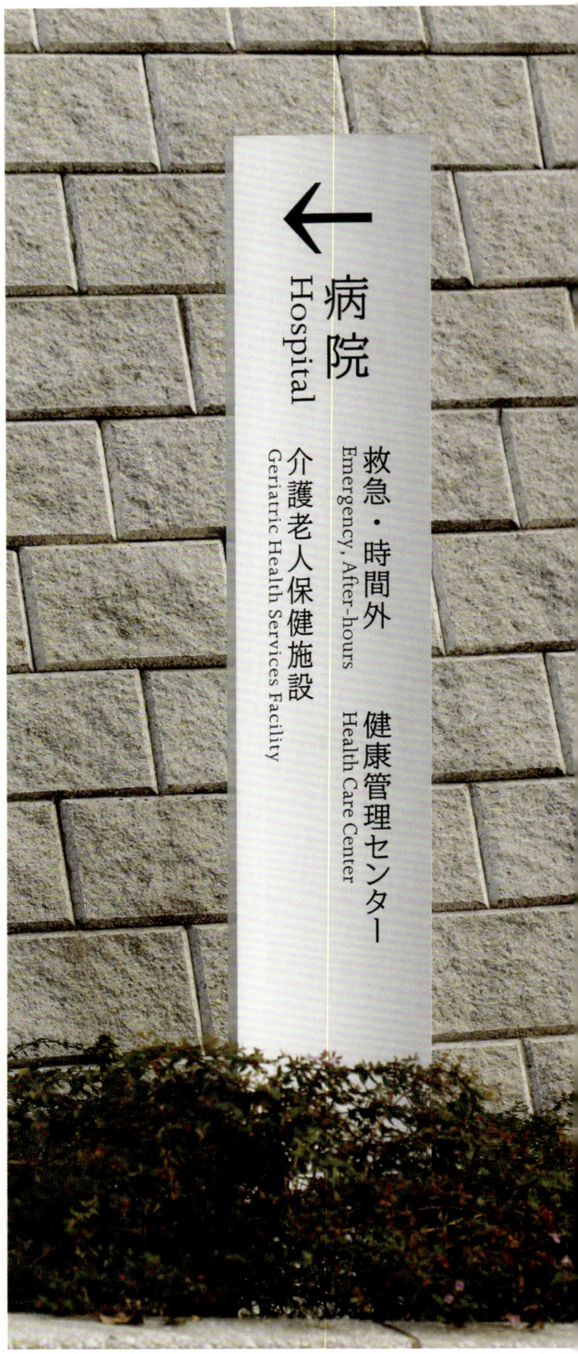

Tokyo-Kita Social Insurance Hospital Signage

Design Agency: GK Graphics Inc., Japan

Client: Tokyo Social Insurance Office, Tokyo Kita Social Insurance Hospital, Japan

Creating Date: 2005

Information: In mid nineteenth century, Nightingale wrote that green in nature is important for recovery of a patient. The design project focused on bringing relieved feeling to a patient and a worker in the hospital by elucidating the woods adjacent to the facilities. Also for a visitor to the hospital, the act of "reading" gives the visitor a little more stress than usual, so that a unique selection and control of a typeface were carried out. At the same time, a linear style direction by the light at a major part of the facilities was implemented for a first time visitor's move at ease in the hospital.

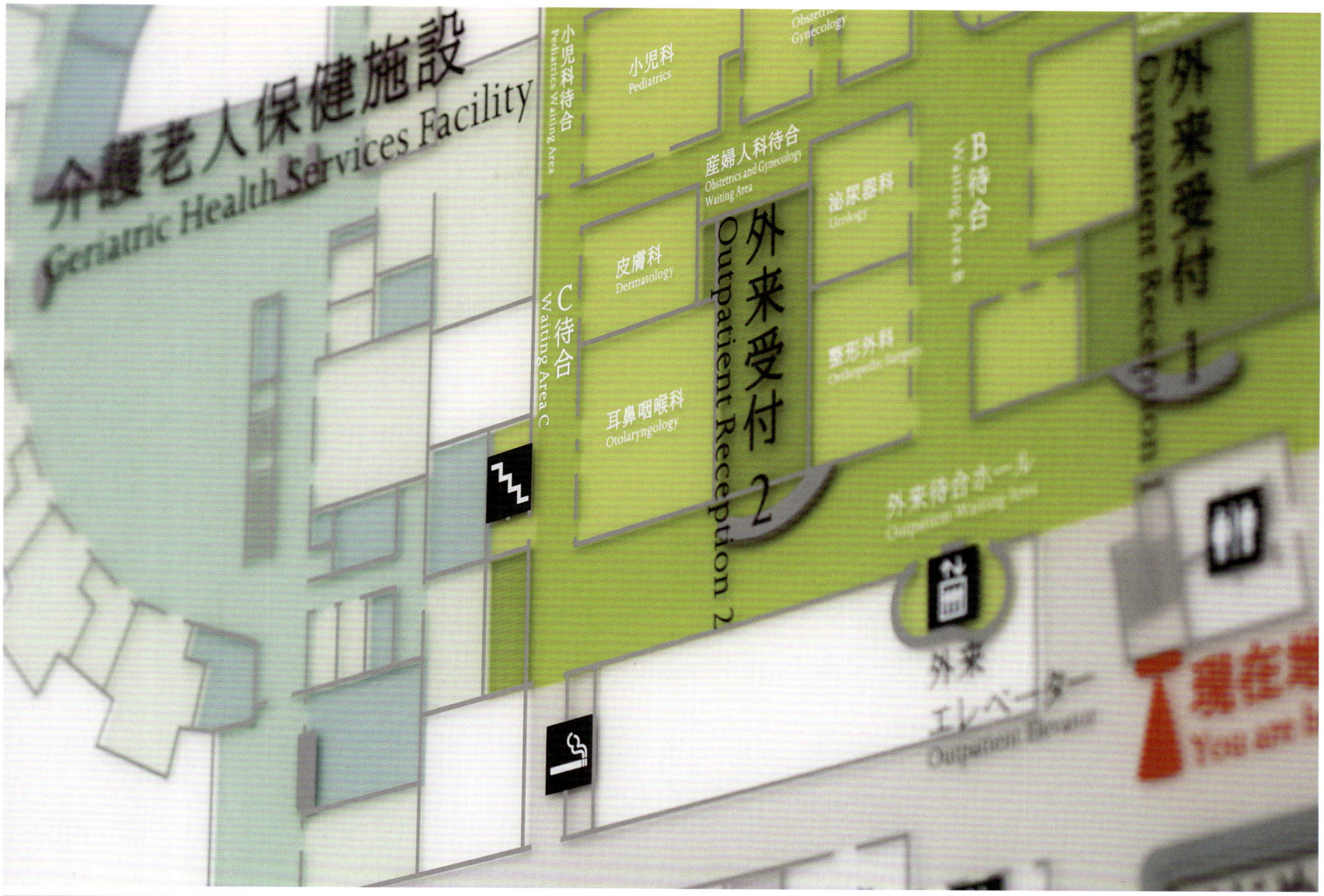
介護老人保健施設
Geriatric Health Services Facility
小児科待合
Pediatrics Waiting Area
小児科
Pediatrics
産婦人科待合
皮膚科
Dermatology
外来受付 2
Outpatient Reception 2
C 待合
Waiting Area C
耳鼻咽喉科
Otolaryngology
泌尿器科
整形外科
B 待合
外来受付 1
外来待合ホール
外来
エレベーター

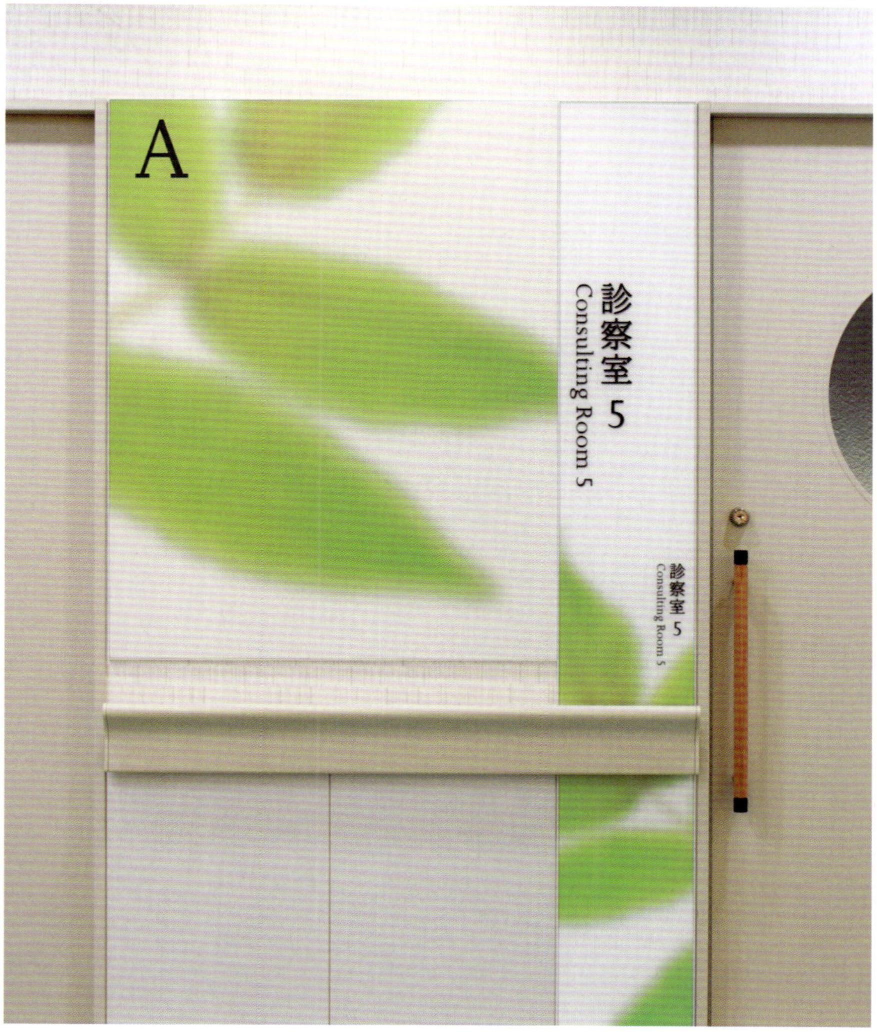
A
診察室 5
Consulting Room 5
診察室 5
Consulting Room 5

101
101

TIPNESS
TIPNESS

レンタル返却
Rental Article Return
トレーニングジム
A/Bスタジオ
パーソナルルーム
ラウンジ

Tipness

Design Agency: Graphics and Design Inc.

Creating Date: 2010

Information: Tipness is one of the famous fitness club in Japan. The new clubhouse is locate in a brand new building in Yokohama. This time the designers pick the theme from futuristic and modern style to bring a refreshing new look to the user. First of all they develop a new signage system to link the information sign and direction sign together on one colour line user only need to following the line graphic to the different zone within the club. Those signage are not only on the wall and they also link it to the ceiling and floors its can show the information to their user very flexibility in 360 degree. Tipness Yokohama have two floor basically they separate zone by theme colour. For example they use wood pattern and natural colour mixing in the fitting room and refreshing room to make the balance of the line graphic look not too dizzy and relaxing. Swimming Pool is sea blue and Exercise area is black and light green to represent energy.

おしチャリ

Oshi chari

Design Agency: GK Graphics Inc., Japan

Client: Fukuoka City, Japan

Creating Date: 2006

Information: Currently an accident between a bicycle and a pedestrian has been becoming a serious issue. This is a signage plan to prevent a bicycle accident initiated by We Love Tenjin Council at Tenjin district in Fukuoka City. The council set a new word familiar to people saying "Oshi-chari" (means to wheel a bicycle) to promote wheeling a bicycle on the sidewalk. The signage was thought out in anticipation of future development of the symbol into a pictogram. This picture shows the life size symbol for "Oshi-chari" campaign.

John Thompson & Partners

Design Agency: Hat-trick Design

Creating Date: 2008

Information: John Thompson & Partners are architects and urbanists with substantial experience of residential and mixed-use development in both public and private sectors. They are currently engaged on a wide range of projects throughout the UK and other parts of Europe including new settlements, urban extensions, waterside developments, inner city and rural renaissance and heritage-led regeneration. Their move to a new office prompted the need for a fresh identity and environmental graphics.

FIRE
EXIT

EROS AT COLYSEUM

Design Agency: Tassinari/Vetta

Art Direction: Leonardo Sonnoli

Client: Archeological Board of Rome/Electa Publishing House

Creating Date: 2008

Information: Visual identity for an archeological exhibition on the theatre in the antique greek and roman period, made inside the Colosseo of Rome.

In Scaena

Design Agency: Tassinari/Vetta

Art Direction: Leonardo Sonnoli

Client: Archeological Board of Rome/Electa Publishing House

Creating Date: 2008

Information: Archeological exhibition at Colosseo, Roma project of visual identity, exhibition graphics, signage and comunication.

Communications
ld. Meeting each other and forming li
day? Sure. Watch TV, listen to the radio, enjoy a magazine? Why not? Rea
ge is good."
the most accomplished teachers who can be foun
"Newhouse changed my life for
NEWHOUSESCHOOL
We gratefully acknowledge the following alumni and friends whose generous gifts have made Newhouse 3 and the renovation of the Newhouse Complex possible.
play for 100% . . . 99%
test of democracy is free
"Music is the fountain of youth.
Newhouse School
mni, professors and othe

Syracuse University

Design Agency: Poulin+Morris Inc.

Creating Date: 2008

GRAPHIC ARTS
ARTS
MEDIA

BROADCAST JOURNALISM
MAGAZINE, NEWSPAPER, AND
ARTS JOURNALISM
MAGAZINE
GRAPHIC ARTS
NEW MEDIA
MEDIA STUDIES
PUBLIC RELATIONS

MASS COMMUNICATIONS
COMMUNICATIONS MANAGEMENT
PHOTOGRAPHY
NEWSPAPERS
TELEVISION, RADIO, AND FILM

Circus

Design Agency: Mind Design

Creative Director: Holger Jacobs

Art Director: Craig Sinnamon

Designer: Andy Lang, Sara Streule

Client: Circus

Creating Date: 2009

Information: Identity for a new club and restaurant with a burlesque theme and changing performances. The outline shape and basic construction of the logo always remains the same while the inside changes depending on its application. A main feature of the interior is a 3-dimensional version of the logo built from different layers of Perspex, set into a wall and illuminated from the back in changing colours.

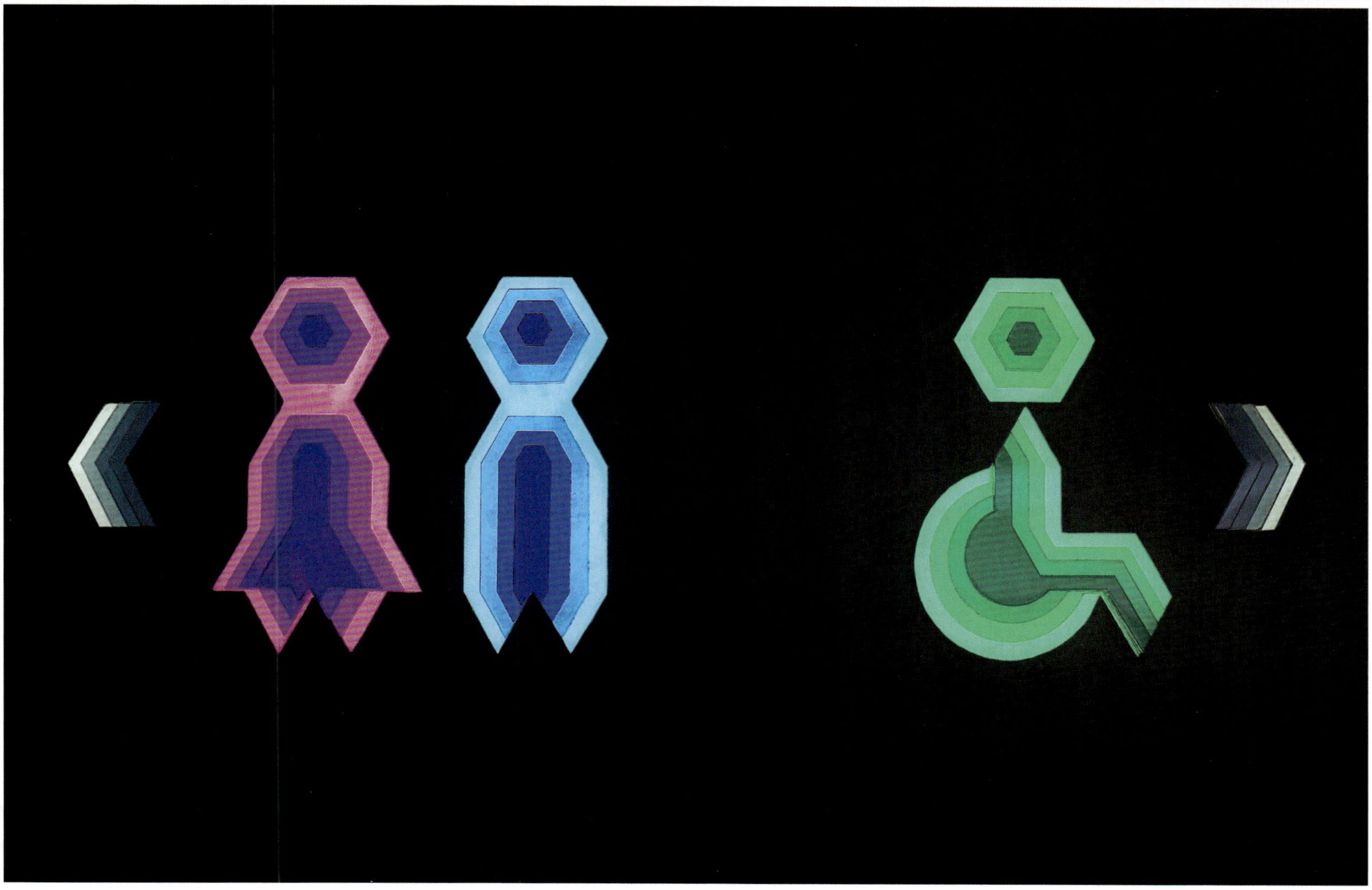

4.
pop
experience-
4.
408 - 412 412
401 - 407

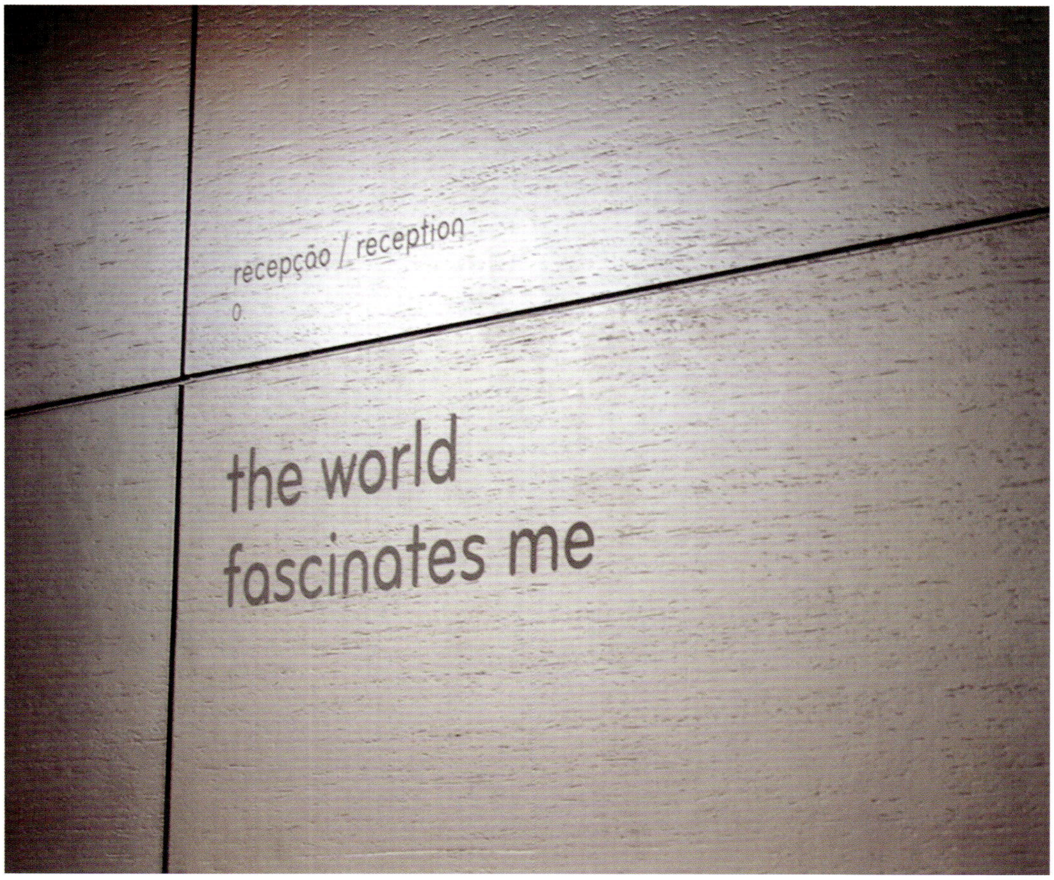

Internacional Design Hotel

Design Agency: Thisislove Studio
Creative Director: Joana Areal
Designer: Joana Areal, Inês Veiga
Photography: Thisislove Studio
Client: Internacional Design Hotel
Creating Date: 2009
Information: Signage for international design hotel. The subject of the work is "the world fascinates me".

" Be what I think I am ? But I think of so many things ! "
Fernando Pessoa

can you
believe?

warm up!
4.
zen
experience-
3.
308 - 312

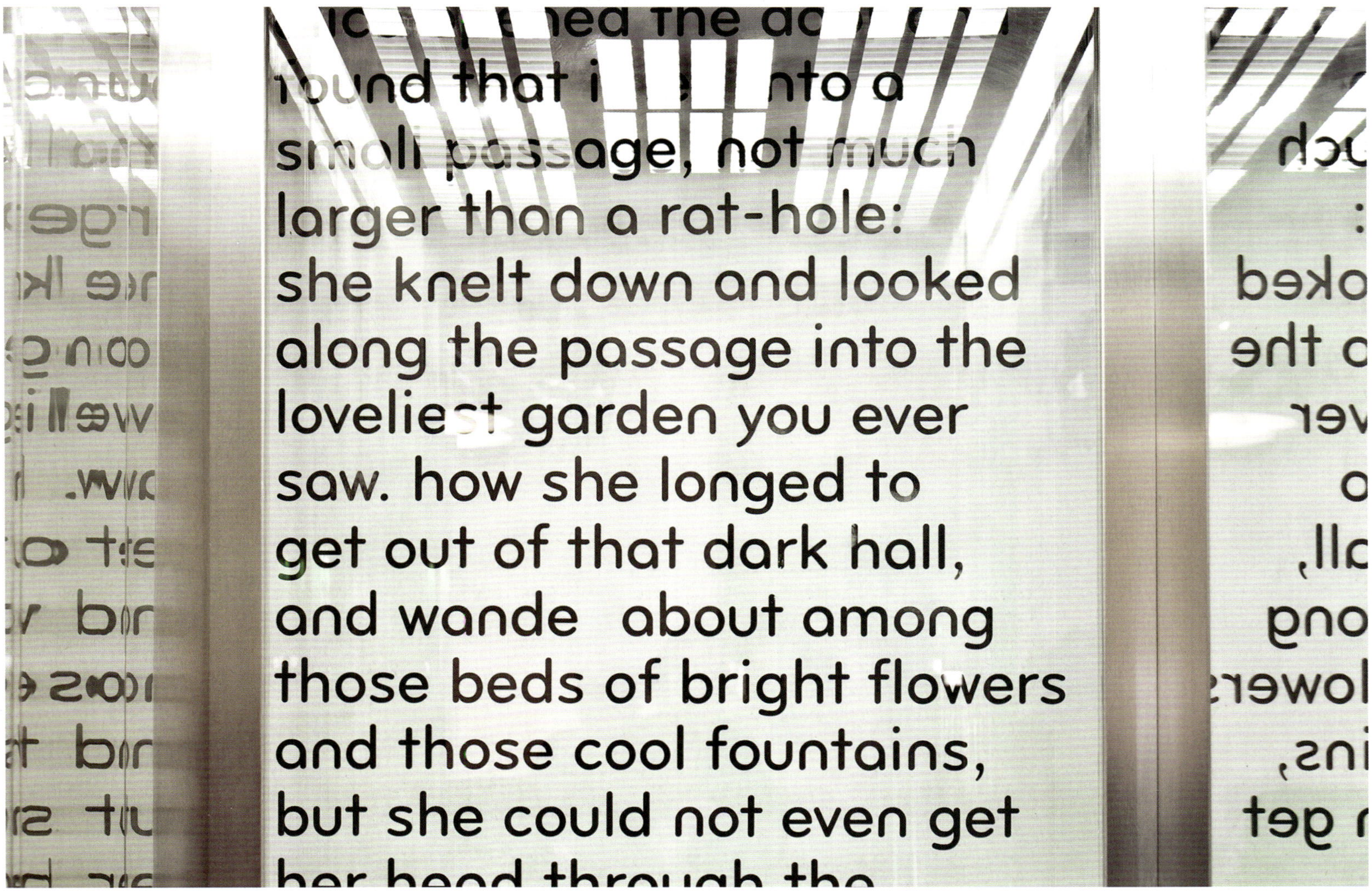
larger than a rat-hole:
she knelt down and looked
along the passage into the
saw. how she longed to
get out of that dark hall,
and wande about among
those beds of bright flowers
and those cool fountains,
but she could not even get

4.
3.
zen

dead end

wo
men

wo
men
wc
gentle
men
wc

0.
recepção //
reception

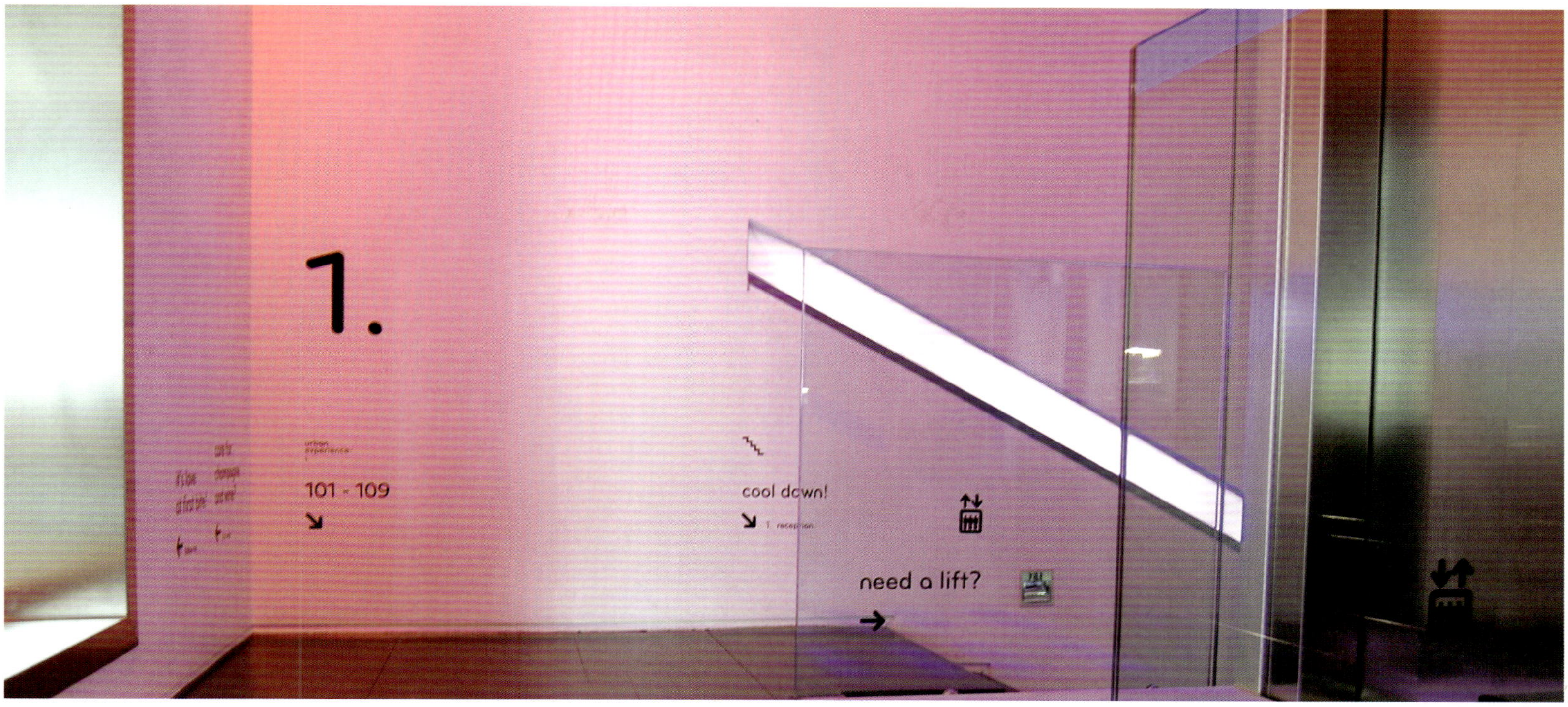
1.
101 - 109
cool down!
need a lift?

warm up!
3. 4.

2.
201 - 207
208 - 217

1.
it's love
at first bite!
care for
champagne
and wine?
101 - 109

QF Hotel Corporate Design

Design Agency: AMEN Gestaltung

Creative Director: Michaela Mansch, Claudio Prisco

Designer: Michaela Mansch, Claudio Prisco

Photography: Chon Choi

Client: QF Hotel

Creating Date: 2010

Information: AMEN Gestaltung was commissioned to develop an integrated concept of corporate design, image folder, guidance system and web design. The guidance system consists of the CD's typography and specially created pictograms composed form parts of the logo. The pictograms and the typography were directly applicated on the walls of the corridors without using signs out of other materials.

HOTEL

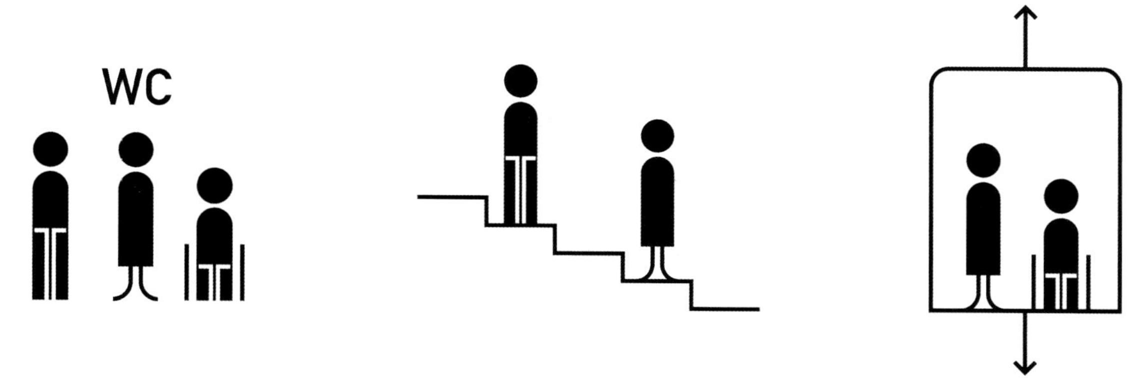

600

2. UG BOUTIQUE SUITE WÄSCHELAGER

3. OG 200 202 204 205 206 207 208 209

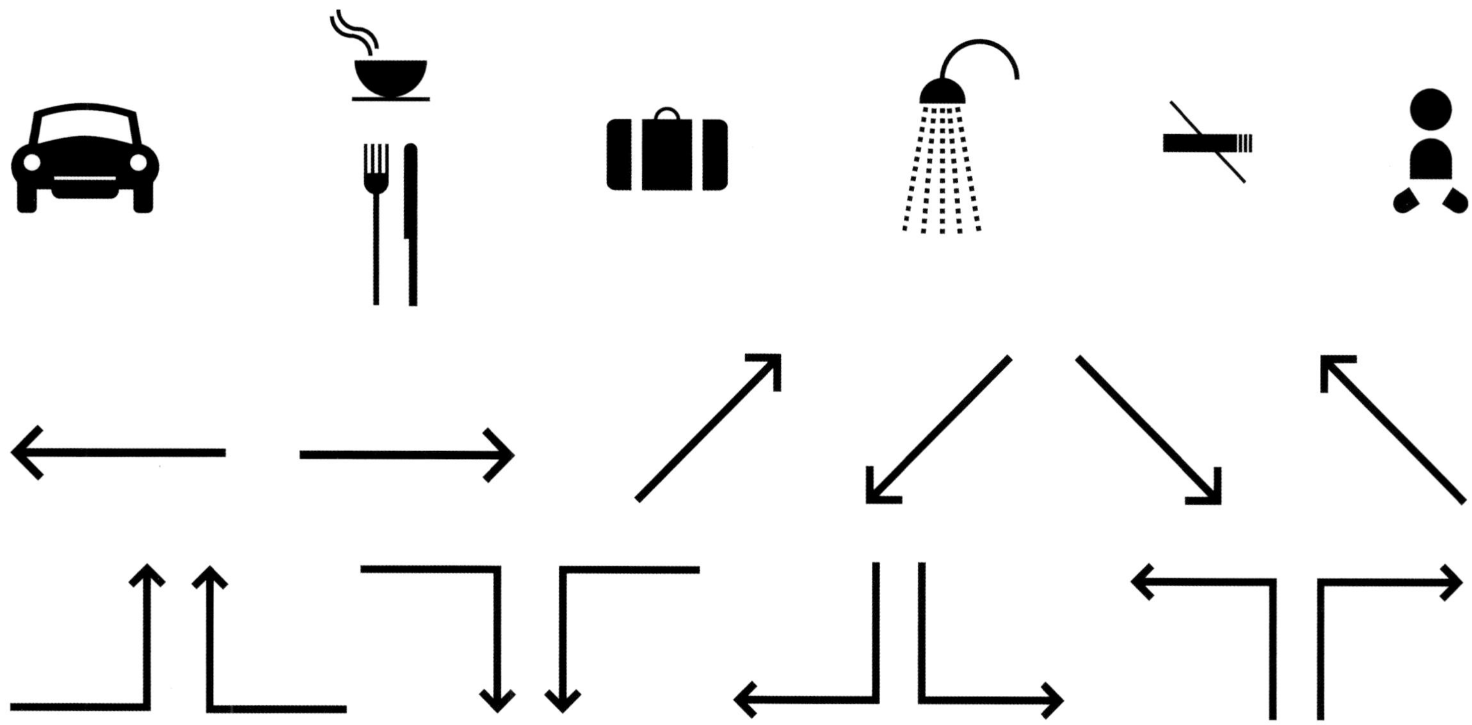

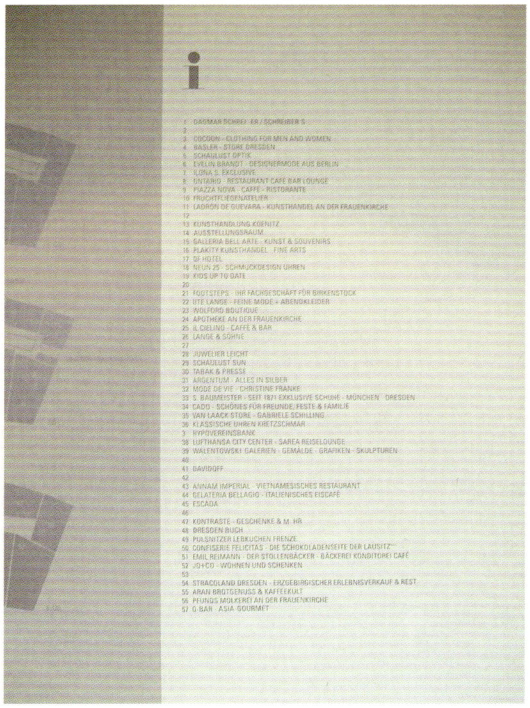

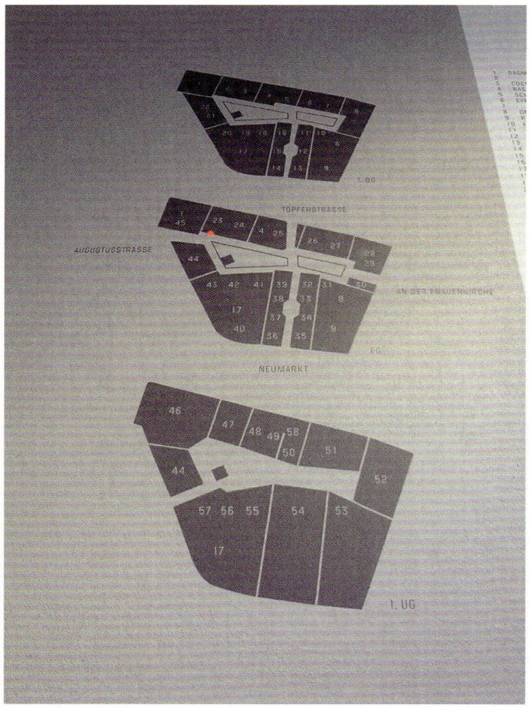

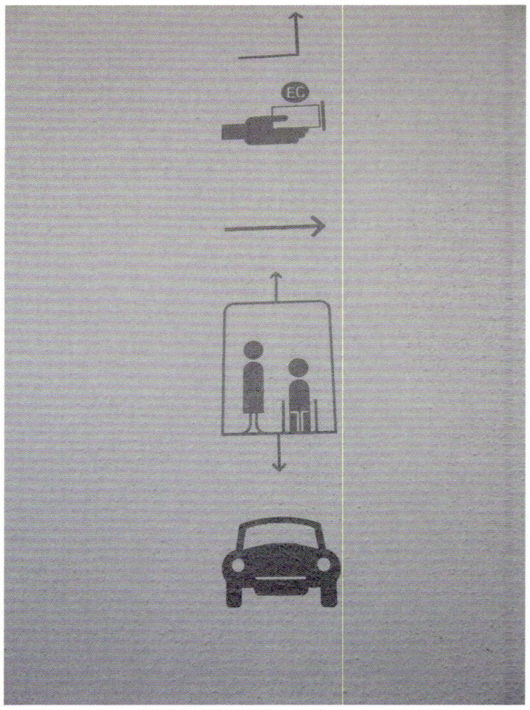
EC

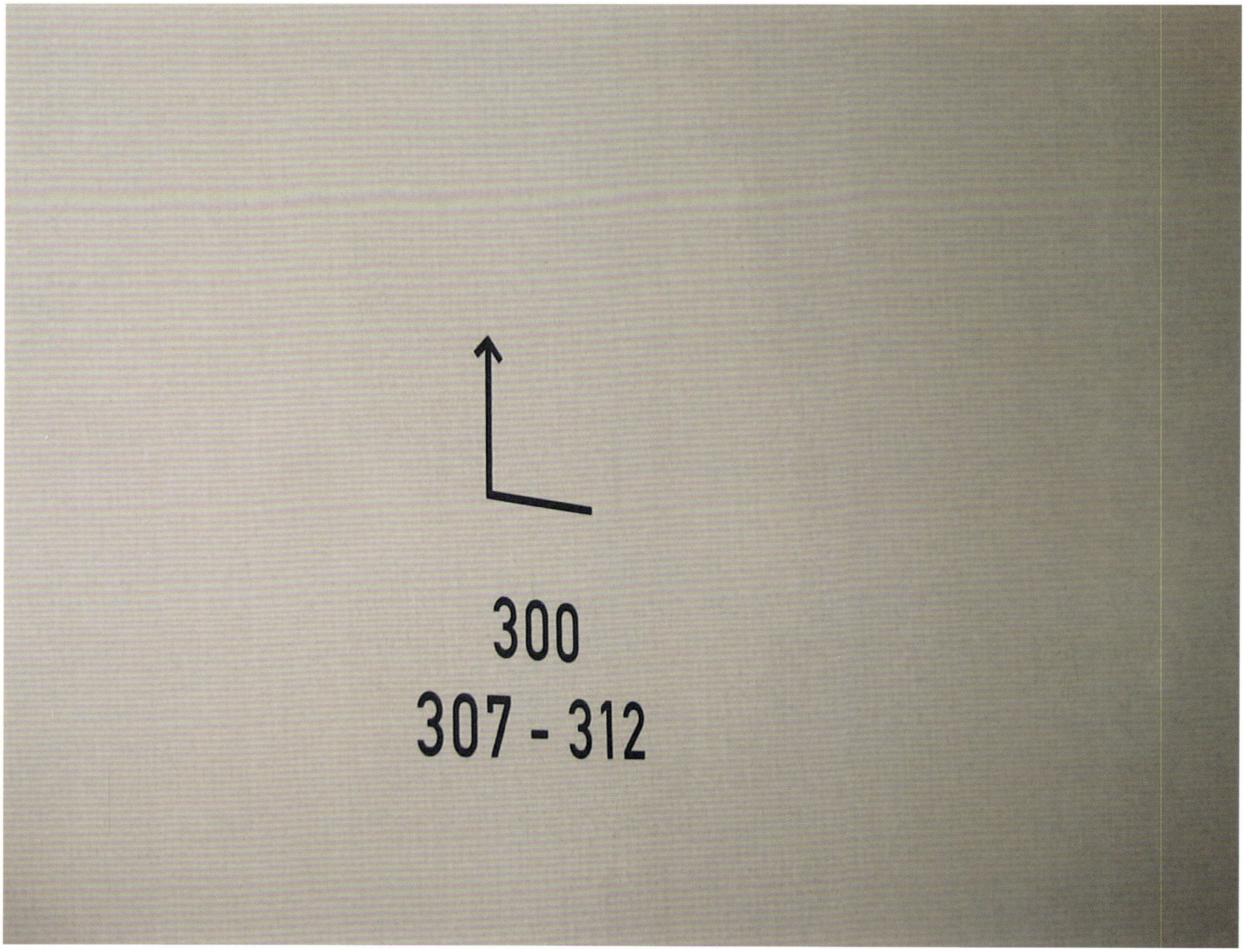
300
307 - 312

3. OG
HOTEL

WC

6. OG
HOTEL

203 - 205

2. UG
REZEPTION

GREENCUBE
ワールド・ロジ大阪フルフィルメントセンター

GREENCUBE

Green Cube

Design Agency: Shinnoske Design

Creative Director: Shinnoske Sugisaki

Designer: Shinsuke Suzuki, Yi Chin Wang, Teppei Yamaguchi

Photography: Taku Fukuda

Client: World Logi Group

Creating Date: 2007

Information: Branding for a logistics solution company. From naming to space experience and open campaign materials was created totally with constancy.

GREENCUBE
GREENCUBE

GREENCUBE
GREENCUBE
はじまる

InfoGALLERY
Control Room
Office
Garden

GREENCUBE
GREENCUBE
はじまる
GREENCUBE
GREENCUBE

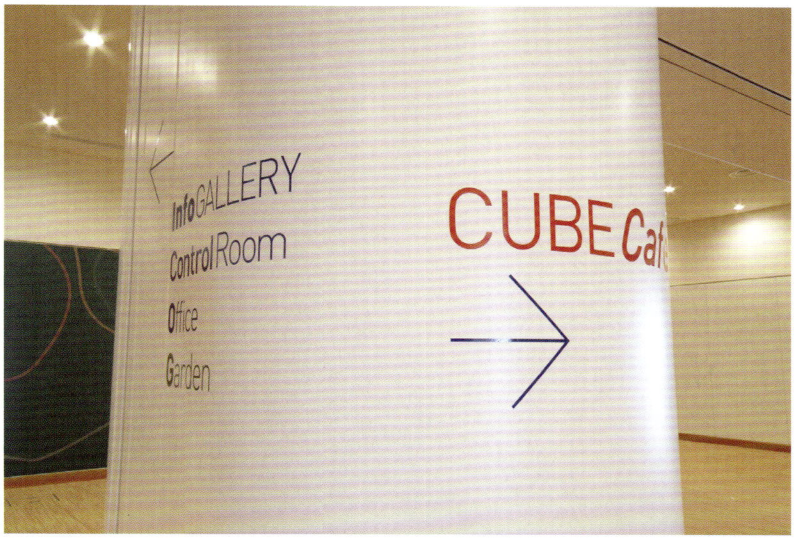
InfoGALLERY
ControlRoom
Office
Garden
CUBE Caf

GREENCUBE
GREENCUBE
はじまる

5
Office

3PL
REAL
3PL
REAL

1
2
3
4
5

Gravis

Design Agency: Eden Design & Communication

Creating Date: 2009

Information: The communication concept and design by Edenspiekermann is flexible and simple. It works in a little Gravis corner of a department store right up to a big double storey 7,500 sqm building, and it creates an unmistakable ambience for the "Digital Lifestyle".The idea of "Digital Lifestyle" has to appeal to customers wherever they happen to be standing or sitting, mostly at the point of sale and online. This is precisely where the brand experience developed by Edenspiekermann starts. The foundations are a new image and word mark, a colour scheme, a typography and layout concept, and an exclusive typeface for pictograms and accentuated text.

GRAVIS
GRAVIS

Service-Center
Schließfächer
WC

Kino Kuniya International

Design Agency: Hiromura Design Office

Client: KINOKUNIYA Co,. Ltd

Creating Date: 2008

breads are made
bon doux
KINOKUNIYA
bon doux
KINOKUNIYA
すし萬

Wine&Liquor
パン

Specialities

markets to find the
crab skipj
a scallops trout barracuda oysters sea bream

NASU GARDEN OUTLET

LOCO MARKET

NASU Garden Outlet

Design Agency: Hiromura Design Office
Client: Seibu Properties Inc.
Creating Date: 2008

NASU GARDEN OUTLET
化粧室
Rest Room
インフォメーション
総合観光案内所
Information, Visitor Center
KIDS GARDEN
LOCO FARM
LOCO MARKET
アクティビティエリア
Activity Area
ACTIVITY AREA
NORTH AREA
MIDDLE AREA
SOUTH AREA
裏側から取り出せます
フロアガイド
Floor Guide

化粧室
Restroom
インフォメーション
総合観光案内所
Information, Visitor Center
Fine Second

P5
N
出口

NASU
GARDEN
OUTLET
NASU
GARDEN
OUTLET
NASU
GARDEN
OUTLET
化粧室
Rest Room
インフォメーション
総合観光案内所
Information, Visitor Center
KIDS
GARDEN
LOCO
FARM
LOCO
MARKET
アクティビティエリア
Activity Area
Fashion Goods
Sports & Outdoor
Lifestyle Goods & Foods
Restaurant & Service
Fashion
ACTIVITY AREA
NORTH AREA
MIDDLE AREA
SOUTH AREA
OPEN
フロアガイド
Floor Guide
OPEN
グルメガイド
Gourmet Guide
OPEN
インフォメーション
Information

Wilderness Park Zürich

Design Agency: Designalltag

Creating Date: 2010

Information: The sign system should guarantee the visitors a pleasant stay in the Park, make them feel secure and ensure the Park becomes established and be experienced visually. The designers wanted a simple, quiet, clean and timeless design that should reflect the dispute between urbanity and wilderness. The elements need a simple geometrical classic shape so that they can contrast clearly to the organic forms of nature. Designalltag developed the sign guidelines and designed the graphic elements. The guidelines cover direction details, security regulations, entrance admittance instructions, information, identification elements, and card material.

Wildnispark Zürich
Langenberg
Alpenmurmeltier
Alpine marmot
Alpensteinbock
Alpine ibex
Braunbär
Brown bear
Damhirsch
Fallow deer
Elch
Moose
Feldhase
Hare
Luchs
Lynx
Przewalskipferd
Przewalski horse
Reh
Roe deer
Rotfuchs
Red fox
Rothirsch
Red deer
Sikahirsch
Sika deer
Wildkatze
Wildcat
Wildschwein
Wild boar
Wisent
European bison
Wolf
Wolf
Eisenbahnlinie
Railway line
Fussweg
Hiking trail
Fahrradweg
Cycle path
Raubtier-Rundweg (ca. 15 min)
Predator Trail
Orelli-Rundweg (ca. 20 min)
Orelli Trail
Langenberg-Rundweg (ca. 60 min)
Langenberg Trail
Treppe/Steilstück
Stair/Steep part
Wald
Forest
Offene Fläche
Open areas
Gewässer
Water
Aussichtspunkt
Panorama point
Gehegeeinblick
Animal viewing platform
Spielplatz
Adliswil/Zürich
Gontenbach
Quellwasser-schloss
Albisstrasse
Buchenegggstr.
Eingang Albisstrasse
Wildnisschule
Shop
Langenberg Zentrum
Betriebs-gebäude
Eingang West
Haupt-eingang
Eingang West
Langenberg
Wildnispark Zürich
Langenberg

Wildnis
park
Zürich
Langenberg
Zürcher
Kantonalbank

Wildnis
park
Zürich
Sihlwald

Parking
Busstation
Toiletten
WC
Sihltal
Bahn
Langnau 40 min
Adliswil 1h 30 min
Zürich Manegg 2h 30 min
Sihluferweg
Wildnisweg
Sihlwald 5 min
Musterort 30 min
47
94

Willkommen im Wildnispark Zürich
Sihlwald
Wildnis
park
Zürich

Bellavita
Eingang / Entredgia
Bellavita Spa
Massage / Massascha
Solarium
Kassenautomat /
Chascha automatica

Rondo
Kongress- und Kulturzentrum
Center da congres e cultura
EG
Pontresina Tourist Information
Schweizer Ski- und
Snowboardschule
Schweizer Bergsteigerschule

Pontresina
Attraktionen / Atracziuns
Sport & Outdoor
Kultur / Cultura
RhB UNESCO Pass
BOCK
AUF ALP LANGUARD
SCENA

Pontresina

Design Agency: Designalltag

Creating Date: 2008

Information: The signage system integrates calm to the environment. There are a lot of different places for shopping, tourist destinations, and train stations. Some places get a lot of tourist while some other places are calm. The reduced design solution pays homage to the village history, and looks confidently towards its bright future. The design is reduced in white and grey colour. This fits in the nature and the village, also when there is a lot of snow in wintertime.

Sino-Singapore Tianjin Eco-city Administrative Committee Office Building

Design Agency: Dongdao

Design Concept: Steel plate with small holes to unify the interface of the signage system and main body of the building. Excellent construction process presents the modern feeling.

Engineering Implement: REEGE

Creating Date: 2008

Information: 1. Sino-Singapore Tianjin Eco-city is a significant project on the strategical level cooperated by China and Singapore governments to improve the ecological environment and construct the ecological civilisation. It is the new bright spot after the cooperation of Suzhou industrial park. It shows the determination of two countries to improve global climate, strengthen environment protection and save resource and energy.

2. Sino-Singapore Tianjin Eco-city locates in the important strategical area of Chinese national development, Tianjin Binhai new area. It is near Tianjin economic and technological development zone, Tianjin port, seashore resort. It is between Tanggu District and Hangu District, 45 kilometres away from city centre of Tianjin, 150 kilometres from Beijing. Its total area is about 31.23 square kilometres, programming resident population of 350,000.

洗手间 Washroom
楼梯间 Stairs Room
116 三号贵宾室 No.3 VIP room
117 四号贵宾室 No.4 VIP room
118 三号会议室 No.3 Meeting Room
113 联合办证大厅
Administration and Certification Center
115 咖啡厅 Cafe
122 邮政局 Post Office
商务中心 Business Center

103
一号会议室
No. 1
Meeting
Room

bibliotheek

jeugd
avontuur

open 070707
openbare bibliotheek amsterdam
openbare bibliotheek amsterdam

Openbare Bibliotheek Amsterdam

Design Agency: Thonik

Creative director: Thonik

Designer: Thonik

Client: Openbare Bibliotheek Amsterdam (OBA)

Creating Date: From 2006 onwards

Information: Thonik designed the visual communication for the public library of Amsterdam. Starting-point for the logo is that the word becomes an image, which is particularly appropriate for a library. Besides the new identity Thonik also designed the signage of the building and together with fashion designer Aziz the cloths of the staff.

Index//